HARRAP

FRENCH
BUSINESS
MANAGEMENT
DICTIONARY

HARRAP

FRENCH
BUSINESS
MANAGEMENT
DICTIONARY

James Coveney

Emeritus Professor of Modern Languages
University of Bath

Sheila J Moore

Senior Lecturer in European Business Studies
Business and Finance School
Farnborough College of Technology

HARRAP

First published in Great Britain 1993
by Chambers Harrap Publishers Ltd
7 Hopetoun Crescent, Edinburgh EH7 4AY

© Chambers Harrap Publishers Ltd 1995

ISBN 0245 60663 7

Previously published in hardback
(ISBN 0245 60603 3)

This edition published 1999

Reprinted 2000

Typeset by Kevin O'Connor Typesetting
Printed in Finland by WSOY

Contents
Table des matières

Introduction

This dictionary is based on a smaller work originally compiled with the aid of a grant from the McKinsey Foundation for Management Research. It is an attempt to fill a gap that clearly exists: the rapid growth of management sciences has resulted in the coining of many terms to describe techniques and concepts which are not easily found in current English-French and French-English dictionaries. The dictionary includes a large number of new terms, many of which have been developed in the financial and information technology sectors.

In general, the dictionary covers the main areas of business management: policy and corporate planning, finance, information technology, marketing, operational research, personnel management, and production.

We have tried to keep a proper balance by not overemphasizing any one area. Moreover, since the scope of the subject is very wide, we have selected only those terms in most frequent use.

We should like to thank M. Pierre Agron, Secretary General of the Comité d'étude des termes techniques français, and his Committee for supplying us with most valuable suggestions regarding equivalents for certain English terms.

We also wish to thank Mme Chantal Pommier of the Paris office of McKinsey, Mr Robert Whiting of the firm's London office, and McKinsey Eurocenter in Brussels for helpful advice and suggestions.

James Coveney
Sheila J. Moore

Introduction

Ce lexique, entièrement révisé et remis à jour, dont la première édition a paru il y a quelques années grâce à l'aide de crédits fournis par la McKinsey Foundation for Management Research, se propose de combler une lacune: le développement rapide des sciences de la gestion de l'entreprise a donné naissance à de nombreux termes pour designer des techniques et des idées nouvelles; ces termes ne se trouvent pas couramment dans les dictionnaires anglais-français ou français-anglais généraux. Le lexique contient un nombre important de termes nouveaux dont beaucoup ont été créés dans les domaines de la finance et de l'informatique.

En général, le lexique comprend les secteurs les plus importants de la gestion de l'entreprise: politique générale de l'entreprise, planification de l'entreprise, informatique, finance, marketing, recherche opérationnelle, direction du personnel, et production. Pour éviter tout déséquilibre nous n'avons donné la préférence à aucun secteur particulier.

Pour le choix des termes la priorité est allée aux concepts vastes et généraux plutôt qu'aux termes très spécialisés qui ont été récemment créés. D'autre part, étant donné l'étendue du domaine étudié, nous avons choisi seulement les termes les plus fréquemment employés.

Beaucoup de termes plus récents ont été ajoutés à la suite de discussions avec des professeurs à Farnborough College of Technology, en particulier Geoff Gravil, Graham Rogers, Jennifer Cairns et Fran Jennings-Clark. Dominique Barnard et Tony Ashwell nous ont aidés à trouver des équivalents français pour certains termes.

Nous remercions M. Pierre Agron, Secrétaire général du Comité d'étude des termes techniques français, ainsi que le Comité, de nous avoir fourni des suggestions utiles pour des équivalents à certains termes anglais.

Enfin, nous remercions Mme Chantal Pommier du bureau de McKinsey & Company, Inc. à Paris, M. Robert Whiting du bureau de McKinsey à Londres, et le McKinsey Eurocenter à Bruxelles de leurs conseils précieux.

James Coveney
Sheila J. Moore

Notes

Where there are alternative translations of a particular term they are listed in alphabetical order except in cases of a common or strongly preferred translation. French terms have been alphabeticized according to the initial letter of their main lexical components (in other words, ignoring partitive articles).

In certain instances we have come up against the untranslatable, where a direct equivalent does not exist for a particular term in the other language. In such cases, an approximate translation has been given in italics.

To help the user we have listed the majority of terms under all the words which occur in that term. Much time could otherwise be wasted in trying to find a term.

Acronyms have been incorporated in the alphabetical listings for each letter.

It should be noted that for words with the alternatives *-ise* or *-ize* and *-isation* or *-ization* the forms *-ize* and *-ization* have been adopted, as English usage is about equally divided between the two, and American practice favours the *-ize*, *-ization*.

In general, however, British English spelling has been used throughout, except in cases connected with computing, such as *analog*, *disk* and *program*, where the American English variant appears to have gained general acceptance as the norm.

The attention of the reader is drawn to a few salient differences between British English and American orthography:

(a) The British English use of *-our* (as in lab*our*) where American usage is *-or* (lab*or*)

(b) The British English use of the final *-re* (as in cent*re*) where American usage is *-er* (cent*er*)

(c) The doubling of certain intervocalic consonants in British English (as in progra*mm*er) where American usage favours a single consonant (progra*m*er)

Finally, the hyphenation of compound terms has proved to be a difficult matter in a book that contains so many new coinages. Compound headwords that are used only as attributive adjectives (such as *stand-alone*) have been hyphenated. Noun compounds have generally been left unhyphenated except in cases where established usage has indicated the need for a hyphen.

Remarques

Lorsqu'un terme possède plusieurs traductions possibles, celles-ci sont données dans l'ordre alphabétique sauf dans les cas où il s'agit d'une traduction courante ou nettement préférée. En ce qui concerne les termes français, seuls les principaux éléments lexicaux sont pris en compte pour l'alphabétisation (en d'autres mots, l'ordre alphabétique ne tient pas compte des articles partitifs).

Dans certains cas nous nous sommes heurtés à des termes intraduisibles pour lesquels il n'existe aucune traduction équivalente dans l'autre langue. En de tels cas une traduction approximative est imprimée en italique.

Afin de faciliter l'utilisation du lexique nous avons fait figurer la plupart des termes sous tous les mots qui les composent. Nous pensons ainsi épargner au lecteur une recherche fastidieuse et une perte de temps considérable.

Les acronymes sont incorporés dans le texte par ordre alphabétique.

Il y a lieu de noter que dans le cas des mots qui s'écrivent soit en *-ise* soit en *-ize*, en *-isation* ou *-ization*, nous avons opté pour les orthographes *-ize* et *-ization*, l'usage anglais balançant entre les deux et la pratique américain préférant les formes *-ize* et *-ization*.

Toutefois, d'une manière générale, le lexique suit l'orthographe de l'anglais britannique sauf dans le cas de mots associés à l'informatique tels que *analog*, *disk* et *program*, où l'orthographe américaine semble être devenue l'orthographe d'usage.

Nous attirons l'attention du lecteur sur quelques différences importantes entre l'orthographe américaine et anglaise:

(a) L'anglais britannique utilise l'orthographe *-our* (comme dans lab*our*) tandis que l'américain préfère *-or* (lab*or*)

(b) L'anglais britannique préfère la terminaison *-re* (comme dans cent*re*) tandis que l'américain utilise *-er* (cent*er*)

(c) En anglais certaines consonnes intervocaliques sont doublées (comme dans progra*mm*er) alors que l'usage américain préfère une seule consonne (progra*m*er)

Enfin, l'emploi du trait d'union dans les mots composés a présenté des difficultés dans une publication contenant tant de néologismes. Des mots-clés composés utilisés seulement comme des adjectifs qualificatifs (p.ex. *stand-alone*) sont écrits avec un trait d'union. Les noms composés sont en général écrits sans trait d'union sauf dans les cas où l'usage établi l'exige.

ENGLISH-FRENCH

A

abandonment: product ...	suppression *(f)* d'un produit
above par	au-dessus du pair *(m)*
absenteeism	absentéisme *(m)*
absorption	absorption *(f)*
absorption costing	méthode *(f)* des coûts d'absorption
	méthode *(f)* des coûts complets
acceptance: brand ...	acceptabilité *(f)* de la marque
acceptance: consumer ...	réceptivité *(f)* des consommateurs
access (to)	accéder à
access: multi-...	accès *(m)* multiple
access: random ...	accès *(m)* sélectif
accountability	ressort *(m)*
accountant: chief ...	chef *(m)* comptable
accounting	comptabilité *(f)*
accounting department	services *(mpl)* comptables
accounting model	modèle *(m)* comptable
accounting period	exercice *(m)* (comptable)
	exercice *(m)* (financier)
	exercice *(m)* (social)
accounting ratio	ratio *(m)* comptable
accounting: cost ...	comptabilité *(f)* analytique
	comptabilité *(f)* de prix de revient
accounting: creative ...	comptabilité *(f)* assouplie
accounting: electronic ... system	ensemble *(m)* électronique de gestion
accounting: management ...	comptabilité *(f)* de gestion
accounting: profit centre ...	comptabilité *(f)* par centres de profit
accounting: responsibility ...	comptabilité *(f)* des sections
accounts department	services *(mpl)* comptables
accounts: consolidated ...	comptes *(m)* consolidés
	comptes *(mpl)* intégrés
accounts: group ...	comptes *(mpl)* de groupe
acquisition	achat *(m)*
	acquisition *(f)*
acquisition profile	profil *(m)* d'acquisition

acquisition: data ...	acquisition *(f)* de données
	saisie *(f)* de données
acquisitions: mergers and ... (M & A)	fusions *(fpl)* et acquisitions *(fpl)*
across-the-board increase	augmentation *(f)* générale
action plan	plan *(m)* d'action
	programme *(m)* d'action
action: industrial ...	action *(f)* revendicative
	mouvements *(mpl)* sociaux
action: unofficial ...	grève *(f)* sauvage
actionable	pour action *(f)*
activate (to)	activer
activity chart	graphique *(m)* des activités
activity sampling	mesure *(f)* du travail par sondage
activity: support ...	fonctions *(fpl)* complémentaires
actualization: self-...	autoréalisation *(f)*
adaptive control	contrôle *(m)* adaptif
add-on equipment	matériel *(m)* complémentaire
added: value ...	valeur *(f)* ajoutée
added: value ... tax (VAT)	taxe *(f)* à la valeur ajoutée (TVA)
administration	administration *(f)*
	gestion *(f)*
administration-production ratio	ratio *(m)* administration-production
administration: financial ...	gestion *(f)* financière
administrative control procedure	procédé *(m)* de contrôle de gestion
administrative expenses	frais *(mpl)* administratifs
administrative overheads	frais *(mpl)* généraux d'administration
administrative theory	théorie *(f)* administrative
ADP (automatic data processing)	TAD (traitement *(m)* automatique des données)
advancement	auto-développement *(m)*
advancement: executive ...	promotion *(f)* des cadres
advantage: competitive ...	avantage *(m)* concurrentiel
advertising agent	agent *(m)* de publicité
advertising appropriation	dotations *(fpl)* budgétaires affectées à la publicité
advertising budget	budget *(m)* de publicité
advertising campaign	campagne *(f)* de publicité
advertising drive	campagne *(f)* de publicité
advertising effectiveness	efficacité *(f)* publicitaire

advertising manager	directeur *(m)* de la publicité
advertising media	média *(mpl)* publicitaires
advertising message	message *(m)* publicitaire
advertising research	études *(fpl)* publicitaires
advertising theme	thème *(m)* publicitaire
advertising: corporate ...	publicité *(f)* de prestige
advertising: point-of-sale ... (POS)	publicité *(f)* sur le lieu de vente (PLV)
advertising: product ...	publicité *(f)* de produit
advertising: subliminal ...	publicité *(f)* subliminale
advisory services	services *(mpl)* de conseil interne
affiliate company	société *(f)* affiliée
	société *(f)* apparentée
after-sales service	service *(m)* après-vente
agenda: hidden ...	programme *(m)* secret
agenda: to be on the ...	être à l'ordre *(m)* du jour
agent: advertising ...	agent *(m)* de publicité
agent: forwarding ...	agent *(m)* expéditeur
	transitaire *(m)*
agent: sole ...	agent *(m)* commercial exclusif
agreement (*written*)	convention *(f)*
agreement: collective bargaining ...	convention *(f)* collective (cc)
agreement: gentleman's ...	accord *(m)* à l'amiable
agreement: productivity ...	contrat *(m)* de productivité
algorithm	algorithme *(m)*
alliance: strategic ...	alliance *(f)* stratégique
allocate (to)	affecter
	allouer
allocation of costs	affectation *(f)* des charges
	imputation *(f)* des charges
allocation of responsibilities	répartition *(f)* des responsabilités
allocation: resource ...	affectation *(f)* des ressources
	allocation *(f)* des ressources
allotment: budget ...	affectation *(f)* budgétaire
allowance: capital ...	déduction *(f)* (fiscale) sur frais d'établissement
allowance: depreciation ...	provision *(f)* pour amortissement
amalgamate (to)	fusionner
amalgamation	absorption *(f)*
	fusion *(f)*

analog computer	ordinateur *(m)* analogique
analog(ue) representation	représentation *(f)* analogique
analysis: break-even ...	étude *(f)* de point mort
analysis: competitor ...	analyse *(f)* des concurrents
analysis: contribution ...	analyse *(f)* des contributions (à la marge)
analysis: cost ...	analyse *(f)* du prix de revient
	étude *(f)* des charges
analysis: cost-benefit ... (CBA)	analyse *(f)* coût-profit
	analyse *(f)* des avantages-coûts
analysis: cost-volume-profit ...	analyse *(f)* volume-coûts-profits
analysis: critical path ... (CPA)	analyse *(f)* du chemin critique
analysis: decision ...	analyse *(f)* de la décision
analysis: depth ...	analyse *(f)* en profondeur
analysis: environmental ...	analyse *(f)* de l'environnement
analysis: financial ...	analyse *(f)* financière
	diagnostic *(m)* financier
analysis: functional ...	analyse *(f)* fonctionnelle (AF)
analysis: input-output ...	analyse *(f)* entrées-sorties
analysis: investment ...	analyse *(f)* des investissements
	étude *(f)* de rentabilité
analysis: job ...	analyse *(f)* par poste de travail
	analyse *(f)* des tâches
analysis: marginal ...	analyse *(f)* marginale
analysis: media ...	analyse *(f)* de média
analysis: morphological ...	analyse *(f)* morphologique
analysis: multiple regression ... (MRA)	analyse *(f)* de régression multiple
analysis: needs ...	analyse *(f)* des besoins
analysis: network ...	analyse *(f)* de réseau
analysis: operations ...	analyse *(f)* des taches
	analyse *(f)* du travail
analysis: part-... training	formation *(f)* par étapes
analysis: problem ...	analyse *(f)* de problème
analysis: product ...	analyse *(f)* de produit
analysis: profit-factor ...	analyse *(f)* des facteurs de profit
analysis: profitability ...	analyse *(f)* de la rentabilité
analysis: project ...	étude *(f)* de projet
analysis: quantitative ...	analyse *(f)* quantitative
analysis: regression ...	analyse *(f)* de régression

analysis: risk ...	analyse *(f)* des risques
analysis: sales ...	analyse *(f)* des ventes
analysis: sensitivity ...	analyse *(f)* de sensibilité
analysis: sequential ...	analyse *(f)* séquentielle
analysis: skills ...	analyse *(f)* des aptitudes
analysis: social ...	analyse *(f)* sociale
analysis: systems ...	analyse *(f)* des systèmes
analysis: training needs ...	analyse *(f)* des besoins en formation
analysis: transactional ... (TA)	analyse *(f)* transactionnelle
analysis: value ... (VA)	analyse *(f)* de la valeur
analysis: variance ...	analyse *(f)* des écarts
analytic accounting	comptabilité *(f)* analytique
analytical training	formation *(f)* par étapes
ancillary operations	services *(mpl)* d'intendance
answerback code	indicatif *(m)*
answerphone	répondeur *(m)* téléphonique
anticipatory response	*anticipation (f) stratégique*
appeal: sales ...	attraction *(f)* commerciale
application: software ...	exploitation *(f)* du logiciel
apportion (to)	partager
	répartir
apportionment	affectation *(f)*
	répartition *(f)*
apportionment: cost ...	répartition *(f)* des charges
appraisal	estimation *(f)*
	évaluation *(f)*
	expertise *(f)*
appraisal: capital expenditure ...	évaluation *(f)* des dépenses d'investissement
appraisal: financial ...	évaluation *(f)* financière
appraisal: investment ...	appréciation *(f)* des investissements
appraisal: market ...	évaluation *(f)* du marché
appraisal: performance ...	appréciation *(f)* des performances
	évaluation *(f)* des résultats
appraisal: resource ...	examen *(m)* des ressources
appraisal: self-...	auto-critique *(f)*
appraisal: staff ...	évaluation *(f)* du personnel
appraise (to)	évaluer
appreciate (to)	augmenter de valeur

appreciation: capital ...	augmentation *(f)* du capital
approach: functional ...	démarche *(f)* fonctionnelle
approach: systems ...	approche *(f)* par la théorie des systèmes
approach: top management ...	optique *(f)* de la direction générale
appropriate (to)	affecter
appropriation: advertising ...	dotations *(fpl)* budgétaires affectées à la publicité
appropriation: budget ...	affectation *(f)* budgétaire allocation *(f)* des fonds
appropriation: marketing ...	dotations *(fpl)* budgétaires affectées au marketing
aptitude test	test *(m)* d'aptitude
arbitrage	arbitrage *(m)*
arbitrageur	arbitragiste *(m)*
arbitration	arbitrage *(m)*
area manager	chef *(m)* de secteur
area network: wide ... ... (WAN)	grand réseau *(m)*
area: growth ...	secteur *(m)* de croissance
area: problem ...	domaine *(m)* problématique zone *(f)* critique
area: product ...	domaine *(m)* de produits
area: sales ...	territoire *(m)* de vente
area: trading ...	territoire *(m)* de vente
arm's length	à distance *(f)*
artificial intelligence	intelligence *(f)* artificielle
assembly line	chaîne *(f)* de montage
assess (to)	évaluer
assessment	appréciation *(f)* évaluation *(f)* assiette *(f)* imposition *(f)*
assessment centre	centre *(m)* d'évaluation de la qualité
assessment: demand ...	évaluation *(f)* de la demande
assessment: problem ...	évaluation *(f)* des problèmes
assessment: project ...	évaluation *(f)* de projet
assessment: quality ...	évaluation *(f)* de la qualité
assessment: risk ...	appréciation *(f)* des risques
asset liability management	gestion *(f)* du bilan

asset management	gestion *(f)* des actifs
asset portfolio	portefeuille *(m)* d'actifs
asset-stripping	cannibalisation *(f)*
	démantèlement *(m)* de l'actif
asset turnover	rotation *(f)* des capitaux
asset value	valeur *(f)* des actifs
assets	actif *(m)*
	avoirs *(mpl)*
	ressources *(fpl)*
assets: capital ...	actif *(m)* immobilisé
assets: current ...	actif *(m)* circulant
	actif *(m)* réalisable
assets: earnings on ...	rendement *(m)* des fonds propres
assets: fixed ...	immobilisations *(fpl)*
	actif *(m)* immobilisé
	capitaux *(mpl)* permanents
	valeurs *(fpl)* immobilisées
assets: hidden ...	actif *(m)* occulte
assets: intangible ...	actif *(m)* immatériel
	valeurs *(fpl)* incorporelles
assets: liquid ...	actif *(m)* disponible
	actif *(m)* négociable
	actif *(m)* réalisable
	liquidités *(fpl)*
assets: net ...	actif *(m)* net
	valeurs *(fpl)* nettes
assets: net current ...	fonds *(m)* de roulement net
assets: quick ...	actif *(m)* disponible
	actif *(m)* négociable
	actif *(m)* réalisable
assets: return on ...	rendement *(m)* des fonds propres
assets: revaluation of ...	réévaluation *(f)* des actifs
assets: tangible ...	valeurs *(fpl)* matérielles
	valeurs *(fpl)* tangibles
assets: wasting ...	immobilisations *(fpl)* défectibles
assignment of expenditure	répartition *(f)* des frais
assignment: job ...	affectation *(f)* des tâches
assistant director	directeur *(m)* adjoint

assistant manager	sous-chef *(m)*
	sous-directeur *(m)*
assistant to manager	adjoint *(m)*
assistant: line ...	attaché *(m)* opérationnel
assistant: staff ...	attaché *(m)* fonctionnel
associate company	société *(f)* affiliée
	société *(f)* apparentée
association: trade ...	association *(f)* professionnelle
assurance: quality ...	contrôle *(m)* de la qualité
at par	au pair *(m)*
attitude survey	enquête *(f)* d'opinion
attitude: user ...	attitudes *(fpl)* des utilisateurs
audiovisual aids	supports *(mpl)* audio-visuels
audit (to)	apurer un compte
	vérifier un compte
audit	audit *(m)*
	contrôle *(m)*
	révision *(f)* comptable
	vérification *(f)* des comptes
audit: efficiency ...	contrôle *(m)* d'efficience
audit: internal ...	audit *(m)* interne
	contrôle *(m)* interne
audit: management ...	contrôle *(m)* de gestion
	diagnostic *(m)* d'évaluation de gestion
audit: manpower ...	inventaire *(m)* des effectifs
audit: operations ...	contrôle *(m)* de gestion
	contrôle *(m)* des opérations
audit: staff ...	inventaire *(m)* des effectifs
auditing: balance sheet ...	contrôle *(m)* du bilan
auditor	commissaire *(m)* aux comptes
	vérificateur *(m)* des comptes
authority structure	structure *(f)* d'autorité
authority: contraction of ...	limitation *(f)* d'autorité
authority: line ...	autorité *(f)* hiérarchique
authorized capital	capital *(m)* nominal
	capital *(m)* social
automate (to)	automatiser
automatic data processing (ADP)	traitement *(m)* automatique des données (TAD)

automation	automation *(f)*
	automatisation *(f)*
automation: office ...	bureautique *(f)*
average	moyenne *(f)*
average cost	coût *(m)* moyen
average revenue	recette *(f)* moyenne
average yield	rendement *(m)* moyen
average: weighted ...	moyenne *(f)* pondérée
awareness level	niveau *(m)* de notoriété
awareness: brand ...	notoriété *(f)* de la marque
awareness: cost ...	connaissance *(f)* des coûts
awareness: market ...	conscience *(f)* du marché

B

back burner: put on the ... ... (to)	mettre en veilleuse *(f)*
back-up facility	installation *(f)* de secours
backlog	arriéré *(m)*
bad-debt losses	pertes *(fpl)* du fait de mauvaises créances
bad debts	créances *(fpl)* douteuses
	mauvaises créances *(fpl)*
balance sheet	bilan *(m)*
balance sheet auditing	contrôle *(m)* du bilan
balanced portfolio	portefeuille *(m)* équilibré
ball game: different ...	autre paire *(f)* de manches
ballpark figure	chiffre *(m)* approximatif
bank rate	taux *(m)* de base bancaire (TBB)
bank: commercial ...	banque *(f)* commerciale
bank: computer ...	banque *(f)* de données
	fichier *(m)* central
bank: data ...	banque *(f)* de données
	fichier *(m)* central
bank: investment ...	banque *(f)* d'investissement
bank: merchant ...	banque *(f)* d'affaires
bar chart	graphique *(m)* à bâtons
	graphique *(m)* en tuyaux d'orgue
bargaining: collective ...	négociations *(fpl)* collectives

bargaining: collective ... agreement	convention *(f)* collective (cc)
bargaining: plant ...	négociations *(fpl)* au niveau local
bargaining: productivity ...	négociations *(fpl)* des contrats de productivité
barrier: non-tariff ... (NTB)	barrière *(f)* non douanière
barrier: tariff ...	barrière *(f)* douanière
barter trade	commerce *(m)* d'échange
base rate	taux *(m)* de base
base year	année *(f)* de référence
base: data ...	base *(f)* de données
batch control	contrôle *(m)* par lots
batch processing	traitement *(m)* par lots
batch production	fabrication *(f)* par lots
batch: economic ... quantity	effectif *(m)* de série économique
bear	baissier *(m)*
bear market	marché *(m)* à la baisse
behaviour: buying ...	comportement *(m)* d'achat
behaviour: consumer ...	comportement *(m)* du consommateur
behaviour: organizational ...	comportement *(m)* de l'homme dans l'organisation
behavioural science	science *(f)* du comportement
below par	au-dessous du pair *(m)*
benchmark	point *(m)* de référence
	repère *(m)*
benefit: cost- ... analysis (CBA)	analyse *(f)* coût-profit
	analyse *(f)* des avantages-coûts
benefits: fringe ...	avantages *(mpl)* annexes
	avantages *(mpl)* sociaux
best-case scenario	hypothèse *(f)* optimiste
bid: leveraged ...	offre *(f)* de rachat par levier
bid: pre-emptive ...	ouverture *(f)* préventive
bid: take-over ... (TOB)	offre *(f)* publique d'achat (OPA)
blackleg	briseur *(m)* de grèves
blue-chip stock	valeur *(f)* de premier ordre
blue-collar worker	travailleur *(m)* manuel
blueprint	projet *(m)*
blue-sky research	recherche *(f)* sans but précis
board control	contrôle *(m)* du conseil d'administration

board meeting	réunion *(f)* du conseil d'administration
board of directors	direction *(f)* générale
board: executive ...	comité *(m)* de direction
	conseil *(m)* d'administration
	conseil *(m)* de direction
boardroom	salle *(f)* du conseil
body language	allure *(f)*
bond: junk ...	junk bond *(m)*
	obligation *(f)* pourrie
bonus	prime *(f)*
bonus scheme	programme *(m)* de primes d'encouragement
bonus: group ...	prime *(f)* collective
	prime *(f)* d'équipe
bonus: premium ...	salaire *(m)* à prime de rendement
book value	valeur *(f)* comptable
boom	boum *(m)*
booster training	recyclage *(m)*
borrowing facility	source *(f)* d'emprunts
bottleneck	goulot *(m)* d'étranglement
bottom line	résultat *(m)* net
bottom out (to)	atteindre son niveau *(m)* le plus bas
bottom-up	de la base au sommet
brains trust	brain-trust *(m)*
brainstorming	brainstorming *(m)*
	remue-méninges *(m)*
branch office	succursale *(f)*
brand	marque *(f)*
brand acceptance	acceptabilité *(f)* de la marque
brand awareness	notoriété *(f)* de la marque
brand image	image *(f)* de marque
brand loyalty	fidélité *(f)* à la marque
brand manager	chef *(m)* de marque
brand name	marque *(f)*
brand portfolio	portefeuille *(m)* de marques
brand positioning	positionnement *(m)* de marques
brand recognition	identification *(f)* d'une marque
brand strategy	stratégie *(f)* de la marque
breakdown: operations ...	décomposition *(f)* des tâches

break even (to)	rentrer dans ses frais
break-even analysis	étude *(f)* de point mort
break-even point	point *(m)* critique
	point *(m)* mort
	seuil *(m)* de rentabilité
break-even quantity	point *(m)* mort
breakthrough	innovation *(f)*
	nouveauté *(f)*
break-up value	valeur *(f)* de récupération
brief (to)	briefer
	fournir des directives *(fpl)* à
briefing	briefing *(m)*
	établissement *(m)* de dossier
broker	courtier *(m)*
broker: software ...	courtier *(m)* en logiciel
brokerage	courtage *(m)*
brokerage fees	frais *(mpl)* de courtage
brown goods	produits *(mpl)* bruns
budget (to)	budgétiser
	établir un budget
budget	budget *(m)*
budget allotment	affectation *(f)* budgétaire
budget appropriation	affectation *(f)* budgétaire
	allocation *(f)* des fonds
budget constraint	contrainte *(f)* budgétaire
budget forecast	prévision *(f)* budgétaire
budget forecasting	prévision *(f)* budgétaire
budget standard	standard *(m)* budgétaire
budget: advertising ...	budget *(m)* de publicité
budget: capital ...	budget *(m)* d'équipement
	budget *(m)* d'investissement
budget: cash ...	budget *(m)* de trésorerie
budget: flexible ...	budget *(m)* flexible
budget: investment ...	budget *(m)* d'investissement
budget: marketing ...	budget *(m)* de marketing
budget: sales ...	budget *(m)* commercial
budget: zero-base ...	budget *(m)* base zéro
budgetary control	contrôle *(m)* budgétaire
budgetary variance	écart *(m)* budgétaire

budgeting	budgétisation *(f)*
	comptabilité *(f)* budgétaire
	établissement *(m)* des budgets
	préparation *(f)* du budget
budgeting control	contrôle *(m)* budgétaire
budgeting: capital ...	budgétisation *(m)* des investissements
	prévision *(f)* des dépenses
	d'investissement
budgeting: cash ...	préparation *(f)* des budgets de
	trésorerie
	prévision *(f)* de trésorerie
budgeting: output ...	*rationalisation (f) des choix budgétaires*
	(RCB)
budgeting: performance ...	*rationalisation (f) des choix budgétaires*
	(RCB)
budgeting: planning, programming,	*rationalisation (f) des choix budgétaires*
... system (PPBS)	*(RCB)*
budgeting: programme ...	*rationalisation (f) des choix budgétaires*
	(RCB)
buffer stock	stock *(m)* tampon
bug	bogue *(f)*
building: team-...	développement *(m)* d'équipe
built-in	incorporé
built-in obsolescence	désuétude *(f)* calculée
bull	haussier *(m)*
bull market	marché *(m)* haussier
bulletin board	panneau *(m)* d'affichage (électronique)
bundling	groupage *(m)*
bureau: computer	façonnier *(m)*
services ...	
bureau: employment ...	agence *(f)* de placement
business corporation	société *(f)* commerciale
business cycle	cycle *(m)* économique
business economist	économiste *(m)* d'entreprise
business forecasting	prévision *(f)* dans l'entreprise
business game	jeu *(m)* d'entreprise
	simulation *(f)* de gestion
business management	gestion *(f)* de l'entreprise
business outlook	conjoncture *(f)*

business policy	politique *(f)* générale de l'entreprise
	politique *(f)* de gestion
business portfolio	portefeuille *(m)* d'activités
business proposition	proposition *(f)* d'affaires
business relations	relations *(fpl)* d'affaires
business strategy	stratégie *(f)* des affaires
business stream	flux *(m)* d'affaires
business system	chaîne *(f)* d'activités
business unit: strategic ...	domaine *(m)* d'activité stratégique
buy in (to)	s'approvisionner de l'extérieur
buy out (to)	désintéresser
buyer: chief ...	chef *(m)* des achats
	chef *(m)* d'approvisionnement
buyer: potential ...	acheteur *(m)* potentiel
buyers' market	marché *(m)* à la baisse
buying behaviour	comportement *(m)* d'achat
buying: impulse ...	achat *(m)* impulsif
buyout	désintéressement *(m)*
buyout: employee ...	rachat *(m)* d'une entreprise par ses employés
buyout: leveraged ... (LBO)	rachat *(m)* par levier
buyout: management ... (MBO)	rachat *(m)* d'une entreprise par ses cadres
buyout: worker ...	rachat *(m)* d'une entreprise par ses employés
buzz-word	mot *(m)* dans le vent
bypass (to)	court-circuiter
by-product	produit *(m)* dérivé
	sous-produit *(m)*
byte	multiplet *(m)*

C

CAD (computer-aided design)	CAO (conception *(f)* assistée par ordinateur)
CAL (computer-aided learning)	EAO (enseignement *(m)* assisté par ordinateur)
CAM (computer-aided manufacturing)	FAO (fabrication *(f)* assistée par ordinateur)

campaign: advertising ...	campagne (f) de publicité
campaign: productivity ...	campagne (f) de productivité
canvass (to)	prospecter
capability	capacité (f)
capacity utilization	utilisation (f) de la capacité
capacity: excess ...	surcapacité (f)
capacity: full ...	plein rendement (m)
capacity: idle ...	capacité (f) inutilisée
capacity: manufacturing ...	capacité (f) de production
capacity: plant ...	capacité (f) de l'usine
capacity: spare ...	capacité (f) inutilisée
capex (capital expenditure)	dépenses (fpl) en capital
capital allowance	déduction (f) (fiscale) sur frais d'établissement
capital appreciation	augmentation (f) du capital
capital assets	actif (m) immobilisé
capital budget	budget (m) d'équipement
	budget (m) d'investissement
capital budgeting	budgétisation (f) des investissements
	prévision (f) des dépenses d'investissement
capital commitment	engagement (m) d'investissement
capital employed	capital (m) investi
capital employed: return on ... ... (ROCE)	rentabilité (f) des capitaux investis (RCI)
capital expenditure (capex)	dépenses (fpl) en capital
capital expenditure appraisal	évaluation (f) des dépenses d'investissement
capital formation	formation (f) de capital
capital gain	augmentation (f) de capital
	plus-value (f)
capital goods	biens (mpl) d'équipement
capital-intensive	capitalistique
capital loss	moins-value (f)
capital-output ratio	ratio (m) d'intensité de capital
capital project evaluation	étude (f) de projet d'investissement
capital raising	mobilisation (f) de fonds

capital rationing	rationnement *(m)* des fonds
capital structure	répartition *(f)* des capitaux
capital: authorized ...	capital *(m)* nominal
	capital *(m)* social
capital: circulating ...	capitaux *(mpl)* circulants
	capitaux *(mpl)* roulants
	fonds *(mpl)* de roulement
capital: issued ...	capital *(m)* émis
	capital *(m)* souscrit
capital: loan ...	capital *(m)* d'emprunt
capital: return on ...	rendement *(m)* de capital
capital: risk ...	capital *(m)* risque
capital: share ...	capital *(m)* actions
capital: venture ...	capital-créateur *(m)*
capital: working ...	fonds *(mpl)* de roulement
capitalist: venture ...	financier *(m)* à risque
capitalization	capitalisation *(f)*
capitalize (to)	capitaliser
care: customer ...	souci *(m)* du client
career planning	plan *(m)* de carrière
car phone	téléphone *(m)* de voiture
cartel	cartel *(m)*
case study	étude *(f)* de cas
cash	espèces *(fpl)*
cash budget	budget *(m)* de trésorerie
cash budgeting	préparation *(f)* des budgets de trésorerie
	prévision *(f)* de trésorerie
cash deal	transaction *(f)* au comptant
cash flow	cash-flow *(m)*
	marge *(f)* brute d'autofinancement (MBA)
	produit *(m)* disponible
cash flow: negative	cash-flow *(m)* négatif
cash forecasting	prévision *(f)* de trésorerie
cash management	gestion *(f)* de trésorerie
cash-poor	pauvre en liquidité *(f)*
cash ratio	coefficient *(m)* de trésorerie
	ratio *(m)* de trésorerie

cash-rich	riche en liquidité *(f)*
cash-strapped	sans liquidité *(f)*
cash: discounted ... flow (DCF)	cash-flow *(m)* actualisé (méthode DCF)
cash: incremental ... flow	cash-flow *(m)* marginal
cash: petty ...	petite caisse *(f)*
CAT (computer-assisted teaching)	enseignement *(m)* automatisé
CBA (cost-benefit analysis)	analyse *(f)* coût-profit
	analyse *(f)* des avantages-coûts
CBT (computer-based training)	enseignement *(m)* assisté par ordinateur (EAO)
ceiling: wage ...	plafonnement *(m)* des salaires
cellphone	téléphone *(m)* sans fil
central processing unit (CPU)	processeur *(m)* central
centralization	centralisation *(f)*
centralize (to)	centraliser
centre: assessment ...	centre *(m)* d'évaluation de la qualité
centre: computer ...	centre *(m)* de calcul
centre: cost ...	centre *(m)* de coûts
centre: profit ...	centre *(m)* de profit
centre: profit ... accounting	comptabilité *(f)* par centres de profit
centre: responsibility ...	centre *(m)* de responsabilité
chain of command	hiérarchie *(f)* de commandement
chain of distribution	circuit *(m)* de distribution
chain of production	chaîne *(f)* de production
chain production	production *(f)* à la chaîne
chain: value ...	chaîne *(f)* de valeur
chairman	président *(m)*
chairman and managing director	président-directeur *(m)* général (PDG)
chairman: deputy ...	vice-président *(m)*
chairman: vice-...	vice-président *(m)*
challenge: job ...	exigences *(fpl)* de poste
change management (management of change)	gestion *(f)* du changement
change: organizational ...	mutation *(f)* des structures
channel: distribution	réseau *(m)* de distribution
channels of communication	canaux *(mpl)* de communication
	liaisons *(fpl)* dans l'entreprise
	voies *(fpl)* de communication

characteristics: job ...	caractéristiques *(fpl)* de poste
chart: activity ...	graphique *(m)* des activités
chart: bar ...	graphique *(m)* à bâtons
	graphique *(m)* en tuyaux d'orgue
chart: flow ...	graphique *(m)* d'acheminement
	graphique *(m)* de circulation
chart: flow process ...	diagramme *(m)* de circulation
chart: management ...	tableau *(m)* de bord
chart: milestone ...	graphique *(m)* des étapes critiques
chart: organization ...	organigramme *(m)*
chart: pie ...	camembert *(m)*
	graphique *(m)* circulaire
chart: Z ...	diagramme *(m)* en Z
	graphique *(m)* en dents de scie
chief accountant	chef *(m)* comptable
chief buyer	chef *(m)* des achats
	chef *(m)* d'approvisionnement
chief executive	directeur *(m)* général
Chinese wall	cloison *(f)* étanche
chip	puce *(f)*
chunk a project (to)	découper un projet en tranches
chunk down (to)	parcelliser
CIM (computer-integrated manufacturing)	FIO (fabrication *(f)* intégrée par ordinateur)
circle: quality ...	cercle *(m)* de qualité
circulating capital	capitaux *(mpl)* circulants
	capitaux *(mpl)* roulants
	fonds *(mpl)* de roulement
classification: job ...	classification *(f)* des fonctions
clearing house	chambre *(f)* de compensation
clerical work measurement (CWM)	chronométrage *(m)* des travaux administratifs
clerical worker	employé *(m)* de bureau
climate: economic ...	conjoncture *(f)*
closed loop	boucle *(f)* fermée
closed shop	pratique *(f)* restrictive de recrutement imposée par les syndicats
closing-down costs	frais *(mpl)* de liquidation
co-determination	codétermination *(f)*

COINS (computerized information system)	système *(m)* d'information par ordinateur
collaborative	coopératif
collateral	gage *(m)*
	nantissement *(m)*
collateral security	nantissement *(m)*
	titre *(m)* déposé en garantie
collective bargaining	négociations *(fpl)* collectives
collective bargaining agreement	convention *(f)* collective (cc)
collusion	collusion *(f)*
command: chain of ...	hiérarchie *(f)* de commandement
command: line of ...	hiérarchie *(f)*
	voie *(f)* hiérarchique
commercial bank	banque *(f)* commerciale
commitment: capital ...	engagement *(m)* d'investissement
commitment: staff ...	engagement *(m)* du personnel
committee: works ...	comité *(m)* d'entreprise (CE)
commodity	produit *(m)*
commodity market	marché *(m)* de matières premières
commodity: primary ...	produit *(m)* de base
common currency	monnaie *(f)* commune
common language	langage *(m)* commun
Common Market	Marché Commun *(m)*
communication: channels of ...	canaux *(mpl)* de communication
	liaisons *(fpl)* dans l'entreprise
	voies *(fpl)* de communication
communication: electronic ...	télématique (f)
communications network	réseau *(m)* de communication
communications theory	théorie *(f)* des communications
company goal	but *(m)* de l'entreprise
company logo	logotype *(m)* de la société
company model	modèle *(m)* de l'entreprise
company objective	objectif *(m)* de l'entreprise
company objectives: overall	objectifs *(mpl)* globaux de l'entreprise
company philosophy	philosophie *(f)* de l'entreprise
company planning	planification *(f)* de l'entreprise
company policy	politique *(f)* de l'entreprise
company profile	profil *(m)* de l'entreprise
company reconstruction	reconstitution *(f)* de la société

company strategy	stratégie (f) de l'entreprise
company structure	structure (f) de l'entreprise
company: affiliate ...	société (f) affiliée
	société (f) apparentée
company: associate ...	société (f) affiliée
	société (f) apparentée
company: holding ...	holding (m)
	société (f) de portefeuille
company: joint-venture ...	co-entreprise (f)
	société (f) d'exploitation en commun
company: parent ...	société (f) mère
company: publicly listed ...	société (f) cotée en bourse
company: quoted ...	société (f) cotée en bourse
company: subsidiary ...	filiale (f)
company: system-managed ...	entreprise (f) dirigée de façon systématisée
company: unlisted ...	société (f) non inscrite à la cote
comparison: inter-firm ...	comparaison (f) inter-entreprises
compartmentalize (to)	compartimenter
compatible	compatible
compensation: executive ...	rémunération (f) des cadres
competence: executive ...	compétence (f) de management
competence: job ...	compétence (f) dans le travail
competency	attribution (f)
competition	concurrence (f)
competition: fair ...	concurrence (f) raisonnable
competition: the ...	compétiteurs (mpl)
competition: unfair ...	concurrence (f) déloyale
competitive	compétitif
	concurrentiel
competitive advantage	avantage (m) concurrentiel
competitive edge	avance (f) sur les concurrents
competitive position	position (f) concurrentielle
competitive price	prix (m) défiant la concurrence
competitive stimulus	stimulant (m) compétitif
competitive strategy	stratégie (f) concurrentielle
competitive tactics	tactique (f) concurrentielle
competitive tendering	soumission (f) concurrentielle
competitive thrust	percée (f) commerciale

competitiveness	compétitivité *(f)*
competitor analysis	analyse *(f)* des concurrents
complex: production …	complexe *(m)* de production
comptroller	contrôleur *(m)* de gestion
	vérificateur *(m)* des comptes
computer	ordinateur *(m)*
computer-aided design (CAD)	conception *(f)* assistée par ordinateur (CAO)
computer-aided learning (CAL)	enseignement *(m)* assisté par ordinateur (EAO)
computer-aided manufacturing (CAM)	fabrication *(f)* assistée par ordinateur (FAO)
computer-assisted teaching (CAT)	enseignement *(m)* automatisé
computer bank	banque *(f)* de données
	fichier *(m)* central
computer-based training (CBT)	enseignement *(m)* assisté par ordinateur (EAO)
computer centre	centre *(m)* de calcul
computer consultant	conseil *(m)* en informatique
computer expert	informaticien *(m)*
computer input	entrée *(f)* de l'ordinateur
	input *(m)* de l'ordinateur
computer-integrated manufacturing (CIM)	fabrication *(f)* intégrée par ordinateur (FIO)
computer language	langage *(m)* machine
computer literate	versé en informatique *(f)*
computer memory	mémoire *(f)* d'ordinateur
computer output	output *(m)* de l'ordinateur
	sortie *(f)* de l'ordinateur
computer program	programme *(m)* d'ordinateur
computer programmer	programmeur *(m)* sur ordinateur
computer programming	programmation *(f)*
computer services	services *(mpl)* en informatique
computer services bureau	façonnier *(m)*
computer simulation	simulation *(f)* par ordinateur
computer storage	mémoire *(f)* (d'un ensemble électronique)
computer terminal	terminal *(m)* d'ordinateur
computer virus	virus *(m)* informatique

computer: analog ...	ordinateur *(m)* analogique
computer: desktop ...	ordinateur *(m)* de bureau
computer: digital ...	calculateur *(m)* numérique
computer: laptop ...	ordinateur *(m)* portatif
computer: personal ... (PC)	ordinateur *(m)* personnel
computerize (to)	automatiser
	informatiser
computerized information system (COINS)	système *(m)* d'information par ordinateur
computerized management	gestion *(f)* automatisée
concept: value ...	concept *(m)* de valeur
conception: product ...	conception *(f)* de produits
conciliate (to)	concilier
conciliation	conciliation *(f)*
conditions (*of a contract*)	cahier *(m)* des charges
conditions of employment	conditions *(fpl)* d'embauche
confidentiality	caractère *(m)* confidentiel
conglomerate	conglomérat *(m)*
consciousness: cost ...	conscience *(f)* des coûts
consensus	consensus *(m)*
consolidated accounts	bilan *(m)* consolidé
consolidation	consolidation *(f)*
	fusion *(f)*
consortium	consortium *(m)*
constraint: budget ...	contrainte *(f)* budgétaire
consult (to)	consulter
consultancy: management ...	cabinet *(m)* de conseil en gestion
consultant	expert-conseil *(m)*
consultant: computer ...	conseil *(m)* en informatique
consultant: management ...	conseil *(m)* en direction
	conseil *(m)* en gestion
	ingénieur-conseil *(m)*
consultation: joint ...	consultations *(fpl)* paritaires
consultative	consultatif
consumer acceptance	réceptivité *(f)* des consommateurs
consumer behaviour	comportement *(m)* du consommateur
consumer durables	produits *(mpl)* de consommation durable
consumer goods	biens *(mpl)* de consommation

consumer goods: fast-moving ... ... (FMG)	biens *(mpl)* de consommation courante
consumer orientation	orientation *(f)* vers le consommateur
consumer price index	indice *(m)* des prix à la consommation
consumer protection	protection *(f)* du consommateur
consumer research	recherche *(f)* des besoins des consommateurs
consumer resistance	résistance *(f)* des consommateurs
consumer-responsive	sensible au consommateur
consumer satisfaction	satisfaction *(f)* du consommateur
consumerism	consommérisme *(m)*
consumers' panel	panel *(m)* de consommateurs
container	conteneur *(m)*
containerization	containeurisation *(f)*
content: work ...	contenu *(m)* du travail
contingencies	faux frais *(mpl)* divers
contingency planning	tenant compte de l'imprévu
contingency reserve	fonds *(mpl)* de prévoyance
contingency theory	théorie *(f)* de la contingence
continuous-flow production	production *(f)* continue
continuous stocktaking	inventaire *(m)* permanent
contract hire	location *(f)* longue durée
contract out (to)	sous-traiter
contract: management ...	contrat *(m)* du management
contract: work by ...	travail *(m)* à forfait
contracting out	prestation *(f)* extérieure de services
contraction of authority	limitation *(f)* d'autorité
contribution analysis	analyse *(f)* des contributions (à la marge)
control	contrôle *(m)*
	contrôle *(m)* de gestion
control information	information *(f)* de contrôle
control: adaptive ...	contrôle *(m)* adaptif
control: administrative ... procedure	procédé *(m)* de contrôle de gestion
control: batch ...	contrôle *(m)* par lots
control: board ...	contrôle *(m)* du conseil d'administration
control: budgetary ...	contrôle *(m)* budgétaire
	contrôle *(m)* de gestion

control: budgeting ...	contrôle *(m)* budgétaire
control: cost ...	contrôle *(m)* des coûts
control: financial ...	contrôle *(m)* financier
control: inventory ...	contrôle *(m)* des stocks
	gestion *(f)* des stocks
control: managerial ...	contrôle *(m)* de direction
control: manufacturing ...	contrôle *(m)* de fabrication
control: numerical ...	commande *(f)* numérique
control: process ...	commande *(f)* de processus
	régulation *(f)* de processus
control: production ...	gestion *(f)* de la production
	régulation *(f)* de la production
	surveillance *(f)* de la production
control: production planning and ...	projet *(m)* et contrôle *(m)* de la production
control: progress ...	contrôle *(m)* de la production
control: quality ... (QC)	contrôle *(m)* de la qualité
control: span of ...	étendue *(f)* des responsabilités
control: statistical ...	contrôle *(m)* statistique
control: stock ...	contrôle *(m)* des stocks
	gestion *(f)* des stocks
control: total quality ... (TQC)	contrôle *(m)* de la qualité globale (CQG)
controller	contrôleur *(m)* de gestion
	vérificateur *(m)* de comptes
controlling interest	participation *(f)* majoritaire
convenience goods	produits *(mpl)* de consommation courante
coordination	coordination *(f)*
core product	produit *(m)* leader
corner	monopole *(m)*
corner (to)	accaparer
corner the market (to)	accaparer le marché
corporate advertising	publicité *(f)* de prestige
corporate culture	culture *(f)* d'entreprise
corporate goal	but *(m)* de l'entreprise
corporate growth	croissance *(f)* de l'entreprise
corporate image	image *(f)* de l'entreprise
corporate mission	vocation *(f)* de la société

corporate model	modèle *(m)* de l'entreprise
corporate objective	objectif *(m)* de l'entreprise
corporate planning	planification *(f)* de l'entreprise
corporate policy	politique *(f)* de l'entreprise
corporate raider	prédateur *(m)*
corporate strategy	stratégie *(f)* de l'entreprise
corporate structure	structure *(f)* de l'entreprise
corporation tax	impôt *(m)* sur les sociétés
corporation: business ...	société *(f)* commerciale
corporatism	corporatisme *(m)*
correlate (to)	mettre en corrélation *(f)*
correlation	corrélation *(f)*
cost accounting	comptabilité *(f)* analytique
	comptabilité *(f)* industrielle
	comptabilité *(f)* de prix de revient
cost allocation	affectation *(f)* des charges
	imputation *(f)* des charges
cost analysis	analyse *(f)* du prix de revient
	étude *(f)* des charges
cost apportionment	répartition *(f)* des charges
cost awareness	connaissance *(f)* des coûts
cost-benefit analysis (CBA)	analyse *(f)* coût-profit
	analyse *(f)* des avantages-coûts
cost centre	centre *(m)* de coûts
cost consciousness	conscience *(f)* des coûts
cost control	contrôle *(m)* des coûts
cost-effective	rentable
cost-effectiveness	coût-efficacité *(m)*
cost-efficient	coût-efficace
	productif
cost factor	élément *(m)* du prix de revient
	facteur *(m)* coût
cost of living	coût *(m)* de la vie
cost of production	coût *(m)* de production
cost-push inflation	inflation *(f)* par les coûts
cost reduction	réduction *(f)* des coûts
cost-sensitive	sensible au coût
cost standard	norme *(f)* de prix de revient
cost structure	structure *(f)* des coûts

cost variance	écart *(m)* des coûts
cost-volume-profit analysis	analyse *(f)* volume-coûts-profits
cost: full-... method	méthode *(f)* des coûts complets
costing	établissement *(m)* des prix de revient
	évaluation *(f)* des coûts
costing: absorption ...	méthode *(f)* des coûts d'absorption
	méthode *(f)* des coûts complets
costing: direct ...	méthode *(f)* des coûts directs
	méthode *(f)* du coût proportionnel
costing: functional ...	*rationalisation (f) des choix budgétaires (RCB)*
costing: marginal ...	comptabilité *(f)* marginale
	méthode *(f)* des coûts marginaux
costing: product ...	comptabilité *(f)* industrielle
costing: standard ...	méthode *(f)* des coûts standards
costs: allocation of ...	affectation *(f)* des charges
	imputation *(f)* des charges
costs: average ...	coûts *(mpl)* moyens
costs: closing-down ...	frais *(mpl)* de liquidation
costs: direct ...	coûts *(mpl)* directs
costs: distribution ...	coûts *(mpl)* de la distribution
costs: estimating systems ...	évaluation *(f)* des coûts de systèmes
costs: fixed ...	coûts *(mpl)* constants
	coûts *(mpl)* fixes
costs: indirect ...	coûts *(mpl)* indirects
costs: managed ...	coûts *(mpl)* contrôlés
costs: marginal ...	coûts *(mpl)* marginaux
costs: opportunity ...	coûts *(mpl)* d'opportunité
costs: replacement ...	coûts *(mpl)* de remplacement
costs: semi-variable ...	charges *(fpl)* semi-variables
costs: set-up ...	frais *(mpl)* d'établissement
costs: standard ...	coûts *(mpl)* standards
costs: start-up ...	frais *(mpl)* de démarrage
costs: variable ...	coûts *(mpl)* variables
costs: unit labour ...	coûts *(mpl)* unitaires du personnel
council: works ...	comité *(m)* d'entreprise (CE)
counselling: employee ...	conseil *(m)* des employés
countertrade	contrepartie *(f)*
cover ratio	taux *(m)* de couverture

coverage: sales ...	couverture *(f)* du marché
CPA (critical path analysis)	analyse *(f)* du chemin critique
CPM (critical path method)	méthode *(f)* du chemin critique
CPU (central processing unit)	processeur *(m)* central
crash	krach *(m)*
crash (to) (*a program*)	se planter
creative accounting	comptabilité *(f)* assouplie
creative marketing	créativité *(f)* commerciale
creative thinking	matière *(f)* grise
	pensée *(f)* créatrice
credit control	contrôle *(m)* de crédit
credit management	gestion *(f)* de crédit
credit rating	réputation *(f)* de solvabilité
	standing *(m)*
credit squeeze	restriction *(f)* du crédit
credit: revolving ...	crédit *(m)* permanent
crisis management	gestion *(f)* des crises
criteria: investment ...	critères *(mpl)* d'investissement
critical mass	masse *(f)* critique
critical path analysis (CPA)	analyse *(f)* du chemin critique
critical path method (CPM)	méthode *(f)* du chemin critique
cross-licensing	concession *(f)* réciproque de licences
culture	culture *(f)*
culture: corporate ...	culture *(f)* d'entreprise
culture: organization ...	culture *(f)* de l'organisation
currency: common ...	monnaie *(f)* commune
currency: parallel ...	monnaie *(f)* parallèle
currency: single ...	monnaie *(f)* unique
current assets	actif *(m)* circulant
	actif *(m)* réalisable
current expenditure	frais *(mpl)* d'exploitation
current liabilities	dettes *(fpl)* à court terme
	exigibilités *(f)*
	passif *(m)* exigible
current ratio	coefficient *(m)* de liquidité
	ratio *(m)* de liquidité
current: net ... assets	fonds *(mpl)* de roulement net
cursor	curseur *(m)*
curve: learning ...	courbe *(f)* d'accoutumance

curve: salary progression ...	courbe *(f)* d'augmentation de salaire
custom and practice	us *(mpl)* et coutumes *(fpl)*
custom-made	fabriqué sur commande *(f)*
customer care	souci *(m)* du client
customer orientation	orientation *(f)* vers le client
customer profile	profil *(m)* de la clientèle
customer service	service *(m)* à la clientèle
customer: prospective ...	prospect *(m)*
customized	personnalisé
cut one's losses (to)	faire la part du feu
cut prices (to)	brader les prix
cut-back: staff ...	réduction *(f)* du personnel
cut-off point	seuil *(m)* de rentabilité
cutting edge	point *(m)* limite
cutting: price- ...	gâchage *(m)* des prix
CWM (clerical work measurement)	chronométrage *(m)* des travaux administratifs
cybernetics	cybernétique *(f)*
cycle: business ...	cycle *(m)* économique
cycle: life ... (*of a product*)	courbe *(f)* de vie *(d'un produit)*
	cycle *(m)* de vie *(d'un produit)*
cycle: trade ...	cycle *(m)* économique
cycle: work ...	cycle *(m)* de travail

D

daisy wheel	marguerite *(f)*
damage limitation	limitation *(f)* des dommages
data acquisition	acquisition *(f)* de données
	saisie *(f)* de données
data bank	banque *(f)* de données
	fichier *(m)* central
data base	base *(f)* de données
data flow chart	organigramme *(m)* de données
data gathering	collecte *(f)* de données
	rassemblement *(m)* de données statistiques
	recueil *(m)* de données statistiques

data processing	informatique *(f)*
	traitement *(m)* des données
data protection	protection *(f)* des données
data retrieval	extraction *(f)* de données
data: automatic ... processing (ADP)	traitement *(m)* automatique des données (TAD)
data: electronic ... processing (EDP)	traitement *(m)* électronique de l'information (TEI)
date: due ...	échéance *(f)*
date: expected ...	date *(f)* au plus tôt
date: latest ...	date *(f)* au plus tard
date: sell-by ...	date *(f)* limite de vente
date: use-by ...	date *(m)* limite de consommation
day shift	équipe *(f)* de jour
DCF (discounted cash flow)	cash-flow *(m)* actualisé
deadline	date *(f)* limite
	délai *(m)*
deal	affaire *(f)*
	marché *(m)*
deal: cash ...	transaction *(f)* au comptant
deal: package ...	panier *(m)*
deal: reach a ... (to)	conclure une affaire
dealer	dépositaire *(m)*
dealing: insider ...	délit *(m)* d'initié
debenture	obligation *(f)*
debottleneck (to)	désengorger
debrief (to)	debriefer
	faire le bilan
debriefing	debriefing *(m)*
	réunion *(f)* de mise au point
debt financing	financement *(m)* par l'emprunt
debt ratio	ratio *(m)* d'endettement
debt-equity ratio	rapport *(m)* dettes-actions
debtor	débiteur *(m)*
debts: bad ...	créances *(fpl)* douteuses
	mauvaises créances *(fpl)*
debug (to)	mettre au point
	dépanner

decentralization	décentralisation *(f)*
decentralize (to)	décentraliser
decentralized management	gestion *(f)* décentralisée
decision analysis	analyse *(f)* de la décision
decision-making	prise *(f)* de décision
decision model	modèle *(m)* de décision
decision process	processus *(m)* de la décision
decision theory	théorie *(f)* des décisions
decision tree	arbre *(m)* de décision
deductible: tax-...	déductible fiscalement
defensive strategy	stratégie *(f)* défensive
deficit financing	financement *(m)* par le déficit
deindustrialization	déindustrialisation *(f)*
delegate (to)	déléguer
delegation	délégation *(f)*
delivery time	délai *(m)* de livraison
demand assessment	évaluation *(f)* de la demande
demand forecasting	prévision *(f)* de la demande
demand-pull inflation	inflation *(f)* par la demande
demanning	dégraissage *(m)*
demerger	défusion *(f)*
democracy: industrial ...	démocratie *(f)* industrielle
demotivate (to)	démotiver
demotivation	démotivation *(f)*
department: accounting ...	services *(mpl)* comptables
department: engineering and design ...	bureau *(m)* d'études
	service *(m)* technique
department: marketing ...	service *(m)* de marketing
department: personnel ...	direction *(f)* du personnel
	service *(m)* du personnel
department: planning ...	bureau *(m)* de planning
	service *(m)* planning
department: research ...	bureau *(m)* d'études
	service *(m)* de recherche
department: sales ...	département *(m)* commercial
	services *(mpl)* commerciaux
departmental head	chef *(m)* d'atelier
departmental management	gestion *(f)* par département
departmental manager	chef *(m)* de service

departmental plan	plan *(m)* de divisions
departmentalization	départementalisation *(f)*
deploy (to)	déployer
deployment	déploiement *(m)*
depreciate (to)	amortir
	diminuer de valeur *(f)*
depreciation allowance	provision *(f)* pour amortissement
depth analysis	analyse *(f)* en profondeur
depth interview	interview *(f)* en profondeur
deputy chairman	vice-président *(m)*
deputy manager	directeur *(m)* adjoint
deputy managing director	directeur *(m)* général adjoint
deregulate (to)	dérégler
deregulation	déréglementation *(f)*
description: job ...	définition *(f)* de fonction
	description *(f)* de poste
design engineering	étude *(f)* de conception
design office	bureau *(m)* d'études
	bureau *(m)* de dessin
design: computer-aided ... (CAD)	conception *(f)* assistée par ordinateur (CAO)
design: engineering and ...	bureau *(m)* d'études
department	service *(m)* technique
design: job ...	conception *(f)* de tâche
design: product ...	conception *(f)* du produit
	dessin *(m)* de produit
design: systems ...	conception *(f)* des systèmes
desk research	recherche *(f)* documentaire
desktop computer	ordinateur *(m)* de bureau
desktop publish (to)	micro-éditer
desktop publishing	micro-édition *(f)*
	publication *(f)* assistée par ordinateur (PAO)
determination: price ...	établissement *(m)* des prix
	fixation *(f)* des prix
developer	promoteur *(m)*
development potential	potentiel *(m)* de développement
development programme	programme *(m)* de développement
development: executive ...	perfectionnement *(m)* des cadres

development: human resource ... (HRD)	développement *(m)* des ressources humaines
development: management ...	formation *(f)* au management perfectionnement *(m)* des cadres
development: new-product ...	développement *(m)* de produits nouveaux
development: organizational ...	développement *(m)* organisationnel
development: product ...	développement *(m)* de produits
development: research and ... (R&D)	recherche *(f)* et développement *(m)* (R et D)
deviation: standard ...	écart *(m)* type
diagnostic routine	programme *(m)* de diagnostic
diagram: flow ...	diagramme *(m)* de circulation organigramme *(m)*
diagram: scatter ...	diagramme *(m)* de dispersion
different ball game	autre paire *(f)* de manches
differential price	prix *(m)* différentiel
differential pricing	fixation *(f)* de prix différents pour un même produit
differential: earnings ...	écart *(m)* de rémunération
differential: price ...	différence *(f)* des prix
differential: wage ...	écarts *(mpl)* salariaux
differentiate (to)	différencier
differentiate: product ... (to)	se différencier
differentiation: product ...	différenciation *(f)* des produits
digital	numérique
digital computer	calculateur *(m)* numérique
digitize (to)	numériser
dilution of equity	dilution *(f)* du bénéfice par action
dilution of labour	adjonction *(f)* de main-d'oeuvre non qualifiée
direct costs	coûts *(mpl)* directs
direct costing	méthode *(f)* des coûts directs méthode *(f)* du coût proportionnel
direct expenses	charges *(fpl)* directes
direct labour	main-d'oeuvre *(f)* directe
direct mail	publicité *(f)* directe
direct marketing	marketing *(m)* direct
direct selling	vente *(f)* directe

director	directeur *(m)*
	dirigeant *(m)*
director: assistant ...	directeur *(m)* adjoint
director: deputy managing ...	directeur *(m)* général adjoint
director: executive ...	directeur *(m)* général
director: financial ...	directeur *(m)* financier
director: managing ... (MD)	président *(m)*-directeur général (PDG)
director: non-executive ...	administrateur *(m)*
director: outside ...	administrateur *(m)*
director: production ...	directeur *(m)* de fabrication
directorate: interlocking ...	direction *(f)* intriquée
directors: board of ...	direction *(f)* générale
disburse (to)	débourser
disbursement	débours *(m)*
discounted cash flow (DCF)	cash-flow *(m)* actualisé
discretion: time span of ...	délai *(m)* de réflexion
discriminate (to)	discriminer
discrimination	discrimination *(f)*
discrimination: positive ...	discrimination *(f)* positive
discrimination: price ...	discrimination *(f)* de prix
diseconomy of scale	déséconomie *(f)* d'échelle
disincentive	effet *(m)* décourageant
disintegration	désincorporation *(f)*
disinvestment	désinvestissement *(m)*
disk	disque *(m)*
disk drive	unité *(f)* de disques
disk: floppy ...	disque *(m)* souple
	disquette *(f)*
disk: hard ...	disque *(m)* dur
disk: Winchester ...	disque *(m)* winchester
dismissal	licenciement *(m)*
dismissal: summary ...	licenciement *(m)* sommaire
dismissal: unfair ...	licenciement *(m)* abusif
dispatching	acheminement *(m)*
	expédition *(f)*
display unit	unité *(f)* d'affichage
display unit: visual ... ... (VDU)	unité *(f)* de visualisation
	visuel *(m)*
disposable income	revenu *(m)* disponible

disposition: source and ... of funds	ressources *(fpl)* et emplois *(mpl)* de capitaux
dispute: industrial ...	conflit *(m)* social
dispute: labour ...	conflit *(m)* du travail
dissolution	dissolution *(f)*
distance learning	télé-enseignement *(m)*
distributed profit	bénéfices *(mpl)* distribués
distribution	distribution *(f)*
distribution channel	réseau *(m)* de distribution
distribution costs	coûts *(mpl)* de la distribution
distribution manager	chef *(m)* de la distribution
distribution network	réseau *(m)* de distribution
distribution planning	planning *(m)* de distribution
distribution policy	politique *(f)* de distribution
distribution: chain of ...	circuit *(m)* de distribution
distribution: frequency ...	distribution *(f)* des fréquences
distribution: physical ... management	gestion *(f)* de la distribution physique
diversification	diversification *(f)*
diversification strategy	stratégie *(f)* de diversification
diversification: product ...	diversification *(f)* des produits
diversify (to)	diversifier
divestment	scission *(f)* d'actif
dividend	dividende *(m)*
dividend policy	politique *(f)* de (versement des) dividendes
division: operating ...	division *(f)* opérationnelle
divisional management	gestion *(f)* cellulaire
	gestion *(f)* par département
doomwatcher	prophète *(m)* de malheur
double taxation relief	suppression *(f)* de la double imposition
down the line	subordonnés *(mpl)*
down-market	bas *(m)* de gamme
downstream	en aval *(m)*
downswing	dégradation *(f)* de l'activité
down time	durée *(f)* d'immobilisation
	temps *(m)* mort
downturn	baisse *(f)*
	ralentissement *(m)*

drift: wage ...	dérive *(f)* des salaires
drip-feeding	goutte à goutte
drive: advertising ...	campagne *(f)* de publicité
drive: disk ...	unité *(f)* de disques
drive: productivity ...	campagne *(f)* de productivité
drive: sales ...	animation *(f)* des ventes
dual sourcing	approvisionnement *(m)* de deux sources
due date	échéance *(f)*
dummy activity	activité *(f)* artificielle
dumping	dumping *(m)*
durables	produits *(mpl)* durables
durables: consumer ...	produits *(mpl)* de consommation durable
dynamic evaluation	analyse *(f)* dynamique
dynamic management model	modèle *(m)* dynamique de gestion
dynamic programming	programmation *(f)* dynamique
dynamics: group ...	dynamique *(f)* de groupe
dynamics: industrial ...	dynamique *(f)* industrielle
dynamics: market ...	dynamique *(f)* de marché
dynamics: product ...	dynamique *(f)* des produits
dysfunction	dysfonctionnement *(m)*

E

e-mail (electronic mail)	courrier *(m)* électronique
early retirement	retraite *(f)* anticipée
earning power	capacité *(f)* bénéficiaire
earnings differential	écart *(m)* de rémunération
earnings on assets	rendement *(m)* des fonds propres
earnings per share (EPS)	bénéfices *(mpl)* par action (BPA)
earnings performance	rentabilité *(f)*
earnings yield	rendement *(m)*
earnings: price-... ratio (P/E)	rapport *(m)* cours-bénéfices
	taux *(m)* de price-earnings
EC (European Community)	CE (Communauté *(f)* Européenne)
econometric	économétrique
economic batch quantity	effectif *(m)* de série économique

economic climate	conjoncture *(f)*
economic intelligence	information *(f)* économique
economic life	durée *(f)* de vie économique
economic manufacturing quantity	quantité *(f)* économique de production
	série *(f)* économique de fabrication
economic mission	mission *(f)* économique
economic order quantity	quantité *(f)* économique à commander
	quantité *(f)* optimale de commande
economic research	études *(fpl)* économiques
economic trend	conjoncture *(f)*
	évolution *(f)* économique
economist: business ...	économiste *(m)* d'entreprise
economy of scale	économie *(f)* d'échelle
economy: motion ...	économie *(f)* des mouvements
ECU (European Currency Unit)	écu *(m)* (Unité *(f)* de Compte Européenne)
ecu: hard ...	écu *(m)* lourd
edge: competitive ...	avance *(f)* sur les concurrents
edge: cutting ...	point *(m)* limite
edge: leading ...	avant-garde *(f)*
EDP (electronic data processing)	TEI (traitement *(m)* électronique de l'information)
effective management	direction *(f)* efficace
effective: cost-...	rentable
effectiveness	efficacité *(f)*
effectiveness: advertising ...	efficacité *(f)* publicitaire
effectiveness: cost-...	coût-efficacité *(m)*
effectiveness: managerial ...	efficacité *(f)* de la direction
effectiveness: organizational ...	efficacité *(f)* organisatrice
efficiency	efficacité *(f)*
	efficience *(f)*
	productivité *(f)*
	rendement *(m)*
efficiency audit	contrôle *(m)* d'efficience *(f)*
efficient	compétent
	efficace
efficient: cost-...	coût-efficace
	productif
effort: sales expansion ...	effort *(m)* d'accroissement des ventes

EFTPOS (electronic funds transfer at point of sale)	transfert *(m)* électronique de fonds au point de vente
elasticity	élasticité *(f)*
electronic accounting system	ensemble *(m)* électronique de gestion
electronic communication	télématique *(f)*
electronic data processing (EDP)	traitement *(m)* électronique de l'information (TEI)
electronic funds transfer at point of sale (EFTPOS)	transfert *(m)* électronique de fonds au point de vente
electronic mail (e-mail)	courrier *(m)* électronique
electronic office	bureau *(m)* électronique
electronic processing	traitement *(m)* informatique
empirical	empirique
employed: capital ...	capital *(m)* investi
employed: return on capital ... (ROCE)	rentabilité *(f)* des capitaux investis (RCI)
employee buyout	rachat *(m)* d'une entreprise par ses employés *(mpl)*
employee counselling	conseil *(m)* des employés
employee relations	relations *(fpl)* avec les employés relations *(fpl)* ouvrières
employees: front-line ...	personnel *(m)* du terrain
employment bureau	agence *(f)* de placement
employment: conditions of ...	conditions *(fpl)* d'embauche
employment: full-time ...	emploi *(m)* à plein temps
employment: part-time ...	travail *(m)* à mi-temps
EMS (European Monetary System)	SME (Système *(m)* Monétaire Européen)
EMU (European Monetary Union)	Union *(f)* Monétaire Européenne
engineer: sales ...	ingénieur *(m)* commercial
engineer: software ...	ingénieur *(m)* en logiciel
engineer: systems ...	ingénieur *(m)* système
engineering	engineering *(m)* ingénierie *(f)*
engineering and design department	bureau *(m)* d'études service *(m)* technique
engineering: design ...	étude *(f)* de conception
engineering: human ...	adaptation *(f)* du travail à l'homme ergonomie *(f)*

engineering: industrial ...	engineering *(m)* industriel
	organisation *(f)* industrielle
engineering: methods ...	étude *(f)* des méthodes
engineering: product ...	étude *(f)* de produit
engineering: production ...	techniques *(fpl)* de la production
engineering: systems ...	engineering *(m)* des systèmes
	mise *(f)* en oeuvre des systèmes
engineering: value ...	analyse *(f)* des coûts
	analyse *(f)* de la valeur
enlargement: job ...	élargissement *(m)* du travail
	extension *(f)* des tâches
enrichment: job ...	enrichissement *(m)* du travail
enterprise	entreprise *(f)*
enterprise: private ...	secteur *(m)* privé
enterprise: public ...	secteur *(m)* public
enterprising	entreprenant
entrepreneurial spirit	esprit *(m)* d'entreprise
environment	environnement *(m)*
environmental analysis	analyse *(f)* de l'environnement *(m)*
environmental forecasting	prévision *(f)* sur l'environnement
environmental scan	balayage *(m)* de l'environnement
EPS (earnings per share)	BPA (bénéfices *(mpl)* par action)
equal employment opportunity	égalité *(f)* des chances *(fpl)* face à l'emploi *(m)*
equal opportunity	égalité *(f)* des chances
equal pay	égalité *(f)* des salaires
equality	égalité *(f)*
equipment leasing	crédit-bail *(m)* immobilier
equipment: add-on ...	matériel *(m)* complémentaire
equipment: peripheral ...	unités *(fpl)* périphériques
equipment: process ... layout	production *(f)* groupée
equity	actif *(m)* net
	actions *(fpl)*
equity market	marché *(m)* des actions
equity: dilution of ...	dilution *(f)* du bénéfice par action
equity: return on ... (ROE)	rendement *(m)* des fonds propres
ergonometrics	mesure *(f)* du travail
ergonomics	adaptation *(f)* du travail à l'homme
	ergonomie *(f)*

ERM (Exchange Rate Mechanism)	mécanisme *(m)* de taux de change
escalation: price ...	flambée *(f)* des prix
espionage: industrial ...	espionnage *(m)* industriel
establishment	effectifs *(mpl)*
estimate: sales ...	estimation *(f)* des ventes
estimating systems costs	évaluation *(f)* des coûts de systèmes
Eurobond	euro-obligation *(f)*
Eurocurrency	eurodevise *(f)*
Eurodollar	eurodollar *(m)*
Euromarket	euromarché *(m)*
European Community (EC)	Communauté *(f)* Européenne (CE)
European Currency Unit (ECU)	Unité *(f)* de Compte Européenne (écu)
European Monetary System (EMS)	Système *(m)* Monétaire Européen (SME)
European Monetary Union (EMU)	Union *(f)* Monétaire Européenne
evaluate (to)	évaluer
evaluation: capital project ...	étude *(f)* de projet d'investissement
evaluation: dynamic ...	analyse *(f)* dynamique
evaluation: job ...	classification *(f)* des emplois
	évaluation *(f)* des emplois
	qualification *(f)* du travail
evaluation: performance ...	appréciation *(f)* des performances
ex gratia **payment**	paiement *(m)* à titre de faveur
exception: management by ...	gestion *(f)* par exception
excess capacity	surcapacité *(f)*
exchange rate	taux *(m)* de change
Exchange Rate Mechanism (ERM)	mécanisme *(m)* de taux de change
exchange rate: forward	taux *(m)* de change à terme
execution: policy ...	exécution *(f)* de la politique
executive	cadre *(m)*
	directeur *(m)*
executive advancement	auto-développement *(m)*
	promotion *(f)* des cadres
executive board	comité *(m)* de direction
	conseil *(m)* d'administration
	conseil *(m)* de direction

executive compensation	rémunération *(f)* des cadres
executive competence	compétence *(f)* de management
executive development	perfectionnement *(m)* des cadres
executive director	directeur *(m)* général
executive manpower strategy	stratégie *(f)* des cadres
executive promotion	promotion *(f)* des cadres
executive remuneration	rémunération *(f)* des cadres
executive search	*assistance (f) au recrutement des cadres*
	executive search (m)
executive training	formation *(f)* des cadres
executive: chief ...	directeur *(m)* général
executive: line ...	dirigeant *(m)* opérationnel
expansion strategy	stratégie *(f)* de croissance
	stratégie *(f)* d'expansion
expansion: sales ... effort	effort *(m)* d'accroissement des ventes
expectations: job ...	perspectives *(fpl)* de carrière
expectations: sales ...	ventes *(fpl)* anticipées
expected date	date *(f)* au plus tôt
expenditure: capital ... (capex)	dépenses *(fpl)* en capital *(m)*
expenditure: current ...	frais *(mpl)* d'exploitation
expense account	frais *(mpl)* de représentation
expenses: administrative ...	frais *(mpl)* administratifs
expenses: direct ...	charges *(fpl)* directes
expenses: indirect ...	charges *(fpl)* indirectes
expenses: operating ...	charges *(fpl)* d'exploitation
expenses: petty ...	menues dépenses *(fpl)*
expenses: recovery of ...	recouvrement *(m)* des dépenses
	récupération *(f)* des frais
expenses: running ...	charges *(fpl)* d'exploitation
	dépenses *(fpl)* de fonctionnement
expert system	système *(m)* expert
expert: computer ...	informaticien *(m)*
exploration: market ...	prospection *(f)* des marchés
exponential smoothing	lissage *(m)* exponentiel
exponential trend	tendance *(f)* exponentielle
extension services	services *(mpl)* logistiques
external relations	relations *(fpl)* extérieures

externalities   extériorités *(fpl)*
externalize (to)   extérioriser

F

facility: borrowing ...   source *(f)* d'emprunts
facsimile   télécopie *(f)*
factor   coefficient *(m)*
                                 facteur *(m)*
                                 indice *(m)*
                                 moyen *(m)* de production
factor: cost ...   élément *(m)* du prix de revient
                                 facteur *(m)* coût
factor: load ...   coefficient *(m)* d'utilisation de la
                                     capacité
                                 facteur *(m)* de charge
                                 indice *(m)* de charge
factor: profit-... analysis   analyse *(f)* des facteurs de profit
factoring   affacturage *(m)*
                                 factorage *(m)*
                                 factoring *(m)*
factors of production   facteurs *(mpl)* de production
factory overheads   frais *(mpl)* généraux de fabrication
failure (*of firm*)   défaillance *(f)* (*de l'entreprise*)
fair competition   concurrence *(f)* raisonnable
fair return   rendement *(m)* équitable
family tree   arbre *(m)* généalogique
fast-moving consumer goods   biens *(mpl)* de consommation courante
  (FMG)
fast-track   parcours *(m)* rapide
                                 voie *(f)* rapide
fax (to)   télécopier
fax   télécopie *(f)*
fax machine   télécopieur *(m)*
feasibility study   étude *(f)* de faisabilité
                                 étude *(f)* préalable
feasible   faisable
                                 réalisable

featherbedding	*limitation (f) des heures de travail pour éviter le chômage*
	subvention *(f)* à une industrie
feedback	feedback *(m)*
	réaction *(f)*
	rétroaction *(f)*
fiddle (to)	traficoter
field research	recherche *(f)* sur le terrain
field testing	test *(m)* sur place
figure: ballpark ...	chiffre *(m)* approximatif
finance (to)	financer
financial administration	gestion *(f)* financière
financial analysis	analyse *(f)* financière
	diagnostic *(m)* financier
financial appraisal	évaluation *(f)* financière
financial control	contrôle *(m)* financier
financial director	directeur *(m)* financier
financial futures	contrat *(m)* à terme d'instruments financiers (CATIF)
financial incentive	incitation *(f)* financière
financial involvement	intéressement *(m)*
financial management	direction *(f)* financière
	gestion *(f)* financière
financial market	place *(f)* financière
financial planning	plan *(m)* financier
financial position	situation *(f)* financière
financial ratio	ratio *(m)* financier
financial review	examen *(m)* financier
financial standard	norme *(f)* financière
financial statement	état *(m)* financier
	rapport *(m)* financier
financial strategy	stratégie *(f)* financière
financial year	exercice *(m)*
financing	financement *(m)*
financing: debt ...	financement *(m)* par l'emprunt
financing: deficit ...	financement *(m)* par le déficit
financing: self-...	autofinancement *(m)*
fire (to)	licencier
	renvoyer

firing: hiring and ...	embauchage *(m)* et renvoi *(m)*
first-line manager	chef *(m)* d'atelier
	contremaître *(m)*
	surveillant *(m)* de premier niveau
fiscal drag	décalage *(m)* fiscal
fiscal policy	politique *(f)* fiscale
fiscal year	année *(f)* budgétaire
	exercice *(m)* financier
fixed assets	actif *(m)* immobilisé
	capitaux *(mpl)* permanents
	immobilisations *(fpl)*
	valeurs *(fpl)* immobilisées
fixed costs	coûts *(mpl)* constants
	coûts *(mpl)* fixes
fixed expenses	frais *(mpl)* fixes
flexible budget	budget *(m)* flexible
flexible firm	firme *(f)* souple et mobile
flexible working hours	horaire *(m)* à la carte
	horaire *(m)* variable
flexitime	horaire *(m)* souple
	horaire *(m)* variable
floppy disk (floppy)	disque *(m)* souple
	disquette *(f)*
flotation	lancement *(m)*
flow chart	graphique *(m)* d'acheminement
	graphique *(m)* de circulation
flow chart: data	organigramme *(m)* de données
flow diagram	diagramme *(m)* de circulation
	organigramme *(m)*
flow line	ligne *(f)* de production
flow process chart	diagramme *(m)* de circulation
	graphique *(m)* d'acheminement
flow production	fabrication *(f)* à la chaîne
flow: cash ...	cash-flow *(m)*
	marge *(f)* brute d'autofinancement (MBA)
	produit *(m)* disponible
flow: continuous-... production	production *(f)* continue

flow: discounted cash ... (DCF)	cash-flow *(m)* actualisé (méthode DCF)
flow: funds	mouvement *(m)* de fonds
flow: incremental cash ...	cash-flow *(m)* marginal
flow: information ...	flux *(m)* de l'information
FMG (fast-moving consumer goods)	biens *(mpl)* de consommation courante
focus (to)	focaliser
focus	point *(m)* focal
follow up (to)	suivre
follow-up	follow-up *(m)*
	rappel *(m)*
	suivi *(m)*
force: sales ...	équipe *(f)* de vente
force: task ...	groupe *(m)* d'intervention
forces: market ...	tendances *(fpl)* de marché
forecast	étude *(f)* prévisionnelle
	prévision *(f)*
forecast: budget ...	prévision *(f)* budgétaire
forecast: market ...	prévision *(f)* du marché
forecast: sales ...	prévision *(f)* des ventes
forecast: technological ...	prévision *(f)* technologique
forecasting	prévision *(f)*
forecasting: budget ...	prévision *(f)* budgétaire
forecasting: business ...	prévision *(f)* dans l'entreprise
forecasting: cash ...	prévision *(f)* de trésorerie
forecasting: demand ...	prévision *(f)* de la demande
forecasting: environmental ...	prévision *(f)* sur l'environnement
forecasting: manpower ...	prévision *(f)* de l'emploi
forecasting: staff ...	prévision *(f)* des effectifs
foreman	chef *(m)* d'équipe
formation: capital ...	formation *(f)* de capital
formulation: policy ...	expression *(f)* de la politique
formulation: strategy ...	élaboration *(f)* des stratégies
forward exchange rate	taux *(m)* de change à terme
forward market	marché *(m)* à terme
forward planning	plan *(m)* à longue échéance
forward rate	taux *(m)* pour les opérations à terme
forward swap	échange *(m)* financier à terme
forwarding	expédition *(f)*

forwarding agent	agent *(m)* expéditeur
	transitaire *(m)*
fractionalize (to)	fractionner
franchise (to)	franchiser
franchise	contrat *(m)* de franchisage
	franchise *(f)*
franchising	franchise *(f)*
freelance (to go)	travailler en indépendant
freeze (to)	bloquer
freeze: wage ...	blocage *(m)* des salaires
frequency distribution	distribution *(f)* des fréquences
friendly: user-...	convivial
fringe benefits	avantages *(mpl)* annexes
	avantages *(mpl)* sociaux
fringe market	marché *(m)* marginal
front-line employees	personnel *(m)* du terrain
full capacity	plein rendement *(m)*
full-cost method	méthode *(f)* des coûts complets
full-time employment	emploi *(m)* à plein temps
full-timer	employé *(m)* qui travaille à plein temps
function	fonction *(f)*
function key	touche *(f)* de fonction
function: managerial ...	fonction *(f)* de direction
functional	fonctionnel
functional analysis	analyse *(f)* fonctionnelle (AF)
functional approach	démarche *(f)* fonctionnelle
functional costing	*rationalisation (f) des choix budgétaires (RCB)*
functional layout	implantation *(f)* fonctionnelle
functional management	gestion *(f)* par fonctions
functional organization	organisation *(f)* fonctionnelle
	organisation *(f)* horizontale
functional relations	liaisons *(fpl)* fonctionnelles
functional responsibility	responsabilité *(f)* fonctionnelle
fund: sinking ...	fonds *(m)* d'amortissement
fund: slush ...	caisse *(f)* noire
funding	financement *(m)*
funds flow	mouvement *(m)* de fonds

funds: source and disposition of ...	ressources *(fpl)* et emplois *(mpl)* de capitaux
futures	contrats *(mpl)* à terme
futures market	marché *(m)* à terme
futures: financial ...	contrat *(m)* à terme d'instruments financiers

G

gain: capital ...	augmentation *(f)* de capital
	plus-value *(f)*
game theory	théorie *(f)* des jeux
game: business ...	jeu *(m)* d'entreprise
	simulation *(f)* de gestion
game: management ...	jeu *(m)* d'entreprise
	simulation *(f)* de gestion
game: zero-sum ...	jeu *(m)* à somme nulle
gap	écart *(m)*
gap study	étude *(f)* des écarts
gateway	passerelle *(f)*
gathering: data ...	collecte *(f)* de données
	rassemblement *(m)* de données
	recueil *(m)* de données
GDP (gross domestic product)	PIB (produit *(m)* intérieur brut)
gearing	effet *(m)* de levier
gearing ratio	ratio *(m)* d'endettement
general management	direction *(f)* générale
general manager	directeur *(m)* général
generate ideas (to)	produire des idées *(fpl)*
generation: product ...	création *(f)* du produit
generic	générique
gentleman's agreement	accord *(m)* à l'amiable
gilt	valeur *(f)* de premier ordre
gilt-edged security	valeur *(f)* de premier ordre
gilt-edged stock	valeur *(f)* de premier ordre
global image	image *(f)* globale
global marketing	marketing *(m)* global
globalization	mondialisation *(f)*
globalize (to)	mondialiser

GM (gross margin)	marge *(f)* brute
GNP (gross national product)	PNB (produit *(m)* national brut)
go public (to)	introduire en bourse
go-getter: be a ... (to)	avoir du punch
go-getting	arrivisme *(m)*
go-slow	grève *(f)* perlée
goal-seeking	recherche *(f)* des buts
goal-setting	établissement *(m)* des buts
	fixation *(f)* des buts
goal: company ...	but *(m)* de l'entreprise
goal: profit ...	but *(m)* de profit
goal: sales ...	objectif *(m)* de vente
goals: hierarchy of ...	hiérarchie *(f)* des objectifs
going rate	taux *(m)* en vigueur
golden handcuffs	menottes *(fpl)* dorées
golden handshake	prime *(f)* de départ
golden hello	pont *(m)* d'or
golden parachute	parapluie *(m)* doré
golden share	action *(f)* préférentielle
goods: brown ...	produits *(mpl)* bruns
goods: capital ...	biens *(mpl)* d'équipement
goods: consumer ...	biens *(mpl)* de consommation
goods: convenience ...	produits *(mpl)* de consommation courante
goods: fast-moving consumer ... (FMG)	biens *(mpl)* de consommation courante
goods: impulse ...	produits *(mpl)* d'appel
	produits *(mpl)* de choc
goods: industrial ...	biens *(mpl)* industriels
goods: investment ...	biens *(mpl)* d'équipement
goods: non-durable ...	produits *(mpl)* non durables
goods: white ...	produits *(mpl)* blancs
goodwill	achalandage *(m)*
	droit *(m)* à la clientèle
	fonds *(m)* commercial
	goodwill *(m)*
grade: salary ...	indice *(m)* de traitement
grapevine	téléphone *(m)* arabe
graphics	traitement *(m)* graphique

green issues	*questions (fpl) ayant rapport à l'environnement*
grey market	marché *(m)* gris
	marché *(f)* parallèle
grid structure	structure *(f)* en grille
grid: managerial ...	grille *(f)* de gestion
grievance	grief *(m)*
grievance procedure	procédure *(f)* pour résoudre des griefs
	procédure prud'hommale
gross domestic product (GDP)	produit *(m)* intérieur brut (PIB)
gross margin (GM)	marge *(f)* brute
gross national product (GNP)	produit *(m)* national brut (PNB)
gross profit	bénéfice *(m)* brut
group accounts	comptes *(mpl)* de groupe
group bonus	prime *(f)* collective
	prime *(f)* d'équipe
group dynamics	dynamique *(f)* de groupe
group incentive	prime *(f)* collective
	prime *(f)* d'équipe
group training	action *(f)* collective de formation
group: product ...	grille *(f)* de produits
	groupe *(m)* de produits
growth area	secteur *(m)* de croissance
growth index	indice *(m)* de croissance
growth industry	industrie *(f)* en croissance rapide
growth potential	potentiel *(m)* de croissance
growth strategy	stratégie *(f)* de croissance
growth: corporate ...	croissance *(f)* de l'entreprise
growth: organic ...	croissance *(f)* organique
growth: personal ...	autodéveloppement *(m)*
	développement *(m)* personnel
guesstimate	estimation *(f)* approximative
	estimation *(f)* au jugé
guidance: vocational ...	orientation *(f)* professionnelle (OP)
guideline	directive *(f)*

H

hacker	pirate *(m)*
hacking	effraction *(f)* informatique
halo effect	effet *(m)* de halo
handcuffs: golden ...	menottes *(fpl)* dorées
handling: information ...	manipulation *(f)* de l'information
	traitement *(m)* de l'information
handling: materials ...	manutention *(f)* (des marchandises)
hands-on	à commande manuelle
hands-on training	formation *(f)* pratique
handshake: golden ...	prime *(f)* de départ
harassment: sexual ...	harcèlement *(m)* sexuel
hard copy	recopie *(f)* d'écran
	vidéotrace *(f)*
hard disk	disque *(m)* dur
hard ecu	écu *(m)* lourd
hard landing	atterrissage *(m)* brutal
hard sell	vente *(f)* agressive
hardware	hardware *(m)*
	matériel *(m)*
harmonization	harmonisation *(f)*
harmonize (to)	harmoniser
hazard: occupational ...	risque *(m)* du métier
hazchem (hazardous chemicals)	produits *(mpl)* chimiques dangereux
head office	administration *(f)* centrale
	siège *(m)* social
head-hunt (to)	faire le search
head-hunter	chasseur *(m)* de têtes
hedge (to)	se couvrir
hedging	hedging *(m)*
	opération *(f)* de couverture
hello: golden ...	pont *(m)* d'or
heuristics	heuristique *(f)*
hidden agenda	programme *(m)* secret
hidden assets	actif *(m)* occulte
hierarchy of goals	hiérarchie *(f)* des objectifs

high-flier	cadre *(m)* à haut potentiel
	star *(m)*
high-tech	technologie *(f)* de pointe
hire (to)	embaucher
hire: contract ...	location *(f)* longue durée
hire: plant ...	location *(f)* d'équipement
hiring and firing	embauchage *(m)* et renvoi *(m)*
histogram	histogramme *(m)*
hive off (to)	rendre indépendant
hold margins (to)	maintenir les marges
holding company	holding *(m)*
	société *(f)* de portefeuille
holidays: staggered ...	étalement *(m)* des vacances
home country	pays *(m)* d'origine
horizontal integration	intégration *(f)* horizontale
host country	pays *(m)* d'accueil
hot money	capitaux *(mpl)* fébriles
house style	style *(m)* de l'entreprise
HRD (human resource development)	développement *(m)* des ressources humaines
HRM (human resource management)	gestion *(f)* des ressources humaines
HRP (human resource planning)	planification *(f)* des ressources humaines
human engineering	adaptation *(f)* du travail à l'homme
	ergonomie *(f)*
human relations	relations *(fpl)* humaines
human resource development (HRD)	développement *(m)* des ressources humaines
human resource management (HRM)	gestion *(f)* des ressources humaines
human resource planning (HRP)	planification *(f)* des ressources humaines
human resources	ressources *(fpl)* humaines
hustle (to)	bousculer
hygiene factors	facteurs *(mpl)* d'hygiène
	facteurs *(mpl)* extrinsèques
hype	hyperbole *(f)*

I

idle capacity	capacité *(f)* inutilisée
image: brand ...	image *(f)* de marque
image: corporate ...	image *(f)* de l'entreprise
image: global ...	image *(f)* globale
image: product ...	image *(f)* de produit
imaging	élaboration *(f)* de l'image
imbalance: trade ...	déséquilibre *(m)* commercial
impact	impact *(m)*
	influence *(f)*
impact: profit ...	incidence *(f)* sur le profit
implement (to)	exécuter
implementation: strategy ...	application *(f)* des stratégies
implication: profit ...	répercussion *(f)* sur les bénéfices
import: parallel ...	importation *(f)* parallèle
improvement: job ...	amélioration *(f)* des tâches
improvement: product ...	amélioration *(f)* de produit
improvement: profit ...	amélioration *(f)* de la rentabilité
impulse buying	achat *(m)* impulsif
impulse goods	produits *(mpl)* d'appel
impulse sale	vente *(f)* de choc
	vente *(f)* d'appel
in-company	interne
in-depth interview	interview *(f)* en profondeur
in-house	interne
in-plant training	formation *(f)* dans l'entreprise
incentive	incitation *(f)*
	stimulant *(m)*
incentive scheme	programme *(m)* de stimulants salariaux
incentive wage	salaire *(m)* au rendement
	salaire *(m)* stimulant
incentive: financial ...	incitation *(f)* financière
incentive: group ...	prime *(f)* collective
	prime *(f)* d'équipe
incentive: tax ...	incitation *(f)* fiscale
income tax	impôt *(m)* sur le revenu
income tax: negative	impôt *(m)* négatif sur le revenu

income: disposable ...	revenu (m) disponible
income: real ...	revenu (m) réel
increase: price ...	majoration (f) de prix
incremental	incrémentiel (ordinateur)
	marginal
	par augmentation (f)
incremental analysis	analyse (f) marginale
incremental cash flow	cash-flow (m) marginal
index number	indice (m)
index: consumer price ...	indice (m) des prix à la consommation
index: growth ...	indice (m) de croissance
index: retail price ... (RPI)	indice (m) des prix de détail
indicator: performance ...	clignotant (m)
	indicateur (m) de performance
indirect costs	coûts (mpl) indirects
indirect expenses	charges (fpl) indirectes
indirect labour	main-d'oeuvre (f) indirecte
induction	accueil (m)
	mise (f) au courant (du personnel)
industrial action	action (f) revendicative
	mouvements (mpl) sociaux
industrial democracy	démocratie (f) industrielle
industrial dispute	conflit (m) social
industrial dynamics	dynamique (f) industrielle
industrial engineering	engineering (m) industriel
industrial espionage	espionnage (m) industriel
industrial goods	biens (mpl) industriels
industrial injury	accident (m) du travail
industrial psychology	psychologie (f) industrielle
industrial relations	relations (fpl) industrielles
	relations (fpl) professionnelles
	relations (fpl) syndicales
industrial safety	sécurité (f) industrielle
industrial security	contre-espionnage (m) industriel
industrial waste	déchets (mpl) industriels
industry: growth ...	industrie (f) en croissance
industry: sunrise ...	industrie (f) en croissance
industry: sunset ...	industrie (f) en déclin
industry: training within ... (TWI)	formation (f) dans l'entreprise

inflation: cost-push ...	inflation *(f)* par les coûts
inflation: demand-pull ...	inflation *(f)* par la demande
inflationary pressure	pression *(f)* inflationniste
informal organization	organisation *(f)* informelle
informatics	informatique *(f)*
information flow	flux *(m)* de l'information
information handling	manipulation *(f)* de l'information
	traitement *(m)* de l'information
information network	réseau *(m)* d'information
information processing	traitement *(m)* de l'information
information retrieval	extraction *(f)* de données
	récupération *(f)* de l'information
information system	système *(m)* d'information
information technology	informatique *(f)*
information theory	théorie *(f)* de l'information
information: computerized ... system	système *(m)* d'information
(COINS)	par ordinateur
information: control ...	information *(f)* de contrôle
information: management ...	information *(f)* d'organisation de la
	gestion
information: management ... system	système *(m)* d'information de
(MIS)	management (SIM)
infrastructure	infrastructure *(f)*
injury: industrial ...	accident *(m)* du travail
innovate (to)	innover
innovative	novateur
input	facteurs *(mpl)* de production
	input *(m)*
	moyens *(mpl)* de production
input (*data*)	données *(fpl)* d'entrée
input-output analysis	analyse *(f)* entrées-sorties
input-output table	tableau *(m)* d'échanges
	inter-industriels
input: computer ...	input *(m)* de l'ordinateur
insider dealing	délit *(m)* d'initié
insider trading	délit *(m)* d'initié
instruction: programmed ...	enseignement *(m)* programmé
intangible assets	actif *(m)* immatériel
	valeurs *(fpl)* incorporelles

integrate (to)	incorporer
	intégrer
integrated management system	système *(m)* intégré de gestion
integrated project management (IPM)	gestion *(f)* intégrée
integrated: computer-... manufacturing (CIM)	fabrication *(f)* intégrée par ordinateur (FIO)
integration	incorporation *(f)*
	intégration *(f)*
intensive production	exploitation *(f)* intensive
intensive: labour-...	consommateur de main-d'oeuvre non-capitalistique
interactive	interactif
interest: controlling ...	participation *(f)* majoritaire
interest: job ...	intérêt *(m)* des tâches
interest: majority ...	participation *(f)* majoritaire
interest: minority ...	participation *(f)* minoritaire
interest: vested ...	droit *(m)* acquis
interface (to)	connecter
	interfacer
interface	interface *(f)*
	jonction *(f)*
inter-firm comparison	comparaison *(f)* inter-entreprises
interlocking directorate	direction *(f)* intriquée
internal audit	audit *(m)* interne
	contrôle *(m)* interne
internal rate of return (IRR)	taux *(m)* de rendement interne
internalize (to)	intérioriser
internationalize (to)	internationaliser
interview: in-depth ...	interview *(f)* en profondeur
intuitive management	management *(m)* intuitif
inventory control	contrôle *(m)* des stocks
	gestion *(f)* des stocks
inventory management	gestion *(f)* des stocks
inventory turnover	rotation *(f)* des stocks
inventory: perpetual ...	inventaire *(m)* tournant
investment analysis	analyse *(f)* des investissements
	étude *(f)* de rentabilité
investment appraisal	appréciation *(f)* des investissements

investment bank	banque *(f)* d'investissement
investment budget	budget *(m)* d'investissement
investment criteria	critères *(mpl)* d'investissement
investment goods	biens *(mpl)* d'équipement
investment management	gestion *(f)* des investissements
investment mix	*origine (f) des capitaux*
investment policy	politique *(f)* d'investissement
investment programme	programme *(m)* d'investissements
investment: offshore ...	investissement *(m)* extraterritorial
investment: return on ... (ROI)	rendement *(m)* des investissements
	rentabilité *(f)* d'investissements
invisibles	invisibles *(mpl)*
involvement: financial ...	intéressement *(m)*
IPM (integrated project management)	gestion *(f)* intégrée
IRR (internal rate of return)	taux *(m)* de rendement interne
issue	émission *(f)*
issue: rights ...	droit *(m)* préférentiel de souscription
issued capital	capital *(m)* émis
	capital *(m)* souscrit
IT (information technology)	informatique *(f)*
iterative	itératif
iterative process	itération *(f)*

J

JIT (just in time)	juste à temps
job analysis	analyse *(f)* des tâches
	analyse *(f)* par poste de travail
job assignment	affectation *(f)* des tâches
job breakdown	décomposition *(f)* des tâches
job challenge	exigences *(fpl)* de poste
job characteristics	caractéristiques *(fpl)* de poste
job classification	classification *(f)* des fonctions
job competence	compétence *(f)* dans le travail
job content	contenu *(m)* du travail
job description	définition *(f)* de fonction
	description *(f)* de poste

job design	conception (f) des tâches
job enlargement	élargissement (m) du travail
	extension (f) des tâches
job enrichment	enrichissement (m) du travail
job evaluation	classification (f) des emplois
	évaluation (f) des emplois
	qualification (f) du travail
job expectations	perspectives (fpl) de carrière
job improvement	amélioration (f) des tâches
job interest	intérêt (m) des tâches
job performance	rendement (m) au travail
job profile	description (f) de fonction
job requirements	exigences (fpl) de poste
job rotation	rotation (f) des postes
job satisfaction	joie (f) au travail
	satisfaction (f) au travail
job security	sécurité (f) de l'emploi
job security agreement	accord (m) sur la sécurité de l'emploi
job-sharing	partage (m) du travail
job simplification	simplification (f) du travail (SdT)
job specification	fixation (f) des tâches
job title	description (f) de poste
job: off-the-… training	formation (f) extérieure
	formation (f) institutionelle
job: on-the-… training	formation (f) sur le tas
	formation (f) sur le terrain
jobbing	courtage (m)
joint consultation	consultations (fpl) paritaires
joint negotiation	négociations (fpl) paritaires
joint representation	démarche (f) collective
joint venture	action (f) concertée
	entreprise (f) conjointe
joint-venture company	société (f) d'exploitation en commun
	co-entreprise (f)
junk bond	junk bond (m)
	obligation (f) pourrie
jurisdiction	domaine (m) d'attributions
	zone (f) de responsabilité
just in time (JIT)	juste à temps

K

key buying factor	facteur *(m)* clé d'achat
key success factor	facteur *(m)* clé de succès
know-how	know-how *(m)*
	savoir-faire *(m)*

L

labour costs: unit	coûts *(mpl)* unitaires du personnel
labour dispute	conflit *(m)* du travail
labour-intensive	consommateur de main-d'oeuvre
	non-capitalistique
labour mobility	mobilité *(f)* de la main-d'oeuvre
labour relations	relations *(fpl)* du travail
	relations *(fpl)* ouvrières
	relations *(fpl)* syndicales
labour turnover	mutation *(f)* de personnel
	rotation *(f)* du personnel
labour: direct ...	main-d'oeuvre *(f)* directe
labour: indirect ...	main-d'oeuvre *(f)* indirecte
labour: semi-skilled ...	main-d'oeuvre *(f)* spécialisée
labour: skilled ...	main-d'oeuvre *(f)* professionnelle
labour: unit ... costs	coûts *(mpl)* unitaires du personnel
labour: unskilled ...	main-d'oeuvre *(f)* non-spécialisée
	ouvriers *(mpl)* non qualifiés
lag	décalage *(m)*
lag response	décalage *(m)*
lag: time ...	décalage *(m)*
LAN (local area network)	réseau *(m)* local
landing: hard ...	atterrissage *(m)* brutal
landing: soft ...	atterrissage *(m)* en douceur
language: common ...	langage *(m)* commun
language: computer ...	langage *(m)* machine
language: machine ...	langage *(m)* machine
laptop computer	ordinateur *(m)* portatif
laser printer	imprimante *(f)* à laser

lateral thinking	pensée *(f)* latérale
latest date	date *(f)* au plus tard
launch: product ...	lancement *(m)* d'un produit
launching	lancement *(m)*
launder (to)	blanchir
laundering	blanchiment *(m)*
lay off (to)	mettre en chômage technique
lay-off	mise *(f)* en chômage technique
layout: functional ...	implantation *(f)* fonctionnelle
layout: plant ... study	étude *(f)* des implantations
layout: process equipment ...	production *(f)* groupée
LBO (leveraged buyout)	rachat *(m)* par levier
lead time	délai *(m)* de livraison
	délai *(m)* de réalisation
	délai *(m)* de suite
leader merchandising	vente *(f)* à perte
leader: loss-...	produit *(m)* d'appel
leader: market ...	innovateur *(m)*
	leader *(m)* du marché
leader: price ...	prix *(m)* directeur
leader: team ...	chef *(m)* d'équipe
leadership	autorité *(f)*
	qualités *(fpl)* de chef
	style *(m)* de direction
leading edge	avant-garde *(f)*
leak: security ...	fuite *(f)*
leapfrog (to)	dépasser
	prendre de l'avance
learning curve	courbe *(f)* d'accoutumance
learning: computer-aided ... (CAL)	enseignement *(m)* assisté par ordinateur (EAO)
learning: distance ...	télé-enseignement *(m)*
learning: programmed ...	enseignement *(m)* programmé
	enseignement *(m)* séquentiel
lease (to)	louer à bail *(m)*
lease or buy (to)	acheter ou louer
lease-lend	prêt-bail *(m)*
leasing	crédit-bail *(m)*
	leasing *(m)*

leasing: equipment ...	crédit-bail *(m)* immobilier
least-cost	moindre coût *(m)*
level playing-field	situation *(f)* à armes égales
level: wage ...	niveau *(m)* des salaires
leverage	effet *(m)* de levier
	leverage *(m)*
	levier *(m)* financier
leveraged bid	offre *(f)* de rachat par levier
leveraged buyout (LBO)	rachat *(m)* par levier
liabilities	engagements *(mpl)*
	passif *(m)*
liabilities: current ...	dettes *(fpl)* à court terme
	exigibilités *(fpl)*
	passif *(m)* exigible
liability: asset ... management	gestion *(f)* du bilan
liberalization	libéralisation *(f)*
licence	licence *(f)*
licence: under ...	sous licence
licensing: cross-...	concession *(f)* réciproque des licences
life cycle (*of a product*)	courbe *(f)* de vie (*d'un produit*)
	cycle *(m)* de vie (*d'un produit*)
life: economic ...	durée *(f)* de vie économique
life: product ...	vie *(f)* d'un produit
life: product ... expectancy	espérance *(f)* de vie d'un produit
life: shelf-...	durée *(f)* de vie
lifestyle	style *(m)* de vie
limitation: damage ...	limitation *(f)* des dommages
line and staff	structure *(f)* line and staff
line and staff organization	organisation *(f)* mixte
line assistant	attaché *(m)* opérationnel
line authority	autorité *(f)* hiérarchique
line executive	dirigeant *(m)* opérationnel
line management	autorité *(f)* hiérarchique
	chefs *(mpl)* directs
line manager	chef *(m)* direct
	directeur *(m)* hiérarchique
line of command	hiérarchie *(f)*
	voie *(f)* hiérarchique

line organization	organisation *(f)* hiérarchique
	organisation *(f)* opérationnelle
	organisation *(f)* verticale
line production	production *(f)* à la chaîne
line relations	liaisons *(fpl)* hiérarchiques
line responsibility	responsabilité *(f)* hiérarchique
line: assembly ...	chaîne *(f)* de montage
line: down the ...	subordonnés *(mpl)*
line: flow ...	ligne *(f)* de production
line: on ...	connecté *(à l'ordinateur)*
line: product ...	gamme *(f)* de produits
	ligne *(f)* de produits
	série *(f)* de produits
line: production ...	chaîne *(f)* de production
line: up the ...	en remontant la hiérarchie *(f)*
linear programming	programmation *(f)* linéaire
linear responsibility	responsabilité *(f)* hiérarchique
liquid assets	actif *(m)* disponible
	actif *(m)* négociable
	actif *(m)* réalisable
	liquidités *(fpl)*
liquidate (to)	liquider
liquidating: self-...	auto-amortissable
liquidation	liquidation *(f)*
liquidity ratio	coefficient *(m)* de liquidité
	taux *(m)* de liquidité
listing	listing *(m)*
literate: computer ...	versé en informatique
load factor	coefficient *(m)* d'utilisation de la capacité
	facteur *(m)* de charge
	indice *(m)* de charge
	taux *(m)* de charge
load: work ...	charge *(f)* de travail
loan capital	capital *(m)* d'emprunt
loan stock	emprunt *(m)* à long terme
loan: parallel ...	emprunt *(m)* parallèle
local area network (LAN)	réseau *(m)* local
local content rules	réglementation *(f)* de contenu local

localization	localisation *(f)*
location: plant ...	localisation *(f)* d'usine
lock-out	lock-out *(m)*
logistic process	processus *(m)* logistique
logistical	logistique
logistics	logistique *(f)*
logo	logotype *(m)*
logo: company ...	logotype *(m)* de la société
long-range planning	planification *(f)* à long terme
long-term planning	planification *(f)* à long terme
loop: closed ...	boucle *(f)* fermée
loss-leader	produit *(m)* d'appel
loss-maker	générateur *(m)* de pertes
loss: capital ...	moins-value *(f)*
losses: bad-debt ...	pertes *(fpl)* du fait de mauvaises créances
low-flier	cadre *(m)* à moindre potentiel
low-tech	peu élaboré
loyalty: brand ...	fidélité *(f)* à la marque
lump sum	somme *(f)* globale

M

M & A (mergers and acquisitions)	fusions *(fpl)* et acquisitions *(fpl)*
machine language	langage *(m)* machine
macro	macro *(m)*
mailbox	boîte *(f)* à lettres
mail merge	publipostage *(m)*
mail order	vente *(f)* par correspondance (VPC)
mail: direct ...	publicité *(f)* directe
mail: electronic ... (e-mail)	courrier *(m)* électronique
mailing	publipostage *(m)*
mainframe	unité *(f)* centrale de traitement
maintenance: planned ...	entretien *(m)* systématique
maintenance: preventive ...	entretien *(m)* préventif
maintenance: productive ...	entretien *(m)* productif
maintenance: resale price ... (RPM)	prix *(mpl)* imposés
maintenance: total plant ...	entretien *(m)* total de l'équipement

majority interest	participation (f) majoritaire
make-or-buy decision	option (f) produire ou acheter
maker: market ...	teneur (m) de marché
malfunction	défaillance (f)
manage (to)	diriger
	gérer
managed costs	coûts (mpl) contrôlés
managed: system-... company	entreprise (f) dirigée de façon systématisée
management	cadres (mpl)
	direction (f)
	encadrement (m)
	gérance (f)
	gestion (f)
	management (m)
	organisation (f)
	personnel (m) dirigeant
management accounting	comptabilité (f) de gestion
management audit	contrôle (m) de gestion
	diagnostic (m) d'évaluation de gestion
management buyout (MBO)	rachat (m) d'une entreprise par ses cadres
management by exception	gestion (f) par exception
management by objectives (MBO)	direction (f) par objectifs (DPO)
management by walking around	management (m) baladeur
management chart	tableau (m) de bord
management competence	compétence (f) de management
management consultancy	cabinet (m) de conseil en gestion
management consultant	conseil (m) en direction
	conseil (m) en gestion
	ingénieur-conseil (m)
management contract	contrat (m) du management
management development	formation (f) au management
	perfectionnement (m) des cadres
management game	jeu (m) d'entreprise
	simulation (f) de gestion
management information	information (f) d'organisation de la gestion

management information system (MIS)	informatique *(f)* de gestion
	système *(m)* d'information de management (SIM)
management potential	potentiel *(m)* des cadres
management practices	procédures *(fpl)* de gestion
management ratio	ratio *(m)* de gestion
management science	science *(f)* de la gestion
management services	*services (m) d'état-major*
	services (m) de conseil interne
	services *(m)* fonctionnels
management staff	personnel *(m)* d'encadrement
	personnel *(m)* dirigeant
management style	style *(m)* managérial
management succession planning	plans *(mpl)* de succession
	plans *(mpl)* de remplacement
management system	système *(m)* de direction
management team	équipe *(f)* de direction
management technique	technique *(f)* de gestion
management theory	théorie *(f)* de la gestion de l'entreprise
management training	formation *(f)* des cadres
management: asset ...	gestion *(f)* des actifs
management: asset liability ...	gestion *(f)* du bilan
management: business ...	gestion *(f)* de l'entreprise
management: cash ...	gestion *(f)* de trésorerie
management: change ... (management of change)	gestion *(f)* du changement
management: computerized ...	gestion *(f)* automatisée
management: credit ...	gestion *(f)* de crédit
management: crisis ...	gestion *(f)* des crises
management: decentralized ...	gestion *(f)* décentralisée
management: departmental ...	gestion *(f)* par département
management: divisional ...	gestion *(f)* cellulaire
	gestion *(f)* par département
management: dynamic ... model	modèle *(m)* dynamique de gestion
management: effective ...	direction *(f)* efficace
management: financial ...	direction *(f)* financière
management: functional ...	gestion *(f)* par fonctions
management: general ...	direction *(f)* générale

management: human resource ... (HRM)	gestion (f)des ressources humaines
management: integrated ... system	système (m) intégré de gestion
management: integrated project ... (IPM)	gestion (f) intégrée
management: intuitive ...	management (m) intuitif
management: investment ...	gestion (f) des investissements
management: line ...	autorité (f) hiérarchique
	chefs (mpl) directs
management: manpower ...	gestion (f) des effectifs
management: market ...	gestion (f) commerciale
management: matrix ...	organisation (f) en matrice
management: middle ...	cadres (mpl) moyens
management: multiple ...	direction (f) multiple
management: office ...	organisation (f) des bureaux
management: operating ...	direction (f) opérationnelle
management: operations ...	gestion (f) des opérations
management: participative ...	direction (f) participative
management: personnel ...	administration (f) du personnel
	direction (f) du personnel
management: physical distribution	gestion (f) de la distribution physique
management: portfolio ...	gestion (f) de portefeuille
management: product ...	gestion (f) de produit
management: production ...	gestion (f) de la production
	organisation (f) de la production
management: programmed ...	direction (f) par programmes
	gestion (f) programmée
management: project ...	project management (m)
management: quality ...	gestion (f) de la qualité
management: resource ...	gestion (f) des ressources
management: safety ...	gestion (f) de la sécurité
management: sales ...	administration (f) des ventes
	direction (f) commerciale
management: scientific ...	gestion (f) scientifique
	organisation (f) scientifique
	organisation (f) scientifique du travail (OST)
management: staff ...	direction (f) du personnel

management: supervisory ...	maitrise *(f)*
management: systems ...	direction *(f)* systématisée
	gestion *(f)* par les systèmes
management: time ...	organisation *(f)* du temps
management: top ...	cadres *(mpl)* dirigeants
	cadres *(mpl)* supérieurs
	haute direction *(f)*
management: top ... approach	optique *(f)* de la direction générale
management: total quality ... (TQM)	gestion *(f)* de la qualité absolue
management: venture ...	gestion *(f)* des risques
manager	chef *(m)*
	directeur *(m)*
	dirigeant *(m)*
	gérant *(m)*
	gestionnaire *(m)*
	responsable *(m)*
manager: advertising ...	directeur *(m)* de la publicité
manager: area ...	chef *(m)* de secteur
manager: assistant ...	sous-chef *(m)*
	sous-directeur *(m)*
manager: assistant to ...	adjoint *(m)*
manager: brand ...	chef *(m)* de marque
manager: departmental ...	chef *(m)* de service
manager: deputy ...	directeur *(m)* adjoint
manager: distribution ...	chef *(m)* de distribution
manager: first-line ...	chef *(m)* d'atelier
	contremaître *(m)*
	surveillant *(m)* de premier niveau
manager: general ...	directeur *(m)* général
manager: line ...	chef *(m)* direct
	directeur *(m)* hiérarchique
manager: marketing ...	directeur *(m)* commercial
	directeur *(m)* du marketing
manager: operations ...	chef *(m)* d'exploitation
manager: owner-...	patron directeur *(m)*
manager: personnel ...	chef *(m)* du personnel
manager: plant ...	chef *(m)* d'établissement
	directeur *(m)* d'usine
manager: procurement ...	chef *(m)* d'approvisionnement

manager: product ...	chef *(m)* de produit
manager: production ...	chef *(m)* de fabrication
manager: project ...	chef *(m)* de projet
manager: purchasing ...	chef *(m)* des achats
manager: sales ...	chef *(m)* de ventes
manager: works ...	chef *(m)* d'établissement
managerial	directorial
	managérial
managerial control	contrôle *(m)* de direction
	contrôle *(m)* de gestion
managerial effectiveness	efficacité *(f)* de la direction
managerial function	fonction *(f)* de direction
managerial grid	grille *(f)* de gestion
managerial structure	hiérarchie *(f)*
managerial style	style *(m)* de direction
managing director (MD)	président *(m)*-directeur général (PDG)
managing director: deputy	directeur *(m)* général adjoint
manning	effectifs *(mpl)*
	personnel *(m)*
manpower	effectifs *(mpl)*
	main-d'oeuvre *(f)*
manpower audit	inventaire *(m)* des effectifs
manpower forecast	prévision *(f)* de l'emploi
manpower forecasting	prévision *(f)* de l'emploi
manpower management	gestion *(f)* des effectifs
manpower planning	planification *(f)* des effectifs
	planification *(f)* de l'emploi
manpower resourcing	recrutement *(m)* et gestion *(f)* des effectifs
manpower: executive ... strategy	stratégie *(f)* des cadres
manufacturing capacity	capacité *(f)* de production
manufacturing control	contrôle *(m)* de fabrication
manufacturing: computer-aided ... (CAM)	fabrication *(f)* assistée par ordinateur (FAO)
manufacturing: computer-integrated (CIM)	fabrication *(f)* intégrée par ordinateur (FIO)
manufacturing: economic ... quantity	quantité *(f)* économique de production
	série *(f)* économique de fabrication

margin of safety	marge *(f)* de sécurité
margin: gross ... (GM)	marge *(f)* brute
margin: net ...	marge *(f)* nette
margin: profit ...	marge *(f)* bénéficiaire
marginal analysis	analyse *(f)* marginale
marginal costs	coûts *(mpl)* marginaux
marginal costing	comptabilité *(f)* marginale
	méthode *(f)* des coûts marginaux
marginal pricing	fixation *(f)* marginale du prix
marginalize (to)	marginaliser
margins: hold ... (to)	maintenir les marges
mark-up	majoration *(f)* (du prix)
	marge *(f)*
market (to)	lancer sur le marché
	trouver un débouché pour
market appraisal	évaluation *(f)* du marché
market awareness	conscience *(f)* du marché
market dynamics	dynamique *(f)* de marché
market exploration	prospection *(f)* des marchés
market forces	tendances *(fpl)* du marché
market forecast	prévision *(f)* du marché
	pronostic *(m)* du marché
market intelligence	information *(f)* commerciale
market leader	innovateur *(m)*
	leader *(m)* du marché
market maker	teneur *(m)* de marché
market management	gestion *(f)* commerciale
market opportunity	créneau *(m)*
market penetration	pénétration *(f)* du marché
market plan	plan *(m)* de marché
market planning	plan *(m)* de marché
market potential	marché *(m)* potentiel
	marché *(m)* tendanciel
market price	prix *(m)* du marché
	prix *(m)* marchand
market profile	profil *(m)* du marché
market prospects	perspectives *(fpl)* commerciales
market rating	cours *(m)* de bourse

market research	analyse *(f)* des marchés
	étude *(f)* du marché
market saturation	saturation *(f)* du marché
market segment	strate *(f)* de marché
market segmentation	segmentation *(f)* des marchés
market-sensitive	sensible au marché
market share	part *(f)* du marché
market structure	structure *(f)* du marché
market study	étude *(f)* de marché
	examen *(m)* des débouchés
market survey	étude *(f)* de marché
market test	test *(m)* de vente
	vente *(f)* expérimentale
market thrust	percée *(f)* commerciale
market trend	orientation *(f)* du marché (à court terme)
	tendance *(f)* du marché (à long terme)
market value	valeur *(f)* marchande
market: bear ...	marché *(m)* à la baisse
market: bull ...	marché *(m)* haussier
market: buyers' ...	marché *(m)* à la baisse
market: commodity ...	marché *(m)* de matières premières
market: down-...	bas *(m)* de gamme
market: equity ...	marché *(m)* des actions
market: financial ...	place *(f)* financière
market: forward ...	marché *(m)* à terme
market: fringe ...	marché *(m)* marginal
market: grey ...	marché *(m)* gris
	marché *(m)* parallèle
market: mature ...	marché *(m)* arrivé à la maturité
market: sellers' ...	marché *(m)* à la hausse
market: single ...	marché *(m)* unique
market: single ... (*of the EC*)	marché *(m)* interne (*de la CE*)
market: stock ...	bourse *(f)*
market: target ...	marché *(m)* cible
market: up-...	haut *(m)*de gamme
marketable	négociable

marketing	commercialisation *(f)*
	marketing *(m)*
marketing appropriation	dotations *(fpl)* budgétaires affectées au marketing
marketing budget	budget *(m)* de marketing
marketing department	service *(m)* de marketing
marketing manager	directeur *(m)* du marketing
marketing mix	formule *(f)* de marketing
	marketing *(m)* mix
marketing research	recherche *(f)* commerciale
marketing strategy	stratégie *(f)* commerciale
	stratégie *(f)* de marché
marketing: creative ...	créativité *(f)* commerciale
marketing: direct ...	marketing *(m)* direct
marketing: global ...	marketing *(m)* global
marketing: test ...	test *(m)* de marché
mass production	fabrication *(f)* en série
	production *(f)* en masse
mass: critical	masse *(f)* critique
massage the figures (to)	habiller le bilan
	manipuler les chiffres *(mpl)*
material: point-of-sale ...	matériel *(m)* de publicité sur le lieu de vente
materials handling	manutention *(f)* (des marchandises)
mathematical programming	programmation *(f)* mathématique
matrix management	organisation *(f)* en matrice
matrix organization	structure *(f)* matricielle
mature market	marché *(m)* arrivé à la maturité
maximization: profit ...	maximisation *(f)* du profit
maximize (to)	maximaliser
MBO (management buyout)	rachat *(m)* d'une entreprise par ses cadres
MBO (management by objectives)	DPO (direction *(f)* par objectifs)
MD (managing director)	PDG (président *(m)*-directeur général)
mean	moyenne *(f)*
meaningful	significatif
measurement: clerical work... (CWM)	chronométrage *(m)* des travaux administratifs
measurement: performance ...	mesure *(f)* de performances

measurement: productivity ...	mesure *(f)* de la productivité
measurement: work ...	mesure *(f)* du travail
media	média *(mpl)*
	supports *(mpl)*
media analysis	analyse *(f)* de média
media selection	sélection *(f)* des média
media: advertising ...	média *(mpl)* publicitaires
median	médiane *(f)*
mediate (to)	agir en médiateur
mediation	médiation *(f)*
meeting: board ...	réunion *(f)* du conseil d'administration
memory	mémoire *(f)*
memory: computer ...	mémoire *(f)* d'ordinateur
memory: random-access ... (RAM)	mémoire *(f)* à accès sélectif
memory: read-only ... (ROM)	mémoire *(f)* morte
	mémoire *(f)* passive
merchandising	commercialisation *(f)*
	merchandising *(m)*
	techniques *(fpl)* marchandes
merchandising: leader ...	vente *(f)* à perte
merchant bank	banque *(f)* d'affaires
merge (to)	amalgamer
	fusionner
merger	fusion *(f)*
mergers and acquisitions (M & A)	fusions *(fpl)* et acquisitions *(fpl)*
merit rating	appréciation *(f)* du mérite
message: advertising ...	message *(m)* publicitaire
methectics	dynamique *(f)* des groupes
method: critical path ... (CPM)	méthode *(f)* du chemin critique
method: full-cost ...	méthode *(f)* des coûts complets
method: points-rating ...	méthode *(f)* de qualification par points
method: present value ...	méthode *(f)* d'actualisation
method: random observation ...	méthode *(f)* des observations instantanées
method: simplex ...	méthode *(f)* du simplexe
methods engineering	étude *(f)* des méthodes
methods study	étude *(f)* des méthodes
methods study department	bureau *(m)* des méthodes

methods: organization and ... (O & M)	méthodes *(fpl)* et organisation
methods: time and ... study	étude *(f)* des temps et des méthodes
micro	micro *(m)*
microchip	puce *(f)*
middle management	cadres *(mpl)* moyens
	maîtrise *(f)*
milestone chart	graphique *(m)* des étapes critiques
minimize risks (to)	minimiser les risques
minimum wage	salaire *(m)* minimum
minority interest	participation *(f)* minoritaire
MIS (management information system)	SIM (système *(m)* d'information de management)
mission statement	définition *(f)* de la mission
mission: corporate ...	vocation *(f)* de la société
mission: economic ...	mission *(f)* économique
mix: investment ...	*origine (f) des capitaux*
mix: marketing ...	formule *(f)* de marketing
	marketing *(m)* mix
mix: product ...	éventail *(m)* de produits
	product-mix *(m)*
mix: promotional ...	moyens *(mpl)* d'action promotionnelle
mix: sales ...	éventail *(m)* de produits
	gamme *(f)* commerciale
mobile phone	téléphone *(m)* mobile
mobile: upwardly ...	dynamique
mobility: labour ...	mobilité *(f)* de la main-d'oeuvre
mobility: staff ...	mobilité *(f)* du personnel
mode	mode *(m)*
model	modèle *(m)*
model: accounting ...	modèle *(m)* comptable
model: corporate ...	modèle *(m)* de l'entreprise
model: decision ...	modèle *(m)* de décision
model: dynamic management ...	modèle *(f)* dynamique de gestion
modem	modem *(m)*
	modulateur-démodulateur *(m)*
modular production	fabrication *(f)* modulaire
modularity	modularité *(m)*
monetarism	monétarisme *(m)*

monetary policy	politique *(f)* monétaire
money supply	masse *(f)* monétaire
monitor (to)	surveiller
monitor performance (to)	contrôler la performance
monitoring: performance ...	contrôle *(m)* de la performance
moonlighting	travail *(m)* au noir
morphological analysis	analyse *(f)* morphologique
motion economy	économie *(f)* des mouvements
motion study	étude *(f)* des mouvements
motion: predetermined ... time system (PMTS)	méthode *(f)* des temps prédéterminés (PMTS)
motion: time and ... study	étude *(f)* des temps et des mouvements
	étude *(f)* des périodes
motivate (to)	animer
	motiver
motivation	motivation *(f)*
motivation: self-...	automotivation *(f)*
motivational	motivationnel
motivational research	étude *(f)* de motivation
motivator	mobile *(m)*
	motivateur *(m)*
motivator: purchasing ...	mobile *(m)* d'achat
motive: profit ...	motivation *(f)* par le profit
mouse	souris *(f)*
MRA (multiple regression analysis)	régression *(f)* multiple
multi-access	accès *(m)* multiple
multimedia training	formation *(f)* plurimédiatique
multiple management	direction *(f)* multiple
multiple regression analysis (MRA)	régression *(f)* multiple
mutual recognition	reconnaissance *(f)* réciproque

N

name of the game	règle *(f)* du jeu
natural wastage	non-remplacement *(m)* des départs
need-to-know basis	en fonction *(f)* des informations à connaître
needs analysis	analyse *(f)* des besoins

needs analysis: training ... ...   analyse *(f)* des besoins en formation
negative cash flow   cash-flow *(m)* négatif
negative income tax   impôt *(m)* négatif sur le revenu
negotiate (to)   négocier
negotiation strategy   stratégie *(f)* de négociation
negotiation: joint ...   négociations *(fpl)* paritaires
net assets   actif *(m)* net
    valeurs *(fpl)* nettes
net current assets   fonds *(m)* de roulement net
net margin   marge *(f)* nette
net present value (NPV)   valeur *(f)* actuelle nette
net profit   bénéfice *(m)* net
net worth   valeur *(f)* nette
network (to)   (inter)connecter
network analysis   analyse *(f)* de réseau
network: communications ...   réseau *(m)* de communication
network: distribution ...   réseau *(m)* de distribution
network: information ...   réseau *(m)* d'information
network: wide area ... (WAN)   grand réseau *(m)*
networking   exploitation *(f)* des contacts d'affaires
    gestion *(f)* de réseau
new-product development   développement *(m)* de produits
    nouveaux
new-product launching   lancement *(m)* de nouveaux produits
niche   créneau *(m)*
night shift   équipe *(f)* de nuit
non-durable goods   produits *(mpl)* non durables
non-executive director   administrateur *(m)*
non-linear programming   programmation *(f)* non-linéaire
non-profit-making   déficitaire
    sans but *(m)* lucratif
non-tariff barrier (NTB)   barrière *(f)* non douanière
non-verbal communication   communication *(f)* non verbale
NPV (net present value)   valeur *(f)* actuelle nette
NTB (non-tariff barrier)   barrière *(f)* non douanière
number-crunching   calcul *(m)*
numerical control   commande *(f)* numérique

O

O & M (organization and methods)	méthodes *(fpl)* et organisation
objective	finalité *(f)*
	objectif *(m)*
objective-setting	définition *(f)* des objectifs
objective: company ...	objectif *(m)* de l'entreprise
objectives: management by ...(MBO)	direction *(f)* par objectifs (DPO)
objectives: overall company ...	objectifs *(mpl)* globaux de l'entreprise
objectives: performance against ...	réalisations *(fpl)* comparées aux projets
observation: random ... method	méthode *(f)* des observations instantanées
obsolescence	obsolescence *(f)*
	vieillissement *(m)*
obsolescence: built-in ...	désuétude *(f)* calculée
obsolescence: planned ...	désuétude *(f)* calculée
occupational hazard	risque *(m)* du métier
off line	non connecté
off-the-job training	formation *(f)* extérieure
	formation *(f)* institutionnelle
office automation	bureautique *(f)*
office management	organisation *(f)* des bureaux
office planning	planification *(f)* des bureaux
office: branch ...	succursale *(f)*
office: electronic ...	bureau *(m)* électronique
office: head ...	administration *(f)* centrale
	siège *(m)* social
officer: training ...	directeur *(m)* de formation
official strike	grève *(f)* officielle
offshore	extraterritorial
offshore investment	investissement *(m)* extraterritorial
on line	connecté *(à l'ordinateur)*
	en ligne *(f)*
on stream	en cours *(m)*
	régime *(m)* de croisière
on-the-job training	formation *(f)* sur le tas
	formation *(f)* sur le terrain

one-off	hors-série
	spécial
ongoing	permanent
open-ended	extensible
	ouvert
	sans limites *(fpl)* fixes
open-plan	non cloisonné
open shop	appartenance *(f)* non obligatoire à un syndicat
operating division	division *(f)* opérationnelle
operating expenses	charges *(fpl)* d'exploitation
operating management	direction *(f)* opérationnelle
operational	opérationnel
operational planning	planification *(f)* des opérations
operational research (OR)	recherche *(f)* opérationnelle (RO)
operations	activités *(fpl)*
	opérations *(fpl)*
operations analysis	analyse *(f)* des tâches
	analyse *(f)* du travail
operations audit	contrôle *(m)* de gestion
	contrôle *(m)* des opérations
operations breakdown	décomposition *(f)* des tâches
operations management	gestion *(f)* des opérations
operations manager	chef *(m)* d'exploitation
operations research (OR)	recherche *(f)* opérationnelle (RO)
operations: ancillary ...	services *(mpl)* d'intendance
operations: hedging ...	opérations *(fpl)* de couverture
opinion survey	enquête *(f)* d'opinion
opportunity costs	coûts *(mpl)* d'opportunité
opportunity: equal employment ...	égalité *(f)* des chances face à l'emploi
opportunity: market ...	créneau *(m)*
opportunity: window of ...	créneau *(m)* favorable
optimization: profit ...	optimisation *(f)* du profit
optimize (to)	optimiser
option: stock ...	option *(f)* d'achat d'actions
option: stock ... plan	plan *(m)* optionnel d'achat d'actions
option: traded ...	option *(f)* négociable
OR (operational research, operations research)	RO (recherche *(f)* opérationnelle)

order: economic ... quantity	quantité *(f)* économique à commander
	quantité *(f)* optimale de commande
organic growth	croissance *(f)* organique
organization and methods (O & M)	méthodes *(fpl)* et organisation
organization chart	organigramme *(m)*
organization culture	culture *(f)* de l'organisation
organization planning	planification *(f)* de l'organisation
organization structure	structure *(f)* d'organisation
organization theory	théorie *(f)* d'organisation
organization: functional ...	organisation *(f)* fonctionnelle
	organisation *(f)* horizontale
organization: informal ...	organisation *(f)* informelle
organization: line ...	organisation *(f)* hiérarchique
	organisation *(f)* opérationnelle
	organisation *(f)* verticale
organization: line and staff ...	organisation *(f)* mixte
organization: matrix ...	structure *(f)* matricielle
organization: staff ...	organisation *(f)* fonctionnelle
	organisation *(f)* horizontale
organizational behaviour	comportement *(m)* de l'homme dans l'organisation
organizational change	mutation *(f)* des structures
organizational development	développement *(m)* organisationnel
organizational effectiveness	efficacité *(f)* organisatrice
organogram	organigramme *(m)*
orientation: consumer ...	orientation *(f)* vers le consommateur
orientation: customer ...	orientation *(f)* vers le client
out of stock	épuisé
out-house	externe
outlook: business ...	conjoncture *(f)*
outlook: profit ...	perspectives *(fpl)* de profit
outplacement	décrutement *(m)*
	outplacement *(m)*
output	chiffre *(m)* d'affaires
	output *(m)*
	production *(f)*
	rendement *(m)*
	résultat *(m)* de sortie

output budgeting	*rationalisation (f) des choix budgétaires (RCB)*
output: capital-... ratio	ratio *(m)* d'intensité de capital
output: input-... analysis	analyse *(f)* entrées-sorties
output: input-... table	tableau *(m)* d'échanges inter-industriels
outside director	administrateur *(m)*
outsourcing	sourcing *(m)*
overall company objectives	objectifs *(mpl)* globaux de l'entreprise
overcapacity	surcapacité *(f)*
overcapitalized	sur-capitalisé
overextended	ayant pris des engagements au-dessus de ses moyens
overheads	frais *(mpl)* généraux (FG)
overheads recovery	couverture *(f)* des frais généraux
overheads: administrative ...	frais *(mpl)* généraux d'administration
overheads: factory ...	frais *(mpl)* généraux de fabrication
overmanned	ayant un excédent de main-d'oeuvre
overmanning	excédent *(m)* de main-d'oeuvre
overprice (to)	mettre un prix trop haut
overstaffed	ayant un personnel trop nombreux
overstaffing	personnel *(m)* trop nombreux
overtime	heures *(fpl)* supplémentaires
owner-manager	patron directeur *(m)*

P

P/E (price-earnings ratio)	rapport *(m)* cours-bénéfices
	taux *(m)* de price-earnings
P/V (profit-volume ratio)	rapport *(m)* profit sur ventes
package deal	contrat *(m)* global
	panier *(m)*
package: software ...	progiciel *(m)*
packaging	conditionnement *(m)*
	emballage *(m)*
palletization	gerbage *(m)*
	palettisation *(f)*
panel: consumers' ...	panel *(m)* de consommateurs
par	pair *(m)*

par: above ...	au-dessus du pair
par: at ...	au pair
par: below ...	au-dessous du pair
parachute: golden ...	parapluie *(m)* doré
parallel currency	monnaie *(f)* parallèle
parallel import	importation *(f)* parallèle
parallel loan	emprunt *(m)* parallèle
parameter	paramètre *(m)*
parametric programming	programmation *(f)* paramétrique
parent company	société *(f)* mère
part-analysis training	formation *(f)* par étapes
part-time employment	emploi *(m)* à mi-temps
	travail *(m)* à mi-temps
part-timer	employé *(m)* qui travaille à mi-temps
participation	participation *(f)*
participation: worker ...	participation *(f)* ouvrière
participative management	direction *(f)* participative
partner	associé *(m)*
partnership	société *(f)* en nom collectif
	association *(f)*
party: working ...	groupe *(m)* de travail
patent	brevet *(m)*
patent trading	échange *(m)* de brevets
pay-as-you-earn (PAYE)	retenue *(f)* de l'impôt sur le revenu à la source
pay-as-you-go	système *(m)* de retenue à la source
pay-off	gains *(mpl)*
	rentabilité *(f)*
	résultats *(mpl)*
pay pause	blocage *(m)* des salaires
pay talks	négociations *(fpl)* salariales
pay: equal ...	égalité *(f)* des salaires
pay: profit-related ...	salaire *(m)* lié aux bénéfices
pay: severance ...	indemnité *(f)* de licenciement
pay: take-home ...	salaire *(m)* net
payback	payback *(m)*
	récupération *(f)* (du capital investi)

payback period	délai *(m)* de récupération
	période *(f)* de récupération
	période *(f)* de remboursement
PAYE (pay-as-you-earn)	retenue *(f)* de l'impôt sur le revenu à la source
payment by results	salaire *(m)* au rendement
payment: *ex gratia* ...	paiement *(m)* à titre de faveur
payroll	registre *(m)* du personnel
PC (personal computer)	ordinateur *(m)* personnel
penetration pricing	politique *(f)* de prix de pénétration par la base
penetration: market ...	pénétration *(f)* du marché
per-share earnings	bénéfices *(mpl)* par action
perform (to)	performer
performance against objectives	réalisations *(fpl)* comparées aux projets
performance appraisal	appréciation *(f)* des performances
	appréciation *(f)* du rendement
	évaluation *(f)* des résultats
performance budgeting	*rationalisation (f) des choix budgétaires (RCB)*
performance evaluation	appréciation *(f)* des performances
performance indicator	clignotant *(m)*
	indicateur *(m)* de performance
performance measurement	mesure *(f)* de performances
performance monitoring	contrôle *(m)* de la performance
performance rating	jugement *(m)* d'allure
performance review	évaluation *(f)* des performances
performance standard	norme *(f)* de rendement
performance: earnings ...	rentabilité *(f)*
performance: job ...	rendement *(m)* au travail
performance: monitor ... **(to)**	contrôler la performance
performance: product ...	comportement *(m)* de produit
performance: profit ...	rendement *(m)*
performance: share price ...	performance *(f)* du prix des actions
performance: standard ...	rendement *(m)* standard
period: accounting	exercice *(m)* (comptable)
	exercice *(m)* (financier)
	exercice *(m)* (social)

peripheral equipment	unités *(fpl)* périphériques
peripherals	périphériques *(mpl)*
perpetual inventory	inventaire *(m)* tournant
personal computer (PC)	ordinateur *(m)* personnel
personal growth	autodéveloppement *(m)*
	développement *(m)* personnel
personnel department	direction *(f)* du personnel
	service *(m)* du personnel
personnel management	administration *(f)* du personnel
	direction *(f)* du personnel
personnel manager	chef *(m)* du personnel
personnel policy	politique *(f)* du personnel
personnel rating	appréciation *(f)* du personnel
	notation *(f)* de la main-d'oeuvre
personnel specification	profil *(m)* de compétences
PERT (programme evaluation and review technique)	méthode *(f)* PERT
pertinence tree	arbre *(m)* de pertinence
petty cash	petite caisse *(f)*
petty expenses	menues dépenses *(fpl)*
phase in (to)	adopter progressivement
phase out (to)	éliminer progressivement
philosophy: company ...	philosophie *(f)* de l'entreprise
physical distribution management	gestion *(f)* de la distribution physique
picket	piquet *(m)* de grève
pie chart	camembert *(m)*
	graphique *(m)* circulaire
piecework	travail *(m)* à la pièce
piggyback	portage *(m)* à l'exportation
pilot production	fabrication *(f)* pilote
	présérie *(f)*
pilot run	présérie *(f)*
pioneer (to)	innover
pioneer product	innovation *(f)*
piracy	pillage *(m)*
plan	plan *(m)*
plan: action ...	plan *(m)* d'action
	programme *(m)* d'action
plan: departmental ...	plan *(m)* de divisions

plan: market ...	plan *(m)* de marché
plan: open-...	non cloisonné
plan: share of production ...	intéressement *(m)*
plan: stock option ...	plan *(m)* optionnel d'achat d'actions
plan: tactical ...	plan *(m)* tactique
planned maintenance	entretien *(m)* systématique
planned obsolescence	désuétude *(f)* calculée
planning	établissement *(m)* des plannings
	plan *(m)*
	planification *(f)*
	planning *(m)*
planning department	bureau *(m)* de planning
	service *(m)* de planification
	service *(m)* planning
planning, programming, budgeting system (PPBS)	*rationalisation (f) des choix budgétaires (RCB)*
planning: career ...	plan *(m)* de carrière
planning: company ...	planification *(f)* de l'entreprise
planning: contingency ...	tenant compte *(m)* de l'imprévu
planning: corporate ...	planification *(f)* de l'entreprise
planning: distribution ...	planning *(m)* de distribution
planning: financial ...	plan *(m)* financier
planning: forward ...	plan *(m)* à longue échéance
planning: human resource ... (HRP)	planification *(f)* des ressources humaines
planning: long-range ...	planification *(f)* à long terme
planning: long-term ...	planification *(f)* à long terme
planning: management succession ...	plans *(mpl)* de succession
	plans *(mpl)* de remplacement
planning: manpower ...	planification *(f)* des effectifs
planning: market ...	plan *(m)* de marché
planning: office ...	planification *(f)* des bureaux
planning: operational ...	planification *(f)* des opérations
planning: organization ...	planification *(f)* de l'organisation
planning: product ...	planification *(f)* du produit
planning: production ...	planning *(m)* de la production
planning: production ... and control	projet *(m)* et contrôle *(m)* de la production
planning: profit ...	planification *(f)* des bénéfices

planning: project ...	plan *(m)* de projet
planning: sales ...	planification *(f)* des ventes
planning: short-term ...	planification *(f)* à court terme
planning: staff ...	planification *(f)* des effectifs
planning: strategic ...	plan *(m)* stratégique
planning: systems ...	planification *(f)* des systèmes
plant bargaining	négociations *(fpl)* au niveau local
plant capacity	capacité *(f)* de l'usine
plant hire	location *(f)* d'équipement
plant layout study	étude *(f)* des implantations
plant location	localisation *(f)* de l'usine
plant maintenance	entretien *(m)* de l'équipement
plant maintenance: total	entretien *(m)* total de l'équipement
plant manager	chef *(m)* d'établissement
	directeur *(m)* d'usine
player: team ...	équipier *(m)*
playing: role-...	jeu *(m)* de rôles
ploughback	autofinancement *(m)*
	bénéfice *(m)* réinvesti
PMTS (predetermined motion time system)	PMTS (méthode *(f)* des temps prédéterminés)
point of sale (POS)	lieu *(m)* de vente (LV)
	point *(m)* de vente
point-of-sale advertising	publicité *(f)* sur le lieu de vente (PLV)
point-of-sale material	matériel *(m)* de publicité sur le lieu de vente
point: break-even ...	point *(m)* critique
	seuil *(m)* de rentabilité
	point *(m)* mort
point: unique selling ... (USP)	promesse *(f)* unique de vente
points-rating method	méthode *(f)* de qualification par points
poison pill	pillule *(f)* empoisonnée
policy execution	exécution *(f)* de la politique
policy formulation	expression *(f)* de la politique
policy: business ...	politique *(f)* générale de l'entreprise
	politique *(f)* de gestion
policy: company ...	politique *(f)* de l'entreprise
policy: distribution ...	politique *(f)* de distribution

policy: dividend ...	politique *(f)* de (versement des) dividendes
policy: investment ...	politique *(f)* d'investissement
policy: personnel ...	politique *(f)* du personnel
policy: pricing ...	politique *(f)* de prix
policy: promotional ...	politique *(f)* de promotion
policy: remittance ...	politique *(f)* à l'égard des remises
policy: sales ...	politique *(f)* de vente
policy: selling ...	politique *(f)* de vente
policy: wage ...	politique *(f)* salariale
pooling arrangements	dispositifs *(mpl)* de mise en commun des ressources
poor: cash ...	pauvre en liquidité
portfolio management	gestion *(f)* de portefeuille
portfolio selection	sélection *(f)* de portefeuille
portfolio: asset ...	portefeuille *(m)* d'actifs
portfolio: balanced ...	portefeuille *(m)* équilibré
portfolio: brand ...	portefeuille *(m)* de marques
portfolio: business ...	portefeuille *(m)* d'activités
portfolio: product ...	portefeuille *(m)* de produits
portfolio: stock ...	portefeuille *(m)* d'actions
POS (point of sale)	LV (lieu *(m)* de vente) point *(m)* de vente
position: competitive ...	position *(f)* concurrentielle
position: financial ...	situation *(f)* financière
positioning	positionnement *(m)*
positioning: brand ...	positionnement *(m)* de marques
positive discrimination	discrimination *(f)* positive
potential buyer	acheteur *(m)* potentiel
potential: development ...	potentiel *(m)* de dévelopement
potential: growth ...	potentiel *(m)* de croissance
potential: management ...	potentiel *(m)* des cadres
potential: market ...	marché *(m)* potentiel marché *(m)* tendanciel
potential: sales ...	potentiel *(m)* de vente
power: earning ...	capacité *(f)* bénéficiaire
PPBS (planning, programming, budgeting system)	*RCB (rationalisation (f) des choix budgétaires)*
PR (public relations)	RP (relations *(fpl)* publiques)

practices: management ...	procédures *(fpl)* de gestion
practices: restrictive ... (*industrial*)	pratiques *(fpl)* restrictives
practices: restrictive ... (*legal*)	ententes *(fpl)*
predator	prédateur *(m)*
predetermined motion time system (PMTS)	méthode *(f)* des temps prédéterminés
pre-emptive bid	ouverture *(f)* préventive
premium	prime *(f)*
premium bonus	salaire *(m)* à prime de rendement
present value method	méthode *(f)* d'actualisation
present value: net ... (NPV)	valeur *(f)* actuelle nette
president	président *(m)*
president: vice-...	sous-directeur *(m)*
	vice-président *(m)*
pressure	pression *(f)*
prestige pricing	politique *(f)* de prix d'écrémage
preventive maintenance	entretien *(m)* préventif
price (to)	fixer le prix
price-cutting	gâchage *(m)* des prix
price determination	établissement *(m)* des prix
	fixation *(f)* des prix
price differential	différence *(f)* des prix
price discrimination	discrimination *(f)* de prix
price-earnings ratio (P/E)	rapport *(m)* cours-bénéfices
	taux *(m)* de price-earnings
price escalation	flambée *(f)* des prix
price-fixing	fixation *(f)* des prix
price increase	majoration *(f)* de prix
price index	indice *(m)* des prix
price index: consumer	indice *(m)* des prix à la consommation
price index: retail ... ... (RPI)	indice *(m)* des prix de détail
price leader	prix *(m)* directeur
price range	échelle *(f)* des prix
price structure	structure *(f)* de prix
price: competitive ...	prix *(m)* défiant la concurrence
price: differential ...	prix *(m)* différentiel
price: market ...	prix *(m)* marchand
	prix *(m)* du marché
price: resale ... maintenance (RPM)	prix *(mpl)* imposés

price: spot ...	prix *(m)* au comptant
price: standard ...	prix *(m)* standard
prices: cut ... (to)	brader les prix *(mpl)*
pricing	établissement *(m)* des prix
	fixation *(f)* des prix
pricing policy	politique *(f)* de prix
pricing strategy	stratégie *(f)* de prix
pricing: differential ...	fixation *(f)* de prix différents pour un même produit
pricing: marginal ...	fixation *(f)* marginale du prix
pricing: penetration ...	politique *(f)* de prix de pénétration par la base
pricing: prestige ...	politique *(f)* de prix d'écrémage
pricing: transfer ...	fixation *(f)* des prix de transfert
primary commodity	produit *(m)* de base
print out (to)	sortir sur imprimante
printout	sortie *(f)* d'imprimante
prioritize (to)	prioritiser
private enterprise	secteur *(m)* privé
privatization	privatisation *(f)*
privatize (to)	privatiser
pro rata	proportionnel
proactive	proactif
proactive strategy	stratégie *(f)* proactive
probability theory	théorie *(f)* des probabilités
problem analysis	analyse *(f)* de problème
problem area	domaine *(m)* problématique
	zone *(f)* critique
problem assessment	évaluation *(f)* des problèmes
problem solving	résolution *(f)* de problèmes
procedural	procédural
procedure	procédure *(f)*
procedure: administrative control	procédé *(m)* de contrôle de gestion
procedure: grievance ...	procédure *(f)* pour résoudre des griefs
	procédure *(f)* prud'hommale
procedures: systems and ...	méthodes *(fpl)* administratives
process (to)	traiter
process control	commande *(f)* de processus
	régulation *(f)* de processus

process costing	comptabilité (f) par fabrication
process equipment layout	production (f) groupée
process: decision ...	processus (m) de la décision
process: flow ... chart	diagramme (m) de circulation
	graphique (m) d'acheminement
process: logistic ...	processus (m) logistique
process: production ...	procédé (m) de fabrication
	processus (m) de production
processing: automatic data... (ADP)	traitement (m) automatique des données (TAD)
processing: batch ...	traitement (m) par lots
processing: central ... unit (CPU)	processeur (m) central
processing: data ...	informatique (f)
	traitement (m) des données
processing: electronic ...	traitement (m) informatique
processing: electronic data ... (EDP)	traitement (m) électronique de l'information (TEI)
processing: information ...	traitement (m) de l'information
processing: word ...	traitement (m) de texte
processor: word ... (WP)	machine (f) à traitement de texte
procurement	approvisionnement (m)
procurement manager	chef (m) d'approvisionnement
product abandonment	suppression (f) d'un produit
product advertising	publicité (f) de produit
product analysis	analyse (f) de produit
	étude (f) de produit
product area	domaine (m) de produits
product conception	conception (f) de produit
product costing	comptabilité (f) industrielle
product design	conception (f) de produit
	dessin (m) du produit
product development	développement (m) de produits
product differentiate (to)	se différencier
product differentiation	différenciation (f) des produits
product diversification	diversification (f) des produits
product dynamics	dynamique (f) des produits
product engineering	étude (f) de produit
product generation	création (f) de produit

product group	grille *(f)* de produits
	groupe *(m)* de produits
product image	image *(f)* de produit
product improvement	amélioration *(f)* de produit
product introduction	lancement *(m)* d'un produit
product launch	lancement *(m)* d'un produit
product life	vie *(f)* d'un produit
product life cycle	courbe *(f)* de vie d'un produit
	cycle *(m)* de vie d'un produit
product life expectancy	espérance *(f)* de vie d'un produit
product line	gamme *(f)* de produits
	ligne *(f)* de produits
	série *(f)* de produits
product management	gestion *(f)* de produit
product manager	chef *(m)* de produit
product mix	éventail *(m)* de produits
	product-mix *(m)*
product performance	comportement *(m)* de produit
product planning	planification *(f)* du produit
product portfolio	portefeuille *(m)* de produits
product profile	profil *(m)* de produit
product profitability	rentabilité *(f)* de produit
product range	éventail *(m)* de produits
product reliability	fiabilité *(f)* de produit
product research	recherche *(f)* de produits
product strategy	stratégie *(f)* de produit
product testing	test *(m)* de produit
product: by-...	sous-produit *(m)*
product: core ...	produit *(m)* leader
product: new- ... development	développement *(m)* de produits nouveaux
product: pioneer ...	innovation *(f)*
product: star ...	produit *(m)* locomotive *(f)*
production	production *(f)*
production complex	complexe *(m)* de production
production control	gestion *(f)* de la production
	régulation *(f)* de la production
	surveillance *(f)* de la production
production costs	coûts *(mpl)* de production

production director	directeur *(m)* de fabrication
production engineering	techniques *(fpl)* de la production
production line	chaîne *(f)* de production
production management	gestion *(f)* de la production
	organisation *(f)* de la production
production manager	chef *(m)* de fabrication
production planning	planning *(m)* de la production
production planning and control	projet *(m)* et contrôle *(m)* de la production
production process	procédé *(m)* de fabrication
	processus *(m)* de production
production run	passage *(m)* de production
production schedule	programme *(m)* de fabrication
production scheduling	programmation *(f)* de la production
production standard	norme *(f)* de production
production target	objectif *(m)* de production
production technique	technique *(f)* de la production
production: batch ...	fabrication *(f)* par lots
production: continuous-flow ...	production *(f)* continue
production: factors of ...	facteurs *(mpl)* de production
production: flow ...	fabrication *(f)* à la chaîne
production: intensive ...	exploitation *(f)* intensive
production: line ...	production *(f)* à la chaîne
production: mass ...	fabrication *(f)* en série
	production *(f)* en masse
production: modular ...	fabrication *(f)* par éléments normalisés
production: pilot ...	fabrication *(f)* pilote
	présérie *(f)*
production: share of ... plan	intéressement *(m)*
productive maintenance	entretien *(m)* productif
productivity	efficience *(f)*
	productivité *(f)*
	rendement *(m)*
	rentabilité *(f)*
productivity agreement	contrat *(m)* de productivité
productivity bargaining	négociations *(fpl)* des contrats de productivité
productivity campaign	campagne *(f)* de productivité

productivity drive	campagne *(f)* de productivité
productivity measurement	mesure *(f)* de la productivité
professionalization	professionnalisation *(f)*
profile: acquisition ...	profil *(m)* d'acquisition
profile: company ...	profil *(m)* de l'entreprise
profile: customer ...	profil *(m)* de la clientèle
profile: job ...	description *(f)* de fonction
profile: market ...	profil *(m)* du marché
profile: product ...	profil *(m)* de produit
profile: risk ...	profil *(m)* de risque
profit	bénéfice *(m)*
	profit *(m)*
profit centre	centre *(m)* de profit
profit centre accounting	comptabilité *(f)* par centres de profit
profit-factor analysis	analyse *(f)* des facteurs de profit
profit goal	but *(m)* de profit
profit impact	incidence *(f)* sur le profit
profit implication	répercussion *(f)* sur les bénéfices
profit improvement	amélioration *(f)* de la rentabilité
profit margin	marge *(f)* bénéficiaire
profit maximization	maximisation *(f)* du profit
profit motive	motivation *(f)* par le profit
profit optimization	optimisation *(f)* du profit
profit outlook	perspective *(f)* de profit
profit performance	rendement *(m)*
profit planning	planification *(f)* des bénéfices
profit projection	projection *(f)* des profits
profit-related pay	salaire *(m)* lié aux bénéfices
profit-sharing	intéressement *(m)*
	participation *(f)* aux bénéfices
profit strategy	stratégie *(f)* de profit
profit target	objectif *(m)* de profit
profit-volume ratio (P/V)	rapport *(m)* profit sur ventes
profit: cost-volume-... analysis	analyse *(f)* volume-coûts-profits
profit: distributed ...	bénéfices *(mpl)* distribués
profit: gross ...	bénéfice *(m)* brut
profit: net ...	bénéfice *(m)* net
profit: undistributed ...	bénéfices *(mpl)* non distribués
profitability	rentabilité *(f)*

profitability analysis	analyse *(f)* de la rentabilité
	étude *(f)* de rentabilité
profitability: product ...	rentabilité *(f)* de produit
profits tax	impôt *(m)* sur les bénéfices
program (to)	programmer
program: computer ...	programme *(m)* d'ordinateur
programme (to)	programmer
programme	programme *(m)*
programme budgeting	*rationalisation (f) des choix budgétaires (RCB)*
programme evaluation and review technique (PERT)	méthode *(f)* PERT
programme package	progiciel *(m)*
programme: development ...	programme *(m)* de développement
programme: investment ...	programme *(m)* d'investissements
programme: trading ...	programme *(m)* de négoce
programmed instruction	enseignement *(m)* programmé
programmed learning	enseignement *(m)* programmé
	enseignement *(m)* séquentiel
programmed management	direction *(f)* par programmes
	gestion *(f)* programmée
programmer: computer ...	programmeur *(m)* sur ordinateur
programming	élaboration *(f)* de programmes
	programmation *(f)*
programming: computer ...	programmation *(f)*
programming: dynamic ...	programmation *(f)* dynamique
programming: linear ...	programmation *(f)* linéaire
programming: mathematical ...	programmation *(f)* mathématique
programming: non-linear ...	programmation *(f)* non-linéaire
programming: parametric ...	programmation *(f)* paramétrique
programming: planning, ..., budgeting system (PPBS)	*rationalisation (f) des choix budgétaires (RCB)*
programming: scientific ...	programmation *(f)* mathématique
progress control	contrôle *(m)* de la production
	surveillance *(f)* de la production
progress: work in ...	travail *(m)* en cours
progression: salary ... curve	courbe *(f)* d'augmentation de salaire
project analysis	étude *(f)* de projet
project assessment	évaluation *(f)* de projet

project management	project management *(m)*
project manager	chef *(m)* de projet
project planning	plan *(m)* de projet
project: capital … evaluation	étude *(f)* de projet d'investissement
project: chunk a … (to)	découper un projet en tranches
project: integrated … management (IPM)	gestion *(f)* intégrée
projection	projection *(f)*
projection: profit …	projection *(f)* des profits
promotion (*personnel*)	promotion *(f)* *(du personnel)*
promotion: executive …	promotion *(f)* des cadres
promotion: sales	promotion *(f)* des ventes
promotional	promotionnel
promotional mix	moyens *(mpl)* d'action promotionnelle
promotional policy	politique *(f)* de promotion
proposal: value …	offre *(f)* de valeur
proposition: business …	proposition *(f)* d'affaires
proposition: unique selling … (USP)	promesse *(f)* unique de vente
prospective customer	prospect *(m)*
prospects: market …	perspectives *(fpl)* commerciales
protection: consumer …	protection *(f)* du consommateur
protection: data …	protection *(f)* des données
protection: turf …	défense *(f)* de son territoire
psychology: industrial …	psychologie *(f)* industrielle
psychometric testing	test *(m)* psychométrique
public enterprise	entreprise *(f)* d'Etat
	secteur *(m)* public
public relations (PR)	relations *(fpl)* publiques (RP)
public utility	service *(m)* public
public: go … (to)	introduire en bourse
publicly listed company	société *(f)* cotée en bourse
publishing: desktop …	micro-édition *(f)*
	publication *(f)* assistée par ordinateur (PAO)
purchasing	achats *(mpl)*
	approvisionnement *(m)*
purchasing manager	chef *(m)* des achats
purchasing motivator	mobile *(m)* d'achat

purchasing power	pouvoir *(m)* d'achat
purchasing power parity	parité *(f)* du pouvoir d'achat

Q

QC (quality control)	contrôle *(m)* de la qualité
	gestion *(f)* de la qualité
quality assessment	évaluation *(f)* de la qualité
quality assurance	contrôle *(m)* de la qualité
quality circle	cercle *(m)* de qualité
quality control (QC)	contrôle *(m)* de la qualité
	gestion *(f)* de la qualité
quality control: total ... ... (TQC)	contrôle *(m)* de la qualité globale (QG)
quality management	gestion *(f)* de la qualité
quality management: total ... ... (TQM)	gestion *(f)* de la qualité absolue
quantitative analysis	analyse *(f)* quantitative
quantity: break-even ...	point *(m)* mort
quantity: economic batch ...	effectif *(m)* de série économique
quantity: economic manufacturing ...	quantité *(f)* économique de fabrication
	série *(m)* économique de fabrication
quantity: economic order ...	quantité *(f)* économique à commander
	quantité *(f)* optimale de commande
queueing theory	théorie *(f)* des files d'attente
quick assets	actif *(m)* disponible
	actif *(m)* négociable
	actif *(m)* réalisable
quick fix	bouclage *(m)* rapide
quota: sales ...	quota *(m)* de ventes
quoted company	société *(f)* cotée en bourse
quotient	quotient *(m)*

R

R & D (research and development)	R et D (recherche *(f)* et développement *(m)*)
raid a company (to)	attaquer une société

raider: corporate ...	prédateur *(m)*
raising: capital ...	mobilisation *(f)* de fonds
RAM (random-access memory)	mémoire *(f)* à accès sélectif
random access	accès *(m)* sélectif
random-access memory (RAM)	mémoire *(f)* à accès sélectif
random observation method	méthode *(f)* des observations instantanées
random sampling	échantillonnage *(m)* aléatoire sondage *(m)* aléatoire
range: price ...	échelle *(f)* des prix
range: product ...	éventail *(m)* de produits
ranking	classement *(m)*
rat race	foire *(f)* d'empoigne panier *(m)* de crabes
rate of return	rentabilité *(f)* taux *(m)* de rendement
rate of return: internal ... ... (IRR)	taux *(m)* de rendement interne
rate: bank ...	taux *(m)* de base bancaire (TBB)
rate: base ...	taux *(m)* de base
rate: forward ...	taux *(m)* pour les opérations à terme
rate: going ...	taux *(m)* en vigueur
rating: credit ...	réputation *(f)* de solvabilité standing *(m)*
rating: market ...	cours *(m)* de bourse
rating: merit ...	appréciation *(f)* du mérite
rating: performance ...	jugement *(m)* d'allure
rating: personnel ...	appréciation *(f)* du personnel notation *(f)* de la main-d'oeuvre
rating: points-... method	méthode *(f)* de qualification par points
ratio: accounting ...	ratio *(m)* comptable
ratio: administration-production ...	ratio *(m)* administration-production
ratio: capital-output ...	ratio *(m)* d'intensité de capital
ratio: cash ...	coefficient *(m)* de trésorerie ratio *(m)* de trésorerie
ratio: cover ...	taux *(m)* de couverture
ratio: current ...	coefficient *(m)* de liquidité
ratio: debt ...	ratio *(m)* d'endettement
ratio: debt-equity ...	rapport *(m)* dettes-actions

ratio: financial ...	ratio *(m)* financier
ratio: gearing ...	ratio *(m)* d'endettement
ratio: liquidity ...	coefficient *(m)* de liquidité
	taux *(m)* de liquidité
ratio: management ...	ratio *(m)* de gestion
ratio: price-earnings ... (P/E)	rapport *(m)* cours-bénéfices
	taux *(m)* de price-earnings
ratio: profit-volume ... (P/V)	rapport *(m)* profit sur ventes
rationale	raisonnement *(m)*
rationalization	rationalisation *(f)*
rationalize (to)	rationaliser
rationing: capital ...	rationnement *(m)* de capitaux
re-evaluation of assets	réévaluation *(f)* des actifs
re-image (to)	changer l'image *(f)*
reach a deal (to)	conclure une affaire
reactive	réactif
reactive strategy	stratégie *(f)* réactive
read-only memory (ROM)	mémoire *(f)* morte
	mémoire *(f)* passive
real income	revenu *(m)* réel
real time	temps *(m)* réel
realize (to) (*profit*)	réaliser *(un portefeuille)*
recognition: brand ...	identification *(f)* d'une marque
recognition: mutual ...	reconnaissance *(f)* réciproque
reconfiguration	reconfiguration *(f)*
reconstruction: company ...	reconstitution *(f)* de la société
record: track ...	antécédents *(mpl)*
recovery of expenses	recouvrement *(m)* des dépenses
	récupération *(f)* des frais
recovery: overhead ...	couverture *(f)* des frais généraux
recruit (to)	recruter
recruitment	embauche *(f)*
	recrutement *(m)*
recycle (to)	recycler
recycling	recyclage *(m)*
redeploy (to)	redéployer
	réorganiser
redeployment	reclassement *(m)* (de main-d'oeuvre)
	réorganisation *(f)*

reduction: cost ...	réduction *(f)* des coûts
reduction: variety ...	normalisation *(f)* quantitative
redundancy	licenciement *(m)*
refocusing	recentrage *(m)*
registered trademark	marque *(f)* déposée
regression analysis	analyse *(f)* de régression
regression analysis: multiple ... ... (MRA)	analyse *(f)* de régression multiple
regulate (to)	réglementer
	régler
regulation	règlement *(m)*
reinvent the wheel (to)	inventer le fil à couper le beurre
relations: business ...	relations *(fpl)* d'affaires
relations: employee ...	relations *(fpl)* avec les employés
	relations *(fpl)* ouvrières
relations: external ...	relations *(fpl)* extérieures
relations: functional ...	liaisons *(fpl)* fonctionnelles
relations: human ...	relations *(fpl)* humaines
relations: industrial ...	relations *(fpl)* industrielles
	relations *(fpl)* professionnelles
relations: labour ...	relations *(fpl)* du travail
	relations *(fpl)* syndicales
relations: line ...	liaisons *(fpl)* hiérarchiques
relations: public ... (PR)	relations *(fpl)* publiques (RP)
reliability	fiabilité *(f)*
reliability: product ...	fiabilité *(f)* de produit
relief: tax ...	dégrèvement *(m)* d'impôt
remittance policy	politique *(f)* à l'égard des remises
remuneration	paiement *(m)*
	rémunération *(f)*
remuneration: executive ...	rémunération *(f)* des cadres
reorganization	restructuration *(f)*
	réorganisation *(f)*
replacement costs	coûts *(mpl)* de remplacement
representation: analog(ue) ...	représentation *(f)* analogique
representation: joint ...	démarche *(m)* collective
representation: worker ...	représentation *(f)* du personnel

representative: trade union ...	délégué *(m)* syndical
requirements: job ...	exigences *(fpl)* de poste
rerun (to)	réexécuter
	repasser
resale price maintenance (RPM)	prix *(mpl)* imposés
research and development (R & D)	recherche *(f)* et développement *(m)* (R et D)
research department	bureau *(m)* d'études
	service *(m)* de recherche
research: advertising ...	études *(fpl)* publicitaires
research: blue-sky ...	recherche *(f)* sans but précis
research: consumer ...	recherche *(f)* des besoins des consommateurs
research: desk ...	recherche *(f)* documentaire
research: economic ...	études *(fpl)* économiques
research: field ...	recherche *(f)* sur le terrain
research: market ...	analyse *(f)* des marchés
	étude *(m)* de marché
research: marketing ...	recherche *(f)* commerciale
research: motivational ...	étude *(f)* de motivation
research: operational ... (OR)	recherche *(f)* opérationnelle (RO)
research: operations ... (OR)	recherche *(f)* opérationnelle (RO)
research: product ...	recherche *(f)* de produits
reserve: contingency ...	fonds *(m)* de prévoyance
resistance: consumer ...	résistance *(f)* des consommateurs
resource allocation	affectation *(f)* des ressources
	allocation *(f)* des ressources
	répartition *(f)* des moyens
resource appraisal	examen *(m)* des ressources
resource management	gestion *(f)* des ressources
resourcing: manpower ...	recrutement *(m)* et gestion *(f)* des effectifs
resourcing: staff ...	recrutement *(m)* et gestion *(f)* des effectifs
response: anticipatory ...	*anticipation (f) stratégique*
response: lag ...	décalage *(m)*
responsibilities: allocation of...	répartition *(f)* des responsabilités
responsibility accounting	comptabilité *(f)* des sections

responsibility centre	centre *(m)* de responsabilité
responsibility: functional ...	responsabilité *(f)* fonctionnelle
responsibility: linear ...	responsabilité *(f)* hiérarchique
responsive: consumer-...	sensible au consommateur
restriction: trade ...	restriction *(f)* sur le commerce
restrictive practices (*industrial*)	pratiques *(fpl)* restrictives
restrictive practices (*legal*)	ententes *(fpl)*
restructure (to)	restructurer
restructuring	restructuration *(f)*
results: payment by ...	salaire *(m)* au rendement
retail price index (RPI)	indice *(m)* des prix de détail
retained profits	bénéfices *(mpl)* non distribués
retire (to)	prendre sa retraite
retirement	retraite *(f)*
retirement: early ...	retraite *(f)* anticipée
retraining	recyclage *(m)*
retrieval: data ...	extraction *(f)* de données
retrieval: information ...	récupération *(f)* de l'information
return	rendement *(m)*
return on assets	rendement *(m)* des fonds propres
return on capital	rendement *(m)* de capital
return on capital employed (ROCE)	rentabilité *(f)* des capitaux investis (RCI)
return on equity (ROE)	rendement *(m)* des fonds propres
return on investment (ROI)	retour *(m)* sur investissement
return on sales	rentabilité *(f)* des ventes
return: fair ...	rendement *(m)* équitable
return: internal rate of ... (IRR)	taux *(m)* de rendement interne
return: rate of ...	rentabilité *(f)*
	taux *(m)* de rendement
revaluation of assets	réévaluation *(f)* des actifs
revenue: average ...	recette *(f)* moyenne
review (to)	réviser
	revoir
review: financial ...	examen *(m)* financier
review: performance ...	évaluation *(f)* des performances
review: salary ...	révision *(f)* des traitements
revolving credit	crédit *(m)* permanent
rich: cash-...	riche en liquidité

rights issue	droit *(m)* préférentiel de souscription
risk analysis	analyse *(f)* des risques
risk assessment	appréciation *(f)* des risques
risk capital	capital *(m)* risque
risk management	gestion *(f)* des risques
risk profile	profil *(m)* de risque
risks: minimize ... (to)	minimiser les risques
robot	robot *(m)*
robotics	robotique *(f)*
robotize (to)	robotiser
robust	solide
ROCE (return on capital employed)	RCI (rentabilité *(f)* des capitaux investis)
ROE (return on equity)	rendement *(m)* des fonds propres
ROI (return on investment)	retour *(m)* sur investissement
role-playing	jeu *(m)* de rôles
role set	*ensemble (m) des attributions*
roll out (to)	introduire globalement
ROM (read-only memory)	mémoire *(f)* morte
	mémoire *(f)* passive
rotation: job ...	rotation *(f)* des postes
round figures: in	en chiffres *(mpl)* ronds
round off (to)	arrondir
	compléter
route (to)	acheminer
	router
routine	programme *(m)*
	routine *(f)*
routine: diagnostic ...	programme *(m)* de diagnostic
routing	acheminement *(m)*
royalty	droits *(mpl)* d'auteur
RPI (retail price index)	indice *(m)* des prix de détail
RPM (resale price maintenance)	prix *(mpl)* imposés
running expenses	charges *(fpl)* d'exploitation
	dépenses *(fpl)* de fonctionnement

S

safety management	gestion *(f)* de la sécurité
safety stock	stock *(m)* de sécurité
	stock *(m)* tampon
safety: industrial ...	sécurité *(f)* industrielle
safety: margin of ...	marge *(f)* de sécurité
salary grade	indice *(m)* de traitement
salary progression curve	courbe *(f)* d'augmentation de salaire
salary review	révision *(f)* des traitements
salary structure	structure *(f)* des salaires
sale: impulse ...	vente *(f)* d'appel
	vente *(f)* de choc
sale: point of ... (POS)	lieu *(m)* de vente (LV)
	point *(m)* de vente
sale: point-of-... advertising	publicité *(f)* sur le lieu de vente (PLV)
sales analysis	analyse *(f)* des ventes
sales appeal	attraction *(f)* commerciale
sales area	territoire *(m)* de vente
sales budget	budget *(m)* commercial
sales coverage	couverture *(f)* du marché
sales department	département *(m)* commercial
	direction *(f)* des ventes
	services *(mpl)* commerciaux
sales drive	animation *(f)* des ventes
sales engineer	ingénieur *(m)* commercial
sales estimate	estimation *(f)* des ventes
sales expansion effort	effort *(m)* d'accroissement des ventes
sales expectations	ventes *(fpl)* anticipées
sales force	équipe *(f)* de vente
sales forecast	prévision *(f)* des ventes
sales goal	objectif *(m)* de vente
sales management	administration *(f)* des ventes
	direction *(f)* commerciale
	direction *(f)* des ventes
	organisation *(f)* des ventes

sales manager	chef *(m)* de ventes
	directeur *(m)* commercial
sales mix	éventail *(m)* de produits
	gamme *(f)* commerciale
sales planning	planification *(f)* des ventes
sales policy	politique *(f)* de vente
sales potential	potentiel *(m)* de vente
sales promotion	promotion *(f)* des ventes
sales quota	quota *(m)* de ventes
sales slump	mévente *(f)*
sales talk	arguments *(mpl)* de vente
sales target	objectif *(m)* de vente
sales territory	territoire *(m)* de vente
sales test	vente *(f)* expérimentale
sales turnover	chiffre *(m)* d'affaires (CA)
sales volume	chiffre *(m)* d'affaires (CA)
	volume *(m)* de ventes
sales: return on ...	rentabilité *(f)* des ventes
sampling: activity ...	mesure *(f)* du travail par sondage
sampling: random ...	échantillonnage *(m)* aléatoire
	sondage *(m)* aléatoire
sampling: statistical ...	échantillonnage *(m)* statistique
satisfaction: consumer ...	satisfaction *(f)* du consommateur
satisfaction: job ...	joie *(f)* au travail
	satisfaction *(f)* au travail
saturation: market ...	saturation *(f)* du marché
scab	briseur *(m)* de grève
scale: diseconomy of ...	déséconomie *(f)* d'échelle
scale: economy of ...	économie *(f)* d'échelle
scale: sliding ...	échelle *(f)* mobile
scan: environmental ...	balayage *(m)* de l'environnement
scanning	lecture *(f)*
	scrutation *(f)*
scatter diagram	diagramme *(m)* de dispersion
scenario	hypothèse *(f)*
scenario: best-case ...	hypothèse *(f)* optimiste
scenario: worst-case ...	hypothèse *(f)* pessimiste
schedule (to)	dresser (un programme)

schedule	calendrier *(m)*
	horaire *(m)*
	plan *(m)* de travail
	programme *(m)*
schedule: production ...	programme *(m)* de fabrication
schedule: work ...	programme *(m)* de travail
scheduling	ordonnancement *(m)*
	programmation *(f)*
scheduling: production ...	programmation *(f)* de la production
scheme: bonus ...	programme *(m)* de primes d'encouragement
scheme: incentive ...	programme *(m)* de stimulants salariaux
scheme: suggestion ...	système *(m)* de suggestions
science: behavioural ...	science *(f)* du comportement
science: management ...	science *(f)* de la gestion
scientific management	gestion *(f)* scientifique
	organisation *(f)* scientifique
	organisation *(f)* scientifique du travail (OST)
scientific programming	programmation *(f)* mathématique
screen (to)	passer au crible
	sélectionner
search: executive ...	*assistance (f) au recrutement des cadres*
	executive search
second guess (to)	*anticiper l'action (f) de quelqu'un*
	décider contre l'avis (m) de quelqu'un
securities	titres *(mpl)*
	valeurs *(fpl)*
securitization	titrisation *(f)*
securitize (to)	titriser
security leak	fuite *(f)*
security: collateral ...	nantissement *(m)*
	titre *(m)* déposé en garantie
security: gilt-edged ...	valeur *(f)* de premier ordre
security: industrial ...	contre-espionnage *(m)* industriel
security: job ...	sécurité *(f)* de l'emploi
security: unlisted ...	valeur *(f)* non cotée
seed money	capital *(m)* de départ
seeking: goal-...	recherche *(f)* des buts

segment (to)	segmenter
segment: market ...	strate (f) de marché
segmentation	segmentation (f)
segmentation: market ...	segmentation (f) des marchés
selection: media ...	sélection (f) des média
selection: portfolio ...	sélection (f) de portefeuille
self-actualization	autoréalisation (f)
self-appraisal	auto-critique (f)
self-liquidating	auto-amortissable
self-motivation	automotivation (f)
sell out (to)	liquider
	réaliser (un portefeuille)
sell-by date	date (f) limite de vente
sell: hard ...	vente (f) agressive
sell: soft ...	promotion (f) (de vente) discrète
sellers' market	marché (m) à la hausse
selling policy	politique (f) de vente
selling: direct ...	vente (f) directe
selling: switch ...	vente (f) à perte
semiconductor	semi-conducteur (m)
semi-skilled labour	main-d'oeuvre (f) spécialisée
semi-variable costs	charges (fpl) semi-variables
	coûts (mpl) semi-variables
sensitive: cost-...	sensible au coût
sensitive: market-...	sensible au marché
sensitivity analysis	analyse (f) de sensibilité
sensitivity training	éducation (f) de la sensibilité
sensitize (to)	sensibiliser
sequential analysis	analyse (f) séquentielle
series: time ...	série (f) chronologique
service: after-sales ...	service (m) après-vente
service: customer ...	service (m) à la clientèle
services: advisory ...	services (mpl) de conseil interne
services: computer	services (mpl) en informatique
services: computer ... bureau	façonnier (m)
services: extension ...	services (mpl) logistiques
services: management ...	*services (mpl) de conseil interne*
	services (mpl) d'état-major
	services (mpl) fonctionnels

set-up costs	frais *(mpl)* d'établissement
severance pay	indemnité *(f)* de licenciement
sexual harassment	harcèlement *(m)* sexuel
share capital	capital *(m)* actions
share of production plan	intéressement *(m)*
share price performance	performance *(f)* du prix des actions
share: earnings per ... (EPS)	bénéfices *(mpl)* par action (BPA)
share: golden ...	action *(f)* préférentielle
share: market ...	part *(f)* du marché
shareholding	actionnariat *(m)*
	possession *(f)* d'actions
sharing: job-...	partage *(m)* du travail
sharing: profit-...	intéressement *(m)*
	participation *(f)* aux bénéfices
sharing: time-...	temps *(m)* partagé
shelf-life	durée *(f)* de vie
shift: day ...	équipe *(f)* de jour
shift: night ...	équipe *(f)* de nuit
shiftwork	travail *(m)* par relais
shipping	expédition *(f)*
shop floor	ateliers *(mpl)*
	ouvriers *(mpl)*
shop steward	délégué *(m)* d'atelier
shop: closed ...	*pratique (f) restrictive de recrutement imposée par les syndicats*
shop: open ...	*appartenance (f) non obligatoire à un syndicat*
short-range planning	planification *(f)* à court terme
short-term planning	planification *(f)* à court terme
shortfall	déficit *(m)*
	manque *(m)*
shortlist (to)	établir une liste restreinte
	sélectionner
shortlist	liste *(f)* restreinte
shut-down	fermeture *(f)*
	immobilisation *(f)*
significant	significatif
simplex method	méthode *(f)* du simplexe

simplification: job ...	simplification *(f)* du travail (SdT)
simplification: work ...	simplification *(f)* du travail (SdT)
simulate (to)	simuler
simulation	simulation *(f)*
simulation: computer ...	simulation *(f)* par ordinateur
single currency	monnaie *(f)* unique
single market	marché *(m)* unique
single market (*of the EC*)	marché *(m)* interne *(de la CE)*
single sourcing	approvisionnement *(m)* d'une source unique
sinking fund	fonds *(m)* d'amortissement
sit-down strike	grève *(f)* sur le tas
skilled labour	main-d'oeuvre *(f)* professionnelle
skills analysis	analyse *(f)* des aptitudes
slack	marge *(f)*
sliding scale	échelle *(f)* mobile
slim down (to)	alléger
slot	créneau *(m)*
slump	récession *(f)*
slump: sales ...	mévente *(f)*
slush fund	caisse *(f)* noire
smart card	carte *(f)* à puce
social analysis	analyse *(f)* sociale
socio-cultural	socio-culturel
socio-economic	socio-économique
sociometric	sociométrique
soft landing	atterrissage *(m)* en douceur
soft sell	promotion *(f)* (de vente) discrète
software	logiciel *(m)*
	software *(m)*
software application	exploitation *(f)* du logiciel
software broker	courtier *(m)* en logiciel
software company	société *(f)* de services d'ingénierie en informatique
	société *(f)* en logiciel
software engineer	ingénieur *(m)* en logiciel
software package	progiciel *(m)*
sole agent	agent *(m)* commercial exclusif
solving: problem ...	résolution *(f)* de problèmes

source and disposition of funds	ressources *(fpl)* et emplois *(mpl)* de capitaux
sourcing	approvisionnement *(m)*
sourcing: dual ...	approvisionnement *(m)* de deux sources
sourcing: single ...	approvisionnement *(m)* d'une source unique
span of control	étendue *(f)* du contrôle
	étendue *(f)* des responsabilités
	éventail *(m)* de contrôle
span: time ... of discretion	délai *(m)* de réflexion
spare capacity	capacité *(f)* inutilisée
specification: job ...	fixation *(f)* des tâches
specification: personnel ...	profil *(m)* de compétences
spellcheck	correcteur *(m)* orthographique
spill-over effect	retombée *(f)*
spin-off effect	retombée *(f)*
spirit: entrepreneurial ...	esprit *(m)* d'entreprise
sponsorship	sponsoring *(m)*
spot price	prix *(m)* au comptant
spreadsheet	feuille *(f)* de calcul électronique
	tableau *(m)* financier
	tableur *(m)*
squeeze: credit ...	restriction *(f)* du crédit
staff	personnel *(m)*
staff and line	structure *(f)* staff and line
staff appraisal	évaluation *(f)* du personnel
staff assistant	attaché *(m)* d'administration
staff audit	inventaire *(m)* des effectifs
staff commitment	engagement *(m)* du personnel
staff cut-back	réduction *(f)* du personnel
staff forecasting	prévision *(f)* des effectifs
staff management	direction *(f)* du personnel
staff manager	chef *(m)* du personnel
staff mobility	mobilité *(f)* du personnel
staff organization	organisation *(f)* fonctionnelle
	organisation *(f)* horizontale
staff planning	planification *(f)* des effectifs

staff resourcing	recrutement *(m)* et gestion *(f)* des effectifs
staff strategy	stratégie *(f)* du potentiel humain
staff transfer	mutation *(f)* dans le personnel
staff turnover	mouvement *(m)* du personnel
	mutation *(f)* du personnel
	rotation *(f)* du personnel
staff: line and ... organization	organisation *(f)* mixte
staff: management ...	personnel *(m)* dirigeant
	personnel *(m)* d'encadrement
staffing	recrutement *(m)* du personnel
stag	loup *(m)*
stagflation	stagflation *(f)*
stagger	décalage *(m)*
staggered holidays	étalement *(m)* des vacances
stake	enjeu *(m)*
stand-alone	autonome
	indépendant
stand-alone word processor	machine *(f)* à traitement de texte autonome
standard	norme *(f)*
	standard *(m)*
standard costing	méthode *(f)* des coûts standards
standard costs	coûts *(mpl)* standards
standard deviation	écart *(m)* type
standard of living	niveau *(m)* de vie
	standard *(m)* de vie
standard performance	rendement *(m)* standard
standard price	prix *(m)* standard
standard time	temps *(m)* de référence
	temps *(m)* standard
standard: budget ...	standard *(m)* budgétaire
standard: cost ...	norme *(f)* de prix de revient
standard: financial ...	norme *(f)* financière
standard: performance ...	norme *(f)* de rendement
standard: production ...	norme *(f)* de production
standardization	normalisation *(f)*
	standardisation *(f)*

standardize (to)	standardiser
	uniformiser
star product	produit *(m)* locomotive *(f)*
start-up	démarrage *(m)*
start-up costs	frais *(mpl)* de démarrage
state of the art	état *(m)* de l'art
	à la pointe du progrès
statement: financial ...	état *(m)* financier
statement: mission ...	définition *(f)* de la mission
statement: vision ...	définition *(f)* de la vision
statistical control	contrôle *(m)* statistique
statistical sampling	échantillonnage *(m)* statistique
status report	état *(m)* d'avancement
	rapport *(m)* sur la solvabilité
stimulus: competitive ...	stimulant *(m)* compétitif
stock control	contrôle *(m)* des stocks
	gestion *(f)* des stocks
stock market	bourse *(f)*
stock option	option *(f)* d'achat d'actions
stock option plan	plan *(m)* optionnel d'achat d'actions
stock portfolio	portefeuille *(m)* d'actions
stock turnover	mouvement *(m)* des stocks
	rotation *(f)* des stocks
stock valuation	évaluation *(f)* des stocks
stock: blue-chip ...	valeur *(f)* de premier ordre
stock: buffer ...	stock *(m)* tampon
stock: gilt-edged ...	valeur *(f)* de premier ordre
stock: safety ...	stock *(m)* de sécurité
	stock *(m)* tampon
stockbroker	courtier *(m)* de bourse
stockbroking	profession *(f)* de courtier de bourse
stocktaking	inventaire *(m)* (des stocks)
stocktaking: continuous ...	inventaire *(m)* permanent
storage	entreposage *(m)*
	magasinage *(m)*
storage: computer ...	mémoire *(f)* (d'un ensemble électronique)
strategic alliance	alliance *(f)* stratégique
strategic business unit	domaine *(m)* d'activité stratégique

strategic interdependence	interdépendance *(f)* des stratégies
strategic plan	plan *(m)* stratégique
strategic planning	plan *(m)* stratégique
strategy formulation	élaboration *(f)* des stratégies
strategy implementation	application *(f)* des stratégies
strategy: brand ...	stratégie *(f)* de la marque
strategy: business ...	stratégie *(f)* des affaires
strategy: competitive ...	stratégie *(f)* concurrentielle
strategy: corporate ...	stratégie *(f)* de l'entreprise
strategy: defensive ...	stratégie *(f)* défensive
strategy: diversification ...	stratégie *(f)* de diversification
strategy: executive manpower ...	stratégie *(f)* des cadres
strategy: expansion ...	stratégie *(f)* d'expansion
strategy: financial ...	stratégie *(f)* financière
strategy: growth ...	stratégie *(f)* de croissance
strategy: marketing ...	stratégie *(f)* commerciale
strategy: negotiation ...	stratégie *(f)* de négociation
strategy: pricing ...	stratégie *(f)* des prix
strategy: proactive ...	stratégie *(f)* proactive
strategy: product ...	stratégie *(f)* de produit
strategy: profit ...	stratégie *(f)* de profit
strategy: reactive ...	stratégie *(f)* réactive
strategy: staff ...	stratégie *(f)* du potentiel humain
strategy: survival ...	stratégie *(f)* de survie
strategy: user ...	stratégie *(f)* de l'utilisateur
stream: business ...	flux *(m)* d'affaires
stream: on ...	en cours *(m)*
	régime *(m)* de croisière
streamline (to)	rationaliser
strengths, weaknesses, opportunities and threats (SWOT) analysis	analyse *(f)* des forces et des faiblesses, des opportunités et des menaces
stress: work ...	tension *(f)* due au travail
strike: official ...	grève *(f)* officielle
strike: sit-down ...	grève *(f)* sur le tas
strike: sympathy ...	grève *(f)* de solidarité
strike: unofficial ...	grève *(f)* sauvage
strike: wildcat ...	grève *(f)* surprise

stripping: asset-...	cannibalisation *(f)*
	démantèlement *(m)* de l'actif
structure (to)	structurer
structure	structure *(f)*
structure : authority ...	structure *(f)* d'autorité
structure: capital ...	répartition *(f)* de capitaux
structure: corporate ...	structure *(f)* de l'entreprise
structure: cost ...	structure *(f)* des coûts
structure: grid ...	structure *(f)* en grille
structure: managerial ...	hiérarchie *(f)*
structure: market ...	structure *(f)* du marché
structure: organization ...	structure *(f)* d'organisation
structure: price ...	structure *(f)* des prix
structure: salary ...	structure *(f)* des salaires
structure: wage ...	structure *(f)* des salaires
structured	structuré
structuring	structuration *(f)*
structuring: work ...	restructuration *(f)* du travail
study: case ...	étude *(f)* de cas
study: feasibility ...	étude *(f)* de faisabilité
	étude *(f)* préalable
study: gap ...	étude *(f)* des écarts
study: market ...	étude *(f)* de marché
	examen *(m)* des débouchés
study: methods ...	étude *(f)* des méthodes
study: motion ...	étude *(f)* des mouvements
study: plant layout ...	étude *(f)* des implantations
study: time ...	chronométrage *(m)*
	étude *(f)* des temps
study: time and methods ...	étude *(f)* des temps et des méthodes
study: time and motion ...	étude *(f)* des temps et des mouvements
study: work ...	étude *(f)* du travail
style: house ...	style *(m)* de l'entreprise
style: management ...	style *(m)* managérial
sub-optimization	sous-optimisation *(f)*
subcontract (to)	sous-traiter
subcontracting	sous-traitance *(f)*
subliminal advertising	publicité *(f)* subliminale
subsidiarity	subsidiarité *(f)*

subsidiary company	filiale *(f)*
succession planning: management ...	plans *(mpl)* de remplacement
	plans *(mpl)* de succession
suggestion scheme	système *(m)* de suggestions
summary dismissal	licenciement *(m)* sommaire
sunrise industry	industrie *(f)* en croissance
sunset industry	industrie *(f)* en déclin
supervise (to)	surveiller
supervision	maîtrise *(f)*
supervisor	agent *(m)* de maîtrise
	surveillant *(m)*
supervisory board	conseil *(m)* de surveillance
supervisory management	maîtrise *(f)*
support activities	fonctions *(fpl)* complémentaires
survey: attitude ...	enquête *(f)* d'opinion
survey: market ...	étude *(f)* de marché
survival strategy	stratégie *(f)* de survie
swap	échange *(m)* financier
swap: forward ...	échange *(m)* financier à terme
switch selling	vente *(f)* à perte
switch trading	*report (m) d'une position d'une*
	échéance sur une autre
SWOT (strengths, weaknesses, opportunities & threats) analysis	analyse *(f)* des forces et des faiblesses, des opportunités et des menaces
sympathy strike	grève *(f)* de solidarité
symposium	colloque *(m)*
syndicate	consortium *(m)*
	syndicat *(m)*
synergism	synergie *(f)*
synergy	synergie *(f)*
system	système *(m)*
system-managed company	entreprise *(f)* dirigée de façon systématisée
system: business ...	chaîne *(f)* d'activités
system: computerized information ... (COINS)	système *(m)* d'information par ordinateur
system: expert ...	système *(m)* expert
system: information ...	système *(m)* d'information

system: integrated management ...	système *(m)* intégré de gestion
system: management ...	système *(m)* de direction
system: management information ... (MIS)	système *(m)* d'information de management (SIM)
	informatique *(f)* de gestion
system: planning, programming, budgeting ... (PPBS)	*rationalisation (f) des choix budgétaires (RCB)*
system: predetermined motion time ... (PMTS)	méthode *(f)* des temps prédéterminés (PMTS)
system: wage ...	système *(m)* des salaires
systematize (to)	systématiser
systems analysis	analyse *(f)* des systèmes
systems and procedures	méthodes *(fpl)* administratives
systems approach	approche *(f)* par la théorie des systèmes
systems design	conception *(f)* des systèmes
systems engineer	ingénieur *(m)* système
systems engineering	engineering *(m)* des systèmes
	mise *(f)* en oeuvre des systèmes
	planification *(f)* des systèmes
systems management	direction *(f)* systématisée
	gestion *(f)* par les systèmes
systems planning	planification *(f)* des systèmes
systems theory	théorie *(f)* des systèmes
systems: estimating ... costs	évaluation *(f)* des coûts de systèmes

T

TA (transactional analysis)	analyse *(f)* transactionnelle
table: input-output ...	tableau *(m)* d'échanges inter-industriels
tactical plan	plan *(m)* tactique
tactical planning	plan *(m)* tactique
tactics: competitive ...	tactique *(f)* concurrentielle
take-home pay	salaire *(m)* net
take-off	décollage *(m)*
take-over	prise *(f)* de contrôle
take-over bid (TOB)	offre *(f)* publique d'achat (OPA)
talk: sales ...	arguments *(mpl)* de vente

talks: pay ...	négociations *(fpl)* salariales
tangible assets	valeurs *(fpl)* matérielles
	valeurs *(fpl)* tangibles
target (to)	cibler
target	objectif *(m)*
target market	marché-cible *(m)*
target-setting	établissement *(m)* des objectifs
	fixation *(f)* des objectifs
target: production ...	objectif *(m)* de production
target: profit ...	objectif *(m)* de profit
targeting	ciblage *(m)*
	fixation *(f)* des objectifs
tariff barrier	barrière *(f)* douanière
tariff barrier: non-... ... (NTB)	barrière *(f)* non douanière
task force	groupe *(m)* d'intervention
tax-deductible	déductible fiscalement
tax incentive	incitation *(f)* fiscale
tax relief	dégrèvement *(m)* d'impôt
tax: corporation ...	impôt *(m)* sur les sociétés
tax: income ...	impôt *(m)* sur le revenu
tax: profits ...	impôt *(m)* sur les bénéfices
tax: value added ... (VAT)	taxe *(f)* à la valeur ajoutée (TVA)
taxation relief: double	suppression *(f)* de la double imposition
teaching: computer-assisted ... (CAT)	enseignement *(m)* automatisé
team-building	développement *(m)* d'équipe
team leader	chef *(m)* d'équipe
team player	équipier *(m)*
tech: high-...	technologie *(f)* de pointe
tech: low-...	peu élaboré
technical manager	directeur *(m)* technique
technique: management ...	technique *(f)* de gestion
technique: production ...	technique *(f)* de la production
technique: programme evaluation and review ... (PERT)	méthode *(f)* PERT
technological forecasting	prévision *(f)* technologique
technology transfer	transfert *(m)* de technologie
technology: information ...	informatique *(f)*
teleconference	téléconférence *(f)*
telemarketing	télémarketing *(m)*

telematics	télématique *(f)*
telesales	télévente *(f)*
	vente *(f)* par téléphone
teletext	vidéotex *(m)* diffusé
tender (to)	faire une soumission
tender	appel *(m)* d'offre (AO)
tendering: competitive ...	soumission *(f)* concurrentielle
terminal	terminal *(m)*
terminal: computer ...	terminal *(m)* d'ordinateur
territory: sales ...	territoire *(m)* de vente
test marketing	test *(m)* de marché
test run	passage *(m)* d'essai
test: aptitude ...	test *(m)* d'aptitude
test: market ...	test *(m)* de vente
	vente *(f)* expérimentale
testing: field ...	test *(m)* sur place
testing: product ...	test *(m)* de produit
testing: psychometric ...	test *(m)* psychométrique
theme: advertising ...	thème *(m)* publicitaire
theory: administrative ...	théorie *(f)* administrative
theory: communications ...	théorie *(f)* des communications
theory: contingency ...	théorie *(f)* de la contingence
theory: decision ...	théorie *(f)* des décisions
theory: game ...	théorie *(f)* des jeux
theory: information ...	théorie *(f)* de l'information
theory: management ...	théorie *(f)* de la gestion de l'entreprise
theory: organization ...	théorie *(f)* d'organisation
theory: probability ...	théorie *(f)* des probabilités
theory: queueing ...	théorie *(f)* des files d'attente
theory: systems ...	théorie *(f)* des systèmes
think-tank	cellule *(f)* de réflexion
	groupe *(m)* de réflexion
think the unthinkable (to)	concevoir l'inconcevable *(m)*
thinking: creative ...	matière *(f)* grise
	pensée *(f)* créatrice
thinking: lateral ...	pensée *(f)* latérale
third party	tiers *(m)*
throughput	débit *(m)*
thrust: competitive ...	percée *(f)* commerciale

time and methods study	étude *(f)* des temps et des méthodes
time and motion study	étude *(f)* des temps et des mouvements
time frame	délai *(m)*
time-lag	décalage *(m)*
time management	organisation *(f)* du temps
time series	série *(f)* chronologique
time-sharing	temps *(m)* partagé
time sheet	feuille *(f)* de présence
time span of discretion	délai *(m)* de réflexion
time study	chronométrage *(m)*
	étude *(f)* des temps
time: down ...	durée *(f)* d'immobilisation
	temps *(m)* mort
time: lead ...	délai *(m)* de livraison
	délai *(m)* de réalisation
	délai *(m)* de suite
time: predetermined motion ... system (PMTS)	méthodes *(fpl)* des temps prédéterminés (PMTS)
time: real ...	temps *(m)* réel
time: standard ...	temps *(m)* de référence
	temps *(m)* standard
time: turnaround ...	délai *(m)* d'exécution
	délai *(m)* de redressement
title: job ...	description *(f)* de poste
TOB (take-over bid)	OPA (offre *(f)* publique d'achat)
toolbox	boîte *(f)* à outils
top management	cadres *(mpl)* dirigeants
	cadres *(mpl)* supérieurs
	direction *(f)* générale
	haute direction *(f)*
top management approach	optique *(f)* de la direction générale
top up (to)	compléter
top-down	du sommet à la base
total plant maintenance	entretien *(m)* total de l'équipement
total quality control (TQC)	contrôle *(m)* de la qualité globale (CQG)
total quality management (TQM)	gestion *(f)* de la qualité absolue
TQC (total quality control)	CQG (contrôle *(m)* de la qualité globale)

TQM (total quality management)	gestion (f) de la qualité absolue
track record	antécedents (mpl)
trade association	association (f) professionnelle
trade cycle	cycle (m) économique
trade imbalance	déséquilibre (m) commercial
trade name	raison (f) sociale
trade off (to)	faire un compromis (m)
	faire un échange (m)
trade-off	compromis (m)
	échange (m)
trade restriction	restriction (f) sur le commerce
trade union	syndicat (m)
trade union representative	délégué (m) syndical
trade: barter ...	commerce (m) d'échange
traded option	option (f) négociable
trademark: registered ...	marque (f) déposée
trading area	secteur (m) de vente
	territoire (m) de vente
trading programme	programme (m) de négoce
trading: insider ...	délit (m) d'initié
trading: patent ...	échange (m) de brevets
trading: switch ...	*report (m) d'une position d'une échéance sur une autre*
trainee turnover	rotation (f) des stagiaires
training	formation (f)
	perfectionnement (m)
training needs	besoins (mpl) en formation
training needs analysis	analyse (f) des besoins en formation
training officer	directeur (m) de formation
training within industry (TWI)	formation (f) dans l'entreprise
training: analytical ...	formation (f) par étapes
training: booster ...	recyclage (m)
training: computer-based ... (CBT)	enseignement (f) assistée par ordinateur (EAO)
training: executive ...	formation (f) des cadres
training: group ...	action (f) collective de formation
training: hands-on ...	formation (f) pratique
training: in-plant ...	formation (f) dans l'entreprise
training: management ...	formation (f) des cadres

training: multimedia ...	formation *(f)* plurimédiatique
training: off-the-job ...	formation *(f)* extérieure
	formation *(f)* institutionnelle
training: on-the-job ...	formation *(f)* sur le terrain
	formation *(f)* sur le tas
training: part-analysis ...	formation *(f)* par étapes
training: sensitivity ...	éducation *(f)* de la sensibilité
training: vocational ...	formation *(f)* professionnelle
transactional	transactionnel
transactional analysis (TA)	analyse *(f)* transactionnelle
transfer pricing	fixation *(f)* des prix de transfert
transfer: technology ...	transfert *(m)* de technologie
transfer: staff ...	mutation *(f)* dans le personnel
transitional	transitionnel
transportation	transport *(m)*
tree: decision ...	arbre *(m)* de décision
tree: family ...	arbre *(m)* généalogique
tree: pertinence ...	arbre *(m)* de pertinence
trend	tendance *(f)*
trend: economic ...	conjoncture *(f)*
	évolution *(f)* économique
trend: exponential ...	tendance *(f)* exponentielle
trend: market ...	orientation *(f)* du marché (à court terme)
	tendance *(f)* du marché (à long terme)
trickle-down theory	*théorie (f) selon laquelle la richesse finit par toucher les plus pauvres*
troubleshooter	dépanneur *(m)*
troubleshooting	dépannage *(m)*
turf protection	défense *(f)* de son territoire
turn around (to)	redresser
turnaround time	délai *(m)* d'exécution
	délai *(m)* de redressement
turnover	chiffre *(m)* d'affaires (CA)
turnover: asset	rotation *(f)* des capitaux
turnover: inventory ...	rotation *(f)* des stocks
turnover: sales ...	chiffre *(m)* d'affaires (CA)
turnover: staff ...	mutation *(f)* du personnel
	rotation *(f)* du personnel

turnover: stock ...	mouvement *(f)* des stocks
	rotation *(f)* des stocks
turnover: trainee ...	rotation *(f)* des stagiaires
TWI (training within industry)	formation *(f)* accélérée dans l'entreprise

U

unbundle (to)	dégrouper
unbundling	dégroupage *(m)*
under licence	sous licence
undercapacity	sous-capacité *(f)*
undercapitalized	sous-capitalisé
undercut (to)	vendre moins cher
undermanned	à court de main-d'oeuvre *(f)*
undermanning	manque *(m)* de main-d'oeuvre
underperform (to)	sous-performer
underprice (to)	mettre un prix trop bas
understaffed	ayant un manque *(m)* de personnel
understaffing	manque *(m)* de personnel
undistributed profit	bénéfices *(mpl)* non distribués
unfair competition	concurrence *(f)* déloyale
unfair dismissal	licenciement *(m)* abusif
unique selling point/proposition (USP)	promesse *(f)* unique de vente
unit labour costs	coûts *(mpl)* unitaires du personnel
unlisted company	société *(f)* non inscrite à la cote
unlisted security	valeur *(f)* non cotée
unofficial action	grève *(f)* sauvage
unofficial strike	grève *(f)* sauvage
unscramble (to)	débrouiller
unskilled labour	main-d'oeuvre *(f)* non-spécialisée
	ouvriers *(mpl)* non qualifiés
unstructured	non structuré
up the line	en remontant la hiérarchie
update (to)	mettre à jour
update	mise *(f)* à jour
up-market	haut *(m)* de gamme
upstream	en amont

upswing	amélioration *(f)* sensible
uptime	temps *(m)* de bon fonctionnement
upturn	reprise *(f)*
upwardly mobile	dynamique
use-by date	date *(f)* limite de consommation
user attitude	attitude *(f)* des utilisateurs
user-friendly	convivial
user strategy	stratégie *(f)* de l'utilisateur
user-unfriendly	non-convivial
USP (unique selling point/proposition)	promesse *(f)* unique de vente
utility: public ...	service *(m)* public
utilization: capacity ...	utilisation *(f)* de la capacité

V

VA (value analysis)	analyse *(f)* de la valeur
valuation: stock ...	évaluation *(f)* des stocks
value added	valeur *(f)* ajoutée
value added tax (VAT)	taxe *(f)* à la valeur ajoutée (TVA)
value analysis (VA)	analyse *(f)* de la valeur
value chain	chaîne *(f)* de valeur
value concept	concept *(m)* de valeur
value engineering	analyse *(f)* de la valeur
	analyse *(f)* des coûts
value proposal	offre *(f)* de valeur
value: asset ...	valeur *(f)* des actifs
value: book ...	valeur *(f)* comptable
value: break-up ...	valeur *(f)* de récupération
value: market ...	valeur *(f)* marchande
value: net present ... (NPV)	valeur *(f)* actuelle nette
value: present ... method	méthode *(f)* d'actualisation
variable costs	coûts *(mpl)* variables
variable costs: semi-... ...	charges *(fpl)* semi-variables
variable expenses	frais *(mpl)* variables
variance	écart *(m)*
	variance *(f)*
variance analysis	analyse *(f)* de variance
	analyse *(f)* des écarts

variance: cost ...	écart *(m)* des coûts
variety reduction	normalisation *(f)* quantitative
VAT (value added tax)	TVA (taxe *(f)* à la valeur ajoutée)
VDU (visual display unit)	unité *(m)* de visualisation
	visuel *(m)*
venture capital	capital-créateur *(m)*
venture capitalist	financier *(m)* à risque
venture management	gestion *(f)* des risques
venture: joint ...	action *(f)* concertée
	entreprise *(f)* conjointe
venture: joint-... company	société *(f)* d'exploitation en commun
	co-entreprise *(f)*
verbal communication	communication *(f)* verbale
verbal communication: non-... ...	communication *(f)* non-verbale
verify (to)	contrôler
	vérifier
vertical integration	intégration *(f)* verticale
vested interest	droit *(m)* acquis
viability	viabilité *(f)*
viable	valable
vice-chairman	vice-président *(m)*
vice-president	sous-directeur *(m)*
video	vidéo *(f)*
viewdata	vidéotex *(m)*
virus: computer ...	virus *(m)* informatique
vision	vision *(f)*
vision statement	définition *(f)* de la vision
visual display unit (VDU)	unité *(m)* de visualisation
	visuel *(m)*
vocational guidance	orientation *(f)* professionnelle (OP)
vocational training	formation *(f)* professionnelle
volume	volume *(m)*
volume: cost-...-profit analysis	analyse *(f)* volume-coûts-profits
volume: profit-... ratio (P/V)	rapport *(m)* profit sur ventes
volume: sales ...	chiffre *(m)* d'affaires (CA)
	volume *(m)* de ventes

W

wage ceiling	plafonnement *(m)* des salaires
wage differential	écarts *(mpl)* salariaux
wage drift	dérive *(f)* des salaires
wage freeze	blocage *(m)* des salaires
wage level	niveau *(m)* des salaires
wage policy	politique *(f)* salariale
wage structure	structure *(f)* des salaires
wage system	système *(m)* des salaires
wage: incentive ...	salaire *(m)* au rendement
	salaire *(m)* stimulant
wage: minimum ...	salaire *(m)* minimum
walking around: management by	management *(m)* baladeur
walkout	grève *(f)* surprise
WAN (wide area network)	grand réseau *(m)*
warehousing	emmagasinage *(m)*
	entreposage *(m)*
	magasinage *(m)*
wastage: natural ...	non-remplacement *(m)* des départs
waste: industrial ...	déchets *(mpl)* industriels
wasting assets	immobilisations *(fpl)* défectibles
weighted average	moyenne *(f)* pondérée
weighting	indemnité *(f)*
well-packaged	bien ficelé
wheeling and dealing	affairisme *(m)*
white-collar (worker)	col *(m)* blanc
white goods	produits *(mpl)* blancs
white knight	chevalier *(m)* blanc
whiz-kid	jeune turc *(m)*
wide area network (WAN)	grand réseau *(m)*
wildcat strike	grève *(f)* surprise
Winchester disk	disque *(m)* winchester
wind down (to)	démanteler
wind up (to)	liquider
winding up	cessation *(f)* de commerce
	liquidation *(f)*
window	viseur *(m)*

window-dressing	truquage *(m)* (du bilan)
window of opportunity	créneau *(m)* favorable
word processing	traitement *(m)* de texte
word processor (WP)	machine *(f)* à traitement de texte
word processor: stand-alone	machine *(f)* à traitement de texte autonome
work by contract	travail *(m)* à forfait
work content	contenu *(m)* du travail
work cycle	cycle *(m)* de travail
work in progress	travail *(m)* en cours
workload	charge *(m)* de travail
work measurement	mesure *(f)* du travail
work schedule	programme *(m)* de travail
work simplification	simplification *(f)* du travail (SdT)
workstation	station *(f)* de travail
work stress	tension *(f)* due au travail
work structuring	restructuration *(f)* du travail
work study	étude *(f)* du travail
work-to-rule	grève *(f)* du zèle
work: clerical ... measurement (CWM)	chronométrage *(m)* des travaux administratifs
worker buyout	rachat *(m)* d'une entreprise par ses employés
worker participation	participation *(f)* ouvrière
worker representation	représentation *(f)* du personnel
working capital	fonds *(m)* de roulement
working hours	horaire *(m)*
working hours: flexible	horaire *(m)* à la carte horaire *(f)* variable
working party	groupe *(m)* de travail
workplace	lieu *(m)* de travail
works committee	comité *(m)* d'entreprise (CE)
works council	comité *(m)* d'entreprise (CE)
works manager	chef *(m)* d'établissement directeur *(m)* d'usine
world-class	de classe *(f)* mondiale
worst-case scenario	hypothèse *(f)* pessimiste
worth: net ...	valeur *(f)* nette
WP (word processor)	machine *(f)* à traitement de texte

write off (to)	passer aux profits *(mpl)* et pertes
write-off	perte *(f)* sèche

Y

yardstick	critère *(m)* d'appréciation
	moyen *(m)* d'évaluation
year: base …	année *(f)* de référence
year: financial …	exercice *(m)*
year: fiscal …	année *(f)* budgétaire
yield	production *(f)*
	rendement *(m)*
yield: average …	rendement *(m)* moyen
yield: earnings …	rendement *(m)*
yuppie	jeune cadre *(m)* dynamique
	yuppie *(m)*

Z

Z chart	diagramme *(m)* en Z
	graphique *(m)* en dents de scie
zero-base budget	budget *(m)* base zéro
zero defects	zéro défaut
zero-rating	exemption *(f)* de la TVA
	taux *(m)* zéro
zero-sum game	jeu *(m)* à somme nulle

FRANCAIS-ANGLAIS

A

absentéisme *(m)*	absenteeism
absolue: gestion *(f)* **de la qualité ...**	total quality management (TQM)
absorption *(f)*	absorption
	amalgamation
absorption: méthode *(f)* **des coûts d'...**	absorption costing
abusif: licenciement *(m)* **...**	unfair dismissal
accaparer	corner (to)
accaparer le marché	corner the market (to)
accéder à	access (to)
acceptabilité *(f)* **de la marque**	brand acceptance
accès *(m)* **multiple**	multi-access
accès *(m)* **sélectif**	random access
accès sélectif: mémoire *(f)* **à ... ...**	random-access memory (RAM)
accident *(m)* **du travail**	industrial injury
accord *(m)* **à l'amiable**	gentleman's agreement
accord *(m)* **sur la sécurité de l'emploi**	job security agreement
accoutumance: courbe *(f)* **d'...**	learning curve
accroissement des ventes: effort *(m)* **d'... ... ...**	sales expansion effort
accueil *(m)*	induction
accueil: pays *(m)* **d'...**	host country
achalandage *(m)*	goodwill
achat *(m)* **impulsif**	impulse buying
achat d'actions: option *(f)* **d'... ...**	stock option
achat: comportement *(m)* **d'...**	buying behaviour
achat: facteur *(m)* **clé d'...**	key buying factor
achat: mobile *(m)* **d'...**	purchasing motivator
achat: offre *(f)* **publique d'... (OPA)**	take-over bid (TOB)
achat: plan *(m)* **optionnel d'... d'actions**	stock option plan
achats: chef *(m)* **des ...**	chief buyer
	purchasing manager

acheminement *(m)*	dispatching
	routing
acheminement: graphique *(m)* d'...	flow process chart
acheminer	route (to)
acheter ou louer	lease or buy (to)
acheteur *(m)* potentiel	potential buyer
acquis: droit *(m)* ...	vested interest
acquisition *(f)*	acquisition
acquisition *(f)* de données	data acquisition
acquisition: profil *(m)* d'...	acquisition profile
acquisitions: fusions *(fpl)* et ...	mergers and acquisitions (M and A)
actif *(m)*	assets
actif *(m)* circulant	current assets
actif *(m)* disponible	liquid assets
	quick assets
actif *(m)* immatériel	intangible assets
actif *(m)* immobilisé	capital assets
	fixed assets
actif *(m)* négociable	liquid assets
	quick assets
actif *(m)* net	net assets
actif *(m)* occulte	hidden assets
actif *(m)* réalisable	current assets
	liquid assets
	quick assets
actif: démantèlement *(m)* de l'...	asset-stripping
actif: scission *(f)* d'...	divestment (*of assets*)
actifs: gestion *(f)* des ...	asset management
actifs: portefeuille *(m)* d'...	asset portfolio
actifs: réévaluation *(f)* des ...	re-evaluation of assets
actifs: valeur *(f)* des ...	asset value
action *(f)* concertée	joint venture
action *(f)* préférentielle	golden share
action *(f)* revendicative	industrial action
action: bénéfices *(mpl)* par ... (BPA)	earnings per share (EPS)
action: plan *(m)* d'...	action plan
actionnariat *(m)*	shareholding
actions: capital *(m)* ...	share capital

actions: marché *(m)* des ...	equity market
actions: option *(f)* d'achat d'...	stock option
actions: performance *(f)* du prix des ...	share price performance
actions: plan *(m)* optionnel d'achat d'...	stock option plan
activer	activate (to)
activité *(f)* artificielle	dummy activity
activités *(fpl)*	operations
activités: chaîne *(f)* d'...	business system
activités: graphique *(m)* des ...	activity chart
activités: portefeuille *(m)* d'...	business portfolio
actualisation: méthode *(f)* d'...	present value method
actualisé: cash flow *(m)* ...	discounted cash flow (DCF)
actuelle: valeur *(f)* ... nette	net present value (NPV)
adaptation *(f)* du travail à l'homme	ergonomics
	human engineering
adaptif: contrôle *(m)* ...	adaptive control
adjoint: directeur *(m)* ...	assistant director
	deputy manager
adjoint: directeur *(m)* général ...	deputy managing director
administrateur *(m)*	non-executive director
	outside director
administratifs: frais *(mpl)* ...	administrative expenses
administration *(f)*	administration
administration *(f)* centrale	head office
administration *(f)* du personnel	personnel management
administration *(f)* des ventes	sales management
administration-production: ratio *(m)* ...	administration-production ratio
administration: conseil *(m)* d'...	board of directors
	executive board
administration: réunion *(f)* du conseil d'...	board meeting
administrative: théorie *(f)* ...	administrative theory
administratives: méthodes *(fpl)* ...	systems and procedures
adopter progressivement	phase in (to)
AF (analyse *(f)* fonctionnelle)	functional analysis
affacturage *(m)*	factoring

affaire *(f)*	deal
affaire: conclure une ...	reach a deal (to)
affaires: chiffre *(m)* d'... (CA)	turnover
	sales volume
affaires: contacts *(mpl)* d' ...	business contacts
	network
affaires: flux *(m)* d'...	business stream
affaires: proposition *(f)* d'...	business proposition
affaires: relations *(fpl)* d'...	business relations
affaires: stratégie *(f)* des ...	business strategy
affairisme *(m)*	wheeling and dealing
affectation *(f)*	allocation
	apportionment
	appropriation
affectation *(f)* budgétaire	budget appropriation
	budget allotment
affectation *(f)* des charges	cost allocation
affectation *(f)* des ressources	resource allocation
affectation *(f)* des tâches	job assignment
affecter	allocate (to)
	appropriate (to)
affichage: panneau *(m)* d'...	bulletin board
(électronique)	
affichage *(m)*: unité d'...	display unit
affiliée: société *(f)* ...	affiliate company
	associate company
agence *(f)* de placement	employment bureau
agent *(m)* commercial exclusif	sole agent
agent *(m)* expéditeur	forwarding agent
agent *(m)* de maîtrise	supervisor
agent *(m)* de publicité	advertising agent
agir en médiateur	mediate (to)
agressive: vente *(f)* ...	hard sell
ajoutée: taxe *(f)* à la valeur ...	value added tax (VAT)
ajoutée: valeur *(f)* ...	value added
aléatoire: échantillonnage *(m)* ...	random sampling
aléatoire: sondage *(m)* ...	random sampling
algorithme *(m)*	algorithm
alléger	slim down (to)

alliance *(f)* stratégique	strategic alliance
allocation *(f)* des fonds	budget appropriations
allocation *(f)* des ressources	resource allocation
allouer	allocate (to)
allure *(f)*	body language
allure: jugement *(m)* d'...	performance rating
amalgamer	merge (to)
amélioration *(f)* de produit	product improvement
amélioration *(f)* de la rentabilité	profit improvement
amélioration *(f)* des tâches	job improvement
amiable: accord *(m)* à l'...	gentleman's agreement
amont: en ...	upstream
amortir	depreciate (to)
amortissable: auto-...	self-liquidating
amortissement: fonds *(m)* d'...	sinking fund
amortissement: provision *(f)* pour ...	depreciation allowance
analogique: ordinateur *(m)* ...	analog computer
analogique: représentation *(f)* ...	analog(ue) representation
analyse *(f)* des aptitudes	skills analysis
analyse *(f)* des avantages-coûts	cost-benefit analysis (CBA)
analyse *(f)* des besoins	needs analysis
analyse *(f)* des besoins en formation	training needs analysis
analyse *(f)* du chemin critique	critical path analysis (CPA)
analyse *(f)* des concurrents	competitor analysis
analyse *(f)* des contributions (à la marge)	contribution analysis
analyse *(f)* coût-profit	cost-benefit analysis (CBA)
analyse *(f)* des coûts	cost analysis
	value engineering
analyse *(f)* de la décision	decision analysis
analyse *(f)* dynamique	dynamic evaluation
analyse *(f)* des écarts	variance analysis
analyse *(f)* entrées-sorties	input-output analysis
analyse *(f)* de l'environnement	environmental analysis
analyse *(f)* des facteurs de profit	profit-factor analysis
analyse *(f)* financière	financial analysis
analyse *(f)* fonctionnelle (AF)	functional analysis

analyse *(f)* des forces et des faiblesses, des opportunités et des menaces	SWOT (strengths, weaknesses, opportunities and threats) analysis
analyse *(f)* des investissements	investment analysis
analyse *(f)* des marchés	market research
analyse *(f)* marginale	incremental analysis
	marginal analysis
analyse *(f)* de média	media analysis
analyse *(f)* morphologique	morphological analysis
analyse *(f)* par poste de travail	job analysis
analyse *(f)* du prix de revient	cost analysis
analyse *(f)* de problème	problem analysis
analyse *(f)* de produit	product analysis
analyse *(f)* en profondeur	in-depth analysis
analyse *(f)* quantitative	quantitative analysis
analyse *(f)* de régression	regression analysis
analyse *(f)* de régression multiple	multiple regression analysis
analyse *(f)* de la rentabilité	profitability analysis
analyse *(f)* de réseau	network analysis
analyse *(f)* des risques	risk analysis
analyse *(f)* de sensibilité	sensitivity analysis
analyse *(f)* séquentielle	sequential analysis
analyse *(f)* sociale	social analysis
analyse *(f)* des systèmes	systems analysis
analyse *(f)* des tâches	job analysis
	operations analysis
analyse *(f)* transactionnelle	transactional analysis (TA)
analyse *(f)* de la valeur	value analysis (VA)
	value engineering
analyse *(f)* de variance	variance analysis
analyse *(f)* des ventes	sales analysis
analyse *(f)* volume-coûts-profits	cost-volume-profit analysis
analytique: comptabilité *(f)* ...	analytic accounting
	cost accounting
animation *(f)*	motivation
animation *(f)* des ventes	sales drive
animer	motivate (to)
	stimulate (to)
année *(f)* budgétaire	fiscal year

année *(f)* de référence	base year
annexes: avantages *(mpl)* ...	fringe benefits
antécedents *(mpl)*	track record
anticipées: ventes *(fpl)* ...	sales expectations
AO (appel *(m)* d'offre)	tender
apparentée: société *(f)* ...	affiliate company
	associate company
appel *(m)* d'offre (AO)	tender
appel: produits *(mpl)* d'...	impulse goods
	loss-leaders
appel: vente *(f)* d'...	impulse sale
application *(f)* de stratégie	strategy implementation
apport *(m)*	contribution *(in a take-over)*
appréciation *(f)*	appraisal
	assessment
appréciation *(f)* des investissements	investment appraisal
appréciation *(f)* du mérite	merit rating
appréciation *(f)* des performances	performance appraisal
	performance evaluation
appréciation *(f)* du personnel	personnel rating
	staff appraisal
appréciation *(f)* des risques	risk assessment
appréciation: critère *(m)* d'...	yardstick
approvisionnement *(m)*	procurement
	purchasing
	sourcing
	supply
approvisionnement *(m)* d'une source unique	single sourcing
approvisionnement *(m)* de deux sources	dual sourcing
approvisionnement: chef *(m)* d'...	procurement manager
approvisionner de l'extérieur (s')	buy in (to)
après-vente: service *(m)* ...	after-sales service
aptitude: test *(m)* d'...	aptitude test
aptitudes: analyse *(f)* des ...	skills analysis
apurer un compte	audit (to)
arabe: téléphone *(m)* ...	grapevine

arbitrage *(m)*	arbitrage
	arbitration
arbitragiste *(m)*	arbitrageur
arbre *(m)* de décision	decision tree
arbre *(m)* généalogique	family tree
arbre *(m)* de pertinence	pertinence tree
arguments *(mpl)* de vente	sales talk
arriéré *(m)*	backlog
arrivisme *(m)*	go-getting
arrondir	round off (to)
art: état *(m)* de l'...	state of the art
artificielle: activité *(f)* ...	dummy activity
artificielle: intelligence *(f)* ...	artificial intelligence
assiette *(f)*	assessment
association *(f)*	partnership
association *(f)* professionnelle	trade association
associé *(m)*	partner
assouplie: comptabilité *(f)* ...	creative accounting
atelier: chef *(m)* d'...	departmental head
	first-line manager
	(shop) foreman
ateliers *(mpl)*	shop-floor
attaché *(m)* fonctionnel	staff assistant
attaché *(m)* opérationnel	line assistant
attaquer une société	raid a company (to)
atterrissage *(m)* brutal	hard landing
atterrissage *(m)* en douceur	soft landing
attitude *(f)* des utilisateurs	user attitude
attraction *(f)* commerciale	sales appeal
attribution *(f)*	competency
au pair	at par
au-dessous du pair	below par
au-dessus du pair	above par
audio-visuels: supports *(mpl)* ...	audiovisual aids
audit *(m)*	audit
audit *(m)* interne	internal audit
augmentation *(f)* du capital	capital appreciation
	capital gain
augmentation *(f)* générale	across-the-board increase

augmenter de valeur	appreciate (to)
auteur: droits *(mpl)* **d'…**	royalty
auto-amortissable	self-liquidating
auto-critique *(f)*	self-appraisal
autodéveloppement *(m)*	advancement
	personal growth
autofinancement *(m)*	ploughback
autofinancement: marge *(f)*	cashflow
brute d'… (MBA)	
automation *(f)*	automation
automatique: traitement *(m)* **… des**	automatic data processing (ADP)
données (TAD)	
automatisation *(f)*	automation
automatisé: enseignement *(m)* **…**	computer-assisted teaching (CAT)
automatiser	automate (to)
	computerize (to)
automotivation *(f)*	self-motivation
autonome	stand-alone
autoréalisation *(f)*	self-actualization
autorité *(f)* **hiérarchique**	line authority
autre paire *(f)* **de manches**	different ball game
aval: en … *(m)*	downstream
avance *(f)* **sur les concurrents**	competitive edge
avancement: état *(m)* **d'…**	progress report
	status report
avant-garde *(f)*	leading edge
avantage *(m)* **concurrentiel**	competitive advantage
avantages *(mpl)* **annexes**	fringe benefits
avantages *(mpl)* **sociaux**	fringe benefits
avantages: analyse *(f)* **des …-coûts**	cost-benefit analysis (CBA)
avoirs *(mpl)*	assets

B

bail *(m)*: **louer à …**	lease (to)
baisse *(f)*	downturn
baisse: marché *(m)* **à la …**	bear market
	buyers' market
baissier *(m)*	bear

baladeur: management *(m)* ...	management by walking around
balayage *(m)* de l'environnement	environmental scan
banque *(f)* d'affaires	merchant bank
banque *(f)* commerciale	commercial bank
banque *(f)* de données	computer bank
	data bank
	data base
banque *(f)* d'investissement	investment bank
barrière *(f)* douanière	tariff barrier
barrière *(f)* non douanière	non-tariff barrier (NTB)
bas *(m)* de gamme	down-market
base *(f)* de données	data base
base: de la ... *(f)* au sommet	bottom-up
base: produit *(m)* de ...	primary commodity
base: taux *(m)* de ...	base rate
base: taux *(m)* de base bancaire (TBB)	bank rate
bâtons: diagramme *(m)* en ...	bar chart
bâtons: graphique *(m)* à ...	bar chart
bénéfice *(m)*	profit
bénéfice *(m)* brut	gross profit
bénéfice *(m)* net	net profit
bénéfice *(m)* réinvesti	ploughback
bénéfices *(mpl)* distribués	distributed profits
bénéfices *(mpl)* non-distribués	retained profits
	undistributed profits
bénéfices *(mpl)* par action (BPA)	earnings per share (EPS)
bénéfices: impôt *(m)* sur les ...	profits tax
bénéfices: participation *(f)* aux ...	profit sharing
bénéfices: planification *(f)* des ...	profit planning
bénéfices: rapport *(m)* cours-...	price-earnings ratio (P/E)
bénéficiaire: capacité *(f)* ...	earning power
bénéficiaire: marge *(f)* ...	profit margin
besoins: analyse *(f)* des ...	needs analysis
besoins en formation: analyse *(f)* des	training needs analysis
bien ficelé	well-packaged
biens *(mpl)* d'équipement	capital goods
	investment goods

biens *(mpl)* de consommation	consumer goods
biens *(mpl)* de consommation courante	fast-moving consumer goods (FMG)
biens *(mpl)* industriels	industrial goods
bilan *(m)*	balance sheet
bilan *(m)* consolidé	consolidated balance sheet
bilan: contrôle *(m)* du ...	balance sheet auditing
bilan: gestion *(f)* du ...	asset liability management
bilan: faire le ...	debrief (to)
bilan: habiller le ...	massage the figures (to)
blanchiment *(m)*	laundering
blanchir	launder (to)
blancs: produits *(mpl)* ...	white goods
blocage *(m)* des salaires	pay pause
	wage freeze
bloquer	freeze (to)
bogue *(f)*	bug
boîte *(f)* à lettres	mailbox
boîte *(f)* à outils	toolbox
bord: tableau *(m)* de ...	management chart
bouclage *(m)* rapide	quick fix
boucle *(f)* fermée	closed loop
boum *(m)*	boom
bourse *(f)*	stockmarket
bourse: société *(f)* cotée en ...	quoted company
	publicly listed company
bourse: cours *(m)* de ...	market rating
bourse: courtier *(m)* de ...	stockbroker
bourse: introduire en ...	go public (to)
bousculer	hustle (to)
BPA (bénéfices *(mpl)* par action)	EPS (earnings per share)
brader les prix	cut prices (to)
brain-trust *(m)*	brains trust
brainstorming *(m)*	brainstorming
brevet *(m)*	patent
brevets: échange *(m)* de ...	patent trading
briefer	brief (to)
briefing *(m)*	briefing

briseur *(m)* **de grèves**	blackleg
	scab
bruns: produits *(mpl)* ...	brown goods
brut: bénéfice *(m)* ...	gross profit
brute: marge *(f)* ...	gross margin (GM)
budget *(m)*	budget
budget *(m)* **base zéro**	zero-base budget
budget *(m)* **commercial**	sales budget
budget *(m)* **d'équipement**	capital budget
budget *(m)* **flexible**	flexible budget
budget *(m)* **d'investissement**	investment budget
budget *(m)* **de marketing**	marketing budget
budget *(m)* **de publicité**	advertising budget
budget *(m)* **de trésorerie**	cash budget
budget: établir un ...	budget (to)
budget: établissement *(m)* **du** ...	budgeting
budget: préparation *(f)* **du** ...	budgeting
budgétaire: affectation *(f)* ...	budget allotment
	budget appropriation
budgétaire: année *(f)* ...	fiscal year
budgétaire: comptabilité *(f)* ...	budgeting
budgétaire: contrainte *(f)* ...	budget constraint
budgétaire: contrôle *(m)* ...	budgetary control
	budgeting control
budgétaire: écart *(m)* ...	budgetary variance
budgétaire: gestion *(f)* ...	budgetary control
budgétaire: prévision *(f)* ...	budget forecasting
	budget forecast
budgétaire: standard *(m)* ...	budget standard
budgétaires: rationalisation *(f)* **des choix** ... **(RCB)**	*planning, programming, budgeting system (PPBS)*
	functional costing
	output budgeting
	performance budgeting
	programme budgeting
budgétisation *(f)*	budgeting
budgétisation *(f)* **des investissements**	capital budgeting
budgétiser	budget (to)
bureau *(m)* **de dessin**	design office

bureau *(m)* **électronique**	electronic office
bureau *(m)* **d'études**	design office
	engineering and design department
	research department
bureau *(m)* **des méthodes**	methods study department
bureau *(m)* **de planning**	planning department
bureau: employé *(m)* **de ...**	clerical worker
bureau: ordinateur *(m)* **de ...**	desktop computer
bureautique *(f)*	office automation
bureaux: organisation *(f)* **des ...**	office management
bureaux: planification *(f)* **des ...**	office planning
but *(m)*	goal
	target
but *(m)* **de l'entreprise**	company goal
	corporate goal
but *(m)* **de profit**	profit goal
buts: fixation *(f)* **des ...**	goal-setting
buts: recherche *(f)* **des ...**	goal-seeking

C

CA (chiffre *(m)* **d'affaires)**	turnover
cabinet *(m)* **de conseil en gestion**	management consultancy
cadre *(m)*	executive
	manager
cadre *(m)* **à haut potentiel**	high-flier
cadre *(m)* **à moindre potentiel**	low-flier
cadre *(m)* **dynamique: jeune ... ...**	yuppie
cadres *(mpl)* **dirigeants**	top management
cadres *(mpl)* **moyens**	middle management
cadres *(mpl)* **supérieurs**	top management
cadres: formation *(f)* **des ...**	executive training
	management training
cadres: perfectionnement *(m)* **des ...**	executive development
	management development
cadres: potentiel *(m)* **des ...**	management potential
cadres: promotion *(f)* **des ...**	executive advancement
	executive promotion

cadres: rémunération *(f)* des ...	executive compensation
	executive remuneration
cadres: stratégie *(f)* des ...	executive manpower strategy
cahier *(m)* des charges	conditions *(of a contract)*
caisse *(f)* noire	slush fund
caisse: petite ... *(f)*	petty cash
calcul: centre *(m)* de ...	computer centre
calcul électronique: feuille *(m)* de ...	spreadsheet
calculateur *(m)* numérique	digital computer
calculée: désuétude *(f)* ...	built-in obsolescence
	planned obsolescence
calendrier *(m)*	schedule
camembert *(m)*	pie chart
campagne *(f)* de productivité	productivity campaign
	productivity drive
campagne *(f)* de publicité	advertising campaign
	advertising drive
canaux *(mpl)* de communication	communication channels
cannibalisation *(f)*	asset-stripping
CAO (conception *(f)* assistée par ordinateur)	CAD (computer-aided design)
capacité *(f)*	capability
	capacity
capacité *(f)* bénéficiaire	earning power
capacité *(f)* inutilisée	idle capacity
	spare capacity
capacité *(f)* de production	manufacturing capacity
capacité *(f)* de l'usine	plant capacity
capacité: sous-... *(f)*	undercapacity
capacité: sur-... *(f)*	overcapacity
capacité: utilisation *(f)* de la ...	capacity utilization
capital *(m)* actions	share capital
capital-créateur *(m)*	venture capital
capital *(m)* de départ	seed money
capital *(m)* émis	issued capital
capital *(m)* d'emprunt	loan capital
capital *(m)* investi	capital employed
capital *(m)* nominal	authorized capital
capital *(m)* à risque	risk capital

capital *(m)* social	authorized capital
capital *(m)* souscrit	issued capital
capital: augmentation *(f)* du ...	capital appreciation
	capital gain
capital: dépenses *(fpl)* en ...	capital expenditure
capital: formation *(f)* de ...	capital formation
capital: récupération *(f)* du ... investi	payback
capital: ratio *(m)* d'intensité de ...	capital-output ratio
capital: rendement *(m)* de ...	return on capital
capitalisation *(f)*	capitalization
capitalisé: sous-...	under-capitalized
capitaliser	capitalize (to)
capitalistique	capital-intensive
capitaux *(mpl)* circulants	circulating capital
capitaux *(mpl)* fébriles	hot money
capitaux *(mpl)* permanents	fixed assets
capitaux *(mpl)* propres	shareholders' equity
capitaux *(mpl)* roulants	circulating capital
capitaux: rationnement *(m)* de ...	capital rationing
capitaux: rentabilité *(f)* des ... investis (RCI)	return on capital employed (ROCE)
capitaux: ressources *(fpl)* et emplois *(mpl)* de ...	source and disposition of funds
caractère *(m)* confidentiel	confidentiality
caractéristiques *(fpl)* de poste	job characteristics
	job description
	job expectations
carrière: perspectives *(fpl)* de ...	career planning
carrière: plan *(m)* de ...	smart card
carte *(f)* à puce	smart card
cartel *(m)*	cartel
cas: étude *(f)* de ...	case study
cash-flow *(m)*	cash flow
cash-flow *(m)* actualisé (méthode DCF)	discounted cash flow (DCF)
cash-flow *(m)* marginal	incremental cash flow
cash-flow *(m)* négatif	negative cash flow
CATIF (contrat *(m)* à terme d'instruments financiers)	financial futures

c.c. (convention *(f)* collective)	collective bargaining agreement
CE (comité *(m)* d'entreprise)	works council
CE (Communauté *(f)* Européenne)	EC (European Community)
cellulaire: gestion *(f)* ...	divisional management
cellule *(f)* de réflexion	think-tank
central: fichier *(m)* ...	computer bank
	data bank
	data base
centrale: administration *(f)* ...	head office
centrale: unité *(f)* ... de traitement	mainframe
centralisation *(f)*	centralization
centraliser	centralize (to)
centre *(m)* de calcul	computer centre
centre *(m)* de coûts	cost centre
centre *(m)* d'évaluation de la qualité	assessment centre
centre *(m)* de profit	profit centre
centre *(m)* de responsabilité	responsibility centre
centre: comptabilité *(f)* par ... de profit	profit centre accounting
cercle *(m)* de qualité	quality circle
cessation *(f)* de commerce	winding up
chaîne *(f)* d'activités	business system
chaîne *(f)* de montage	assembly line
chaîne *(f)* de production	chain of production
	production line
chaîne *(f)* de valeur	value chain
chaîne: fabrication *(f)* à la ...	flow production
chaîne: production *(f)* à la ...	chain production
	line production
chambre *(f)* de compensation	clearing house
chances: égalité *(f)* des ...	equal opportunity
change: taux *(m)* de ...	exchange rate
change: taux *(m)* de ... à terme	forward exchange rate
changement: gestion *(f)* du ...	change management (management of change)
changer l'image *(f)*	re-image (to)
charge *(m)* de travail	workload
charge: facteur *(m)* de ...	load factor

charge: indice *(m)* de ...	load factor
charge: taux *(m)* de ...	load factor
charges *(fpl)* d'exploitation	operating expenses
	running expenses
charges *(fpl)* directes	direct expenses
charges *(fpl)* indirectes	indirect expenses
charges *(fpl)* variables	variable costs
charges *(fpl)* semi-variables	semi-variable costs
charges: affectation *(f)* des ...	allocation of costs
charges: cahier *(m)* des ...	conditions (*of a contract*)
charges: étude *(f)* des ...	cost analysis
charges: imputation *(f)* des ...	allocation of costs
charges: répartition *(f)* des ...	cost apportionment
chasseur *(m)* de têtes	head-hunter
chef *(m)*	manager
chef *(m)* des achats	chief buyer
	purchasing manager
chef *(m)* d'approvisionnement	chief buyer
	procurement manager
chef *(m)* d'atelier	departmental head
	first-line manager
chef *(m)* comptable	chief accountant
chef *(m)* direct	line manager
chef *(m)* de la distribution	distribution manager
chef *(m)* d'équipe	foreman
	team leader
chef *(m)* d'établissement	plant manager
	works manager
chef *(m)* d'exploitation	operations manager
chef *(m)* de fabrication	production manager
chef *(m)* de marque	brand manager
chef *(m)* du personnel	personnel manager
	staff manager
chef *(m)* de produit	product manager
chef *(m)* de projet	project manager
chef *(m)* de secteur	area manager
chef *(m)* de service	departmental manager
chef *(m)* de ventes	sales manager
chef: sous-... *(m)*	assistant manager

chemin *(m)* critique: analyse *(f)* du	critical path analysis (CPA)
chemin *(m)* critique: méthode *(f)* du	critical path method (CPM)
chevalier *(m)* blanc	white knight
chiffre *(m)* d'affaires (CA)	sales volume
	turnover
chiffre *(m)* repère	benchmark
chiffres: manipuler les ...	massage the figures (to)
chiffres ronds: en	in round figures
chimiques: produits *(mpl)* ... dangereux	hazchem (hazardous chemicals)
choc: vente *(f)* de ...	impulse sale
choix *(mpl)* budgétaires: rationalisation *(f)* des ... ...(RCB)	*planning, programming, budgeting system (PPBS)*
	functional costing
	output budgeting
	performance budgeting
	programme budgeting
chômage: mettre en ... *(m)* technique	lay off (to)
chronologique: série *(f)* ...	time series
chronométrage *(m)*	time study
chronométrage *(m)* des travaux administratifs	clerical work measurement (CWM)
ciblage *(m)*	targeting
cible *(f)*	target
cible: marché-... *(m)*	target market
cibler	target (to)
circuit *(m)* de distribution	chain of distribution
circulaire: graphique *(m)* ...	pie chart
circulant: actif *(m)* ...	current assets
circulants: capitaux *(mpl)* ...	circulating capital
circulation: graphique *(m)* de ...	flow chart
classe mondiale: de	world-class
classement *(m)*	ranking
classification *(f)* des emplois	job evaluation
classification *(f)* des fonctions	job classification
clé: facteur *(m)* ... d'achat	key buying factor
clé: facteur *(m)* ... de succès	key success factor

client: orientation *(f)* vers le ...	customer orientation
client: souci *(m)* du ...	customer care
clientèle: profil *(m)* de la ...	customer profile
clientèle: service *(m)* à la ...	customer service
clignotant *(m)*	performance indicator
cloison *(f)* étanche	Chinese wall
cloisonné: non ...	open-plan
co-entreprise *(f)*	joint-venture company
codétermination *(f)*	co-determination
coefficient *(m)* de liquidité	current ratio
coefficient *(m)* de trésorerie	cash ratio
	liquidity ratio
coefficient *(m)* d'utilisation de la capacité	load factor
col *(m)* blanc	white-collar (worker)
collecte *(f)* de données	data gathering
collective: convention *(f)* ... (c.c.)	collective bargaining agreement
collective: démarche *(f)* ...	joint representation
collective: prime *(f)* ...	group bonus
	group incentive
collectives: négociations *(fpl)* ...	collective bargaining
colloque *(m)*	symposium
collusion *(f)*	collusion
comité *(m)* de direction	board of directors
	executive board
comité *(m)* d'entreprise (CE)	works committee
	works council
commande *(f)* numérique	numerical control
commande *(f)* de processus	process control
commande: fabriqué sur ... *(f)*	custom-made
	customized
commande: quantité *(f)* optimale de ...	economic order quantity
commande *(f)* manuelle: à	hands-on
commandement: hiérarchie *(f)* de ...	chain of command
commander: quantité *(f)* économique à ...	economic order quantity
commerce *(m)* d'échange	barter trade

commerce: restriction *(f)* sur le ...	trade restriction
commercial: agent *(m)* ... exclusif	sole agent
commercial: budget *(m)* ...	sales budget
commercial: département *(m)* ...	sales department
commercial: directeur *(m)* ...	sales manager
commercial: ingénieur *(m)* ...	sales engineer
commerciale: attraction *(f)* ...	sales appeal
commerciale: créativité *(f)* ...	creative marketing
commerciale: direction *(f)* ...	sale management
commerciale: gamme *(f)* ...	sales mix
commerciale: gestion *(f)* ...	sales management
commerciale: information *(f)* ...	market intelligence
commerciale: percée *(f)* ...	market thrust
commerciale: recherche *(f)* ...	marketing research
commerciale: société *(f)* ...	business corporation
commerciale: stratégie *(f)* ...	marketing strategy
commerciales: perspectives *(fpl)* ...	market prospects
commercialisation *(f)*	selling
	marketing
commerciaux: services *(mpl)* ...	sales department
commissaire *(m)* aux comptes	auditor
commun: langage *(m)* ...	common language
commun: société *(f)* d'exploitation en ...	joint-venture company
Communauté *(f)* Européenne (CE)	European Community (EC)
commune: monnaie *(f)* ...	common currency
communication *(f)* non verbale	non-verbal communication
communication *(f)* verbale	verbal communication
communication: canaux *(mpl)* de ...	channels of communication
communication: voies *(f)* de ...	channels of communication
communications: réseau *(m)* de ...	communications network
communications: théorie *(f)* des ...	communications theory
comparaison *(f)* inter-entreprises	inter-firm comparison
compartimenter	compartmentalize (to)
compatible	compatible
compensation: chambre *(f)* de ...	clearing house
compétence *(f)* de management	executive competence
	management competence
compétence *(f)* dans le travail·	job competence

compétent	efficient
compétiteurs *(mpl)*	the competition
compétitif	competitive
compétitif: stimulant *(m)* ...	competitive stimulus
compétitivité *(f)*	competitiveness
complémentaire: matériel *(m)* ...	add-on equipment
complémentaires: fonctions *(fpl)* ...	support activities
complets: méthode *(f)* des coûts ...	absorption costing
	full-cost method
compléter	round off (to)
	top up (to)
complexe *(m)* de production	production complex
comportement *(m)* d'achat	buying behaviour
comportement *(m)* du consommateur	consumer behaviour
comportement *(m)* de produit	product performance
comportement: science *(f)* du ...	behavioural science
compromis: faire un ...	trade off (to)
comptabilité *(f)*	accounting
	accounting department
comptabilité *(f)* analytique	cost accounting
comptabilité *(f)* assouplie	creative accounting
comptabilité *(f)* budgétaire	budgeting
comptabilité *(f)* par centres de profit	profit centre accounting
comptabilité *(f)* par fabrication	process costing
comptabilité *(f)* de gestion	management accounting
comptabilité *(f)* industrielle	analytic accounting
	product costing
comptabilité *(f)* de prix de revient	cost accounting
comptabilité *(f)* des sections	responsibility accounting
comptabilité *(f)* marginale	marginal costing
comptable: chef *(m)* ...	chief accountant
comptable: modèle *(m)* ...	accounting model
comptable: ratio *(m)* ...	accounting ratio
comptable: valeur *(f)* ...	book value
comptables: services *(mpl)* ...	accounting department
	accounts department
comptant: prix *(m)* au ...	spot price
comptant: transaction *(f)* au ...	cash deal
compte: apurer un ...	audit (to)

comptes *(mpl)* consolidés	consolidated accounts
comptes *(mpl)* de groupe	group accounts
comptes *(mpl)* intégrés	consolidated accounts
comptes: commissaire *(m)* aux ...	auditor
comptes: vérificateur *(m)* de ...	auditor
	comptroller
	controller
comptes: vérification *(f)* de ...	audit
	auditing
concept *(m)* de valeur	value concept
conception *(f)* assistée par ordinateur (CAO)	computer-aided design (CAD)
conception *(f)* du produit	product conception
	product design
conception *(f)* des systèmes	systems design
conception *(f)* des tâches	job design
conception: étude *(f)* de ...	design engineering
concertée: action *(f)* ...	joint venture
concession *(f)* réciproque de licences	cross-licensing
concevoir l'inconcevable *(m)*	think the unthinkable (to)
conciliation	conciliation
concilier	conciliate (to)
conclure une affaire	reach a deal (to)
concurrence *(f)*	competition
concurrence *(f)* déloyale	unfair competition
concurrence *(f)* raisonnable	fair competition
concurrentiel	competitive
concurrentiel: avantage *(m)* ...	competitive advantage
concurrentielle: position *(f)* ...	competitive position
concurrentielle: soumission *(f)* ...	competitive tendering
concurrentielle: tactique *(f)* ...	competitive tactics
concurrents: analyse *(f)* des ...	competitor analysis
concurrents: avance *(f)* sur les ...	competitive edge
conditionnement *(m)*	packaging
conditions *(fpl)* d'embauche	conditions of employment
confidentiel: caractère *(m)* ...	confidentiality
conflit *(m)* du travail	labour dispute
conflit *(m)* social	industrial dispute
conglomérat *(m)*	conglomerate

conjoncture *(f)*	business outlook
	economic climate
	economic trend
connaissance *(f)* des coûts	cost awareness
connecté *(à l'ordinateur)*	on line
connecté: non ...	off line
connecter	interface (to)
conscience *(f)* des coûts	cost consciousness
conscience *(f)* du marché	market awareness
conseil *(m)* d'administration	board of directors
	executive board
conseil *(m)* de direction	board of directors
	executive board
conseil *(m)* en direction	management consultant
conseil *(m)* des employés	employee counselling
conseil *(m)* de gestion	board of directors
conseil *(m)* en gestion	management consultant
conseil *(m)* en informatique	computer consultant
conseil *(m)* de prud'hommes	*conciliation board*
conseil *(m)* de surveillance	supervisory board
conseil: expert-... *(m)*	consultant
conseil: ingénieur-... *(m)*	management consultant
conseil: réunion *(f)* du ...	board meeting
d'administration	
conseil: salle *(f)* du ...	boardroom
conseil: services *(mpl)* de ... interne	advisory services
conseil en gestion: cabinet *(m)* de ...	management consultancy
consensus *(m)*	consensus
consolidation *(f)*	consolidation
consolidé: bilan *(m)* ...	consolidated balance sheet
consolidés: comptes *(mpl)* ...	consolidated accounts
consommateur: comportement *(m)*	consumer behaviour
du ...	
consommateur: orientation *(f)* vers	consumer orientation
le ...	
consommateur: protection *(f)* du ...	consumer protection
consommateur: satisfaction *(f)* du ...	consumer satisfaction
consommateur: sensible au ...	consumer-responsive
consommateurs: panel *(m)* de ...	consumers' panel

consommateurs: recherche *(f)* des besoins des ...	consumer research
consommateurs: réceptivité *(f)* des ...	consumer acceptance
consommateurs: résistance *(f)* des ...	consumer resistance
consommation: biens *(mpl)* de ...	consumer goods
consommation: produits *(mpl)* de ... durable	consumer durables
consommation courante: biens *(mpl)* de	fast-moving consumer goods (FMG)
consommation courante: produits *(mpl)* de	convenience goods
consommérisme *(m)*	consumerism
consortium *(m)*	consortium
	syndicate
consultatif	consultative
consultations *(fpl)* paritaires	joint consultation
consulter	consult (to)
consulting *(m)*	consultancy
contacts *(mpl)* d'affaires	business contacts
	network
containeurisation *(f)*	containerization
conteneur *(m)*	container
contenu *(m)* du travail	job content
	work content
contenu local: réglementation *(f)* de	local content rules
contingence: théorie *(f)* de la ...	contingency theory
continue: production *(f)* ...	continuous-flow production
contrainte *(f)* budgétaire	budget constraint
contrat *(m)* de franchisage	franchise
contrat *(m)* global	package deal
contrat *(m)* du management	management contract
contrat *(m)* de productivité	productivity agreement
contrat *(m)* à terme d'instruments financiers (CATIF)	financial futures
contrats *(mpl)* à terme	futures
contre-espionnage *(m)* industriel	industrial security
contremaître *(m)*	first-line manager
	foreman

contrepartie *(f)*	countertrade
contributions: analyse *(f)* des ... (à la marge)	contribution analysis
contrôle *(m)*	audit
	control
contrôle *(m)* adaptif	adaptive control
contrôle *(m)* du bilan	balance sheet auditing
contrôle *(m)* budgétaire	budgetary control
	budgeting control
contrôle *(m)* du conseil d'administration	board control
contrôle *(m)* des coûts	cost control
contrôle *(m)* du crédit	credit control
contrôle *(m)* de direction	managerial control
contrôle *(m)* d'efficience	efficiency audit
contrôle *(m)* de fabrication	manufacturing control
contrôle *(m)* financier	financial control
contrôle *(m)* de gestion	budgetary control
	management audit
	managerial control
	operations audit
contrôle *(m)* interne	internal audit
contrôle *(m)* par lots	batch control
contrôle *(m)* des opérations	operations audit
contrôle *(m)* de la performance	performance monitoring
contrôle *(m)* de la production	progress control
contrôle *(m)* de la qualité	quality assurance
	quality control (QC)
contrôle *(m)* de la qualité globale (CQG)	total quality control (TQC)
contrôle *(m)* statistique	statistical control
contrôle *(m)* des stocks	inventory control
	stock control
contrôle: éventail *(m)* de ...	span of control
contrôle: information *(f)* de ...	control information
contrôle: prise *(f)* de ...	take-over
contrôlée: grève non-...	wildcat strike
contrôler la performance	monitor performance (to)
contrôlés: coûts *(mpl)* ...	managed costs

contrôleur *(m)* de gestion	comptroller
	controller
convention *(f)*	agreement (*written*)
convention *(f)* collective (cc)	collective bargaining agreement
convivial	user-friendly
convivial: non-...	user-unfriendly
coopératif	collaborative
coordination *(f)*	coordination
corporatisme *(m)*	corporatism
correcteur *(m)* orthographique	spellcheck
corrélation *(f)*	correlation
correspondance: vente *(f)* par ... (VPC)	mail order
cote: société *(f)* non inscrite à la ...	unlisted company
cotée: société *(f)* ... en bourse	publicly listed company
	quoted company
cotée: valeur *(f)* non ...	unlisted security
courbe *(f)* d'accoutumance	learning curve
courbe *(f)* d'augmentation de salaire	salary progression curve
courbe *(f)* de vie (d'un produit)	product life cycle
courrier *(m)* électronique	electronic mail (e-mail)
cours *(m)* de bourse	market rating
cours: en ...	on stream
cours: rapport *(m)* ...-bénéfices	price-earnings ratio (P/E)
cours: travail *(m)* en ...	work in progress
court terme: dettes *(fpl)* à ...	current liabilities
court terme: planification *(f)* à ...	short-range planning
	short-term planning
courtage *(m)*	brokerage
	jobbing
courtage: frais *(mpl)* de ...	brokerage fees
court-circuiter	bypass (to)
courtier *(m)*	broker
courtier *(m)* de bourse	stockbroker
courtier *(m)* en logiciel	software broker
côut *(m)* de la vie	cost of living
coût: analyse *(f)* ...-profit	cost-benefit analysis (CBA)
coût: méthode *(f)* du ... proportionnel	direct costing

coût: facteur *(m)* ...	cost factor
coût: moindre ...	least-cost
coût: sensible au ...	cost-sensitive
coût-efficace	cost-efficient
coût-efficacité *(m)*	cost-effectiveness
coûts d'absorption: méthode *(f)* des	absorption costing
coûts complets: méthode *(f)* des	absorption costing
	full-cost method
coûts *(mpl)* constants	fixed costs
coûts *(mpl)* contrôlés	managed costs
coûts *(mpl)* directs	direct costs
coûts *(mpl)* de la distribution	distribution costs
coûts *(mpl)* fixes	fixed costs
coûts *(mpl)* indirects	indirect costs
coûts *(mpl)* marginaux	marginal costs
coûts *(mpl)* moyens	average costs
coûts *(mpl)* d'opportunité	opportunity costs
coûts *(mpl)* de production	costs of production
coûts *(mpl)* de remplacement	replacement costs
coûts *(mpl)* semi-variables	semi-variable costs
coûts *(mpl)* standards	standard costs
coûts *(mpl)* unitaires du personnel	unit labour costs
coûts *(mpl)* variables	variable costs
coûts: analyse *(f)* des ...	value engineering
coûts: analyse *(f)* volumes-...-profits	cost-volume-profit analysis
coûts: centre *(m)* de ...	cost centre
coûts: connaissance *(f)* des ...	cost awareness
coûts: conscience *(f)* des ...	cost consciousness
coûts: contrôle *(m)* des ...	cost control
coûts: écart *(m)* des ...	cost variance
coûts: inflation *(f)* par les ...	cost-push inflation
coûts: méthode *(f)* des ... directs	direct costing
coûts: méthode *(f)* des ... marginaux	marginal costing
coûts: méthode *(f)* des ... standards	standard costing
coûts: réduction *(f)* des ...	cost reduction
coûts: structure *(f)* des ...	cost structure
couverture *(f)* des frais généraux	overheads recovery
couverture *(f)* du marché	sales coverage

couverture: opération (f) de ...	hedging (operation)
couverture: taux (m) de ...	cover ratio
couvrir: se ...	hedge (to)
créances (fpl) douteuses	bad debts
créances: mauvaises ... (fpl)	bad debts
création (f) des produits	product generation
créativité (f) commerciale	creative marketing
crédit (m) permanent	revolving credit
crédit-bail (m)	leasing
crédit-bail (m) immobilier	equipment leasing
crédit: contrôle (m) du ...	credit control
crédit: gestion (f) de ...	credit management
crédit: restriction (f) du ...	credit squeeze
créneau (m)	market opportunity
	niche
	slot
créneau (m) favorable	window of opportunity
crible: passer au ...	screen (to)
crises: gestion (f) des ...	crisis management
critère (m) d'appréciation	yardstick
critères (mpl) d'investissement	investment criteria
critique: auto-... (f)	self-appraisal
critique: masse (f) ...	critical mass
critique: point (m) ...	breakeven point
critique: zone (f) ...	problem area
critiques: graphique (m) des étapes ...	milestone chart
croissance (f) de l'entreprise	corporate growth
croissance (f) organique	organic growth
croissance: indice (m) de ...	growth index
croissance: industrie (f) en ...	growth industry
	sunrise industry
croissance: potentiel (m) de ...	growth potential
croissance: secteur (m) de ...	growth area
croissance: stratégie (f) de ...	expansion strategy
	growth strategy
culture (f)	culture
culture (f) d'entreprise	corporate culture
culture (f) de l'organisation	organization culture
curseur (m)	cursor

cybernétique *(f)*	cybernetics
cycle *(m)* économique	business cycle
	trade cycle
cycle *(m)* de travail	work cycle
cycle *(m)* de vie d'un produit	product life cycle

D

date *(f)* au plus tard	latest date
date *(f)* au plus tôt	expected date
date *(f)* limite	deadline
date *(f)* limite de consommation	use-by date
date *(f)* limite de vente	sell-by date
débiteurs *(mpl)*	debtors
débouché: trouver un ... pour	market (to)
débouchés: examen *(m)* des ...	market study
débours *(m)*	disbursement
débourser	disburse (to)
debriefer	debrief (to)
debriefing *(m)*	debriefing
débrouiller	unscramble (to)
décalage *(m)*	stagger
	time-lag
décalage *(m)* fiscal	fiscal drag
décentralisation *(f)*	decentralization
décentralisée: gestion *(f)* ...	decentralized management
décentraliser	decentralize (to)
déchets *(mpl)* industriels	industrial waste
décision: analyse *(f)* de la ...	decision analysis
décision: arbre *(m)* de ...	decision tree
décision: modèle *(m)* de ...	decision model
décision: prise *(f)* de ...	decision-making
décision: processus *(m)* de la ...	decision process
décisions : préparation *(f)* des ...	preparing decisions
décisions: théorie *(f)* des ...	decision theory
déclin: industrie *(f)* en ...	sunset industry
décollage *(m)*	take-off
décomposition *(f)* des tâches	job breakdown

découper un projet en tranches	chunk a project (to)
décrutement (m)	outplacement
déductible fiscalement	tax-deductible
déduction (f) (fiscale) sur frais d'établissement	capital allowance
défaillance (f)	malfunction
défaillance (f) (de l'entreprise)	failure (of firm)
défaut: zéro (m) ...	zero defects
défectibles: immobilisations (fpl) ...	wasting assets
défense (f) de son territoire	turf protection
défensive: stratégie (f) ...	defensive strategy
déficit (m)	deficit
	shortfall
déficit: financement (m) par le ...	deficit financing
déficitaire	non-profit-making
définition (f) de fonction	job description
définition (f) des objectifs	objective-setting
définition (f) de la mission	mission statement
définition (f) de la vision	vision statement
défusion (f)	demerger
dégradation (f) de l'activité	downswing
dégraissage (m)	demanning
dégrèvement (m) d'impôt	tax relief
dégroupage (m)	unbundling
dégrouper	unbundle (to)
déindustrialisation (f)	deindustrialization
délai (m)	deadline
	time frame
délai (m) d'exécution	turnaround time
délai (m) de livraison	delivery time
	lead time
délai (m) de réalisation	lead time
délai (m) de récupération	payback period
délai (m) de redressement	turnaround time
délai (m) de réflexion	time span of discretion
délai (m) de suite	lead time
délégation (f)	delegation
délégué (m) d'atelier	shop steward
délégué (m) syndical	trade union representative

déléguer	delegate (to)
délit *(m)* d'initié	insider dealing
déloyale: concurrence *(f)* ...	unfair competition
demande: évaluation *(f)* de la ...	demand assessment
demande: inflation *(f)* par la ...	demand-pull inflation
demande: prévision *(f)* de la ...	demand forecasting
démantèlement *(m)* de l'actif	asset-stripping
démanteler	wind down (to)
démarche *(f)* collective	joint representation
démarche *(f)* fonctionnelle	functional approach
démarrage *(m)*	start-up
démarrage: frais *(mpl)* de ...	start-up costs
démocratie *(f)* industrielle	industrial democracy
démotivation *(f)*	demotivation
démotiver	demotivate (to)
dents de scie: graphique *(m)* en ...	Z chart
dépannage *(m)*	troubleshooting
dépanner	debug (to)
dépanneur *(m)*	troubleshooter
départ: capital *(m)* de ...	seed money
départ: prime *(f)* de ...	golden handshake
départs *(mpl)* naturels	natural wastage
département *(m)* commercial	sales department
département: gestion *(f)* par ...	departmental management
	divisional management
départementalisation *(f)*	departmentalization
dépasser	leapfrog (to)
dépenses *(fpl)* en capital	capital expenditure (capex)
dépenses *(fpl)* de fonctionnement	running expenses
dépenses *(fpl)* d'investissement	capital expenditure
dépenses *(fpl)* d'investissement: évaluation *(f)* des	capital expenditure appraisal
dépenses: menues *(fpl)* ...	petty expenses
dépenses: recouvrement *(m)* des ...	recovery of expenses
déploiement *(m)*	deployment
déployer	deploy (to)
déposée: marque *(f)* ...	registered trademark
dépositaire *(m)*	dealer
déréglementation *(f)*	deregulation

dérégler	deregulate (to)
dérive *(f)* des salaires	wage drift
dérivé: produit *(m)* ...	by-product
description *(f)* de fonction	job profile
description *(f)* de poste	job description
	job title
déséconomie *(f)* d'échelle	diseconomy of scale
désengorger	debottleneck (to)
déséquilibre *(m)* commercial	trade imbalance
désincorporation *(f)*	disintegration
désintéressement *(m)*	buyout
désintéresser	buy out (to)
désinvestissement *(m)*	disinvestment
dessin *(m)* du produit	product design
dessin: bureau *(m)* de ...	design office
désuétude *(f)* calculée	built-in obsolescence
	planned obsolescence
détail: indice *(m)* des prix de ...	retail price index (RPI)
dettes *(fpl)* à court terme	current liabilities
dettes-actions: rapport *(m)* ...	debt-equity ratio
développement *(m)* d'équipe	team-building
développement *(m)* organisationnel	organizational development
développement *(m)* personnel	personal growth
développement *(m)* de produits	product development
développement *(m)* de produits nouveaux	new-product development
développement *(m)* des ressources humaines	human resource development (HRD)
développement: programme *(m)* de ...	development programme
développement: potentiel *(m)* de ...	development potential
développement: recherche *(f)* et ... (R et D)	research and development (R & D)
diagnostic *(m)* d'évaluation de gestion	management audit
diagnostic *(m)* financier	financial analysis
diagnostic: programme *(m)* de ...	diagnostic routine
diagramme *(m)* en bâtons	bar chart
diagramme *(m)* de circulation	flow chart
	flow process chart

diagramme *(m)* **de dispersion**	scatter diagram
diagramme *(m)* **en Z**	Z chart
différenciation *(f)* **des produits**	product differentiation
différencier	differentiate (to)
différentiel: prix *(m)* ...	differential price
diminuer de valeur *(f)*	depreciate (to)
direct: chef *(m)* ...	line manager
direct: marketing *(m)* ...	direct marketing
directe: main-d'oeuvre *(f)* ...	direct labour
directe: publicité *(f)* ...	direct mail
directe: vente *(f)* ...	direct selling
directes: charges *(fpl)* ...	direct expenses
directs: coûts *(mpl)* ...	direct costs
directeur *(m)*	director
	executive
	manager
directeur *(m)* **adjoint**	assistant director
	deputy manager
directeur *(m)* **commercial**	marketing manager
	sales manager
directeur *(m)* **de fabrication**	production director
directeur *(m)* **financier**	financial director
directeur *(m)* **de formation**	training officer
directeur *(m)* **général**	chief executive
	executive director
	general manager
	managing director (MD)
directeur *(m)* **général adjoint**	deputy managing director
directeur *(m)* **hiérarchique**	line manager
directeur *(m)* **du marketing**	marketing manager
directeur *(m)* **de la publicité**	advertising manager
directeur *(m)* **technique**	technical manager
	works manager
directeur *(m)* **d'usine**	plant manager
	works manager
directeur: patron-... *(m)*	owner manager
directeur: prix *(m)* ...	price leader
directeur: sous-... *(m)*	assistant manager
directeur: sous-... *(m)*	vice-president

direction *(f)*	administration
	management
direction *(f)* commerciale	sales management
direction *(f)* efficace	effective management
direction *(f)* financière	financial management
direction *(f)* générale	board of directors
	general management
	top management board
direction *(f)* intriquée	interlocking directorate
direction *(f)* multiple	multiple management
direction *(f)* par objectifs (DPO)	management by objectives (MBO)
direction *(f)* opérationnelle	operating management
direction *(f)* du personnel	personnel department
	personnel management
	staff management
direction *(f)* par programmes	programmed management
direction *(f)* participative	participative management
direction *(f)* systématisée	systems management
direction *(f)* des ventes	sales department
	sales management
direction: comité *(m)* de ...	board of directors
	executive board
direction: conseil *(m)* de ...	executive board
direction: conseil *(m)* en ...	management consultant
direction: contrôle *(m)* de ...	managerial control
direction: efficacité *(f)* de la ...	managerial effectiveness
direction: équipe *(f)* de	management team
direction: fonction *(f)* de ...	managerial function
direction: haute *(f)* ...	top management
direction: optique *(f)* de la ... générale	top management approach
direction: style *(m)* de ...	management style
	leadership
direction: système *(m)* de ...	management system
directive *(f)*	directive
	guideline
directives *(fpl)*: fournir des ... à	brief (to)
directoire *(m)*	board of directors
directorial	managerial

directs: coûts *(mpl)* ...	direct costs
directs: méthode *(f)* des coûts ...	direct costing
dirigeant *(m)*	director
	executive
	manager
dirigeant *(m)* opérationnel	line executive
dirigeant: personnel *(m)* ...	management staff
dirigeants: cadres *(mpl)* ...	top management
diriger	manage (to)
discrète: promotion *(f)* de vente ...	soft sell
discrimination *(f)*	discrimination
discrimination *(f)* positive	positive discrimination
discrimination *(f)* de prix	price discrimination
discriminer	discriminate (to)
dispersion: diagramme *(m)* de ...	scatter diagram
disponible: actif *(m)* ...	liquid assets
	quick assets
disponible: produit *(m)* ...	cash flow
disponible: revenu *(m)* ...	disposable income
disque *(m)*	disk
disque *(m)* dur	hard disk
disque *(m)* souple	floppy disk (floppy)
disque *(m)* winchester	Winchester disk
disques: unité *(f)* de ...	disk drive
disquette *(f)*	floppy disk (floppy)
dissolution *(f)*	shut-down
distance: à ...	arm's length
distribués: bénéfices *(mpl)* ...	distributed profit
distribués: bénéfices *(mpl)* non-...	retained profit
	undistributed profit
distribution *(f)*	distribution
distribution *(f)* des fréquences	frequency distribution
distribution: chef *(m)* de la ...	distribution manager
distribution: circuit *(m)* de ...	chain of distribution
distribution: coûts *(mpl)* de la ...	distribution costs
distribution: planning *(m)* de ...	distribution planning
distribution: politique *(f)* de ...	distribution policy
distribution: réseau *(m)* de ...	distribution channel
	distribution network

distribution physique: gestion *(f)* de la ...	physical distribution management
diversification *(f)*	diversification
diversification *(f)* des produits	product diversification
diversification: stratégie *(f)* de ...	diversification strategy
diversifier	diversify (to)
dividende *(m)*	dividend
division *(f)* opérationnelle	operating division
divisions: plan *(m)* de ...	departmental plan
	departmental planning
documentaire: recherche *(f)* ...	desk research
domaine *(m)* problématique	problem area
domaine *(m)* de produits	product area
dommages: limitation *(f)* des ...	damage limitation
données *(fpl)* d'entrée	input (data)
données: acquisition *(f)* de ...	data acquisition
données: banque *(f)* de ...	computer bank
	data bank
	data base
données: base *(f)* de ...	data base
données: collecte *(f)* de ...	data gathering
données: extraction *(f)* de ...	data retrieval
données: organigramme *(m)* de ...	data flowchart
données: protection *(f)* des ...	data protection
données: récupération *(f)* de ...	data retrieval
données: saisie *(f)* de ...	data acquistion
données: traitement *(m)* automatique des ... (TAD)	automatic data processing (ADP)
données statistiques: rassemblement *(m)* de ...	data gathering
données statistiques: recueil *(m)* de ...	data gathering
doré: parapluie *(m)* ...	golden parachute
dorées: menottes *(fpl)* ...	golden handcuffs
dotations *(fpl)* budgétaires affectées au marketing	marketing appropriation
dotations *(fpl)* budgétaires affectées à la publicité	advertising appropriation
douanière: barrière *(f)* ...	tariff barrier
douanière: barrière *(f)* non ...	non-tariff barrier (NTB)

double imposition: suppression *(f)* **de la … …**	double taxation relief
douteuses: créances *(fpl)* **…**	bad debts
DPO (direction *(f)* **par objectifs)**	MBO (management by objectives)
dresser *(un programme)*	schedule (to)
droit *(m)* **acquis**	vested interest
droit *(m)* **à la clientèle**	goodwill
droit *(m)* **préférentiel de souscription**	rights issue
droits *(mpl)* **d'auteur**	royalty
dumping *(m)*	dumping
dur: disque *(m)* **…**	hard disk
durables: produits *(mpl)* **non …**	non-durable products
durables: produits *(mpl)* **…**	durables
durée *(f)* **d'immobilisation**	down time
durée *(f)* **de vie**	shelf-life
durée *(f)* **de vie économique**	economic life
dynamique *(f)* **de groupe**	group dynamics
	methectics
dynamique *(f)* **industrielle**	industrial dynamics
dynamique *(f)* **de marché**	market dynamics
dynamique *(f)* **des produits**	product dynamics
dynamique: analyse *(f)* **…**	dynamic analysis
dynamique: programmation *(f)* **…**	dynamic programming
dysfonctionnement *(m)*	dysfunction

E

écart *(m)*	divergence
	gap
	variance
écart *(m)* **budgétaire**	budgetary variance
écart *(m)* **des coûts**	cost variance
écart *(m)* **de rémunération**	earnings differential
écart *(m)* **type**	standard deviation
écarts: analyse *(f)* **des …**	variance analysis
échange *(m)*	trade-off
échange *(m)* **de brevets**	patent trading
échange *(m)* **financier**	swap

échange *(m)* financier à terme	forward swap
échange: commerce *(m)* d' …	barter trade
échange: faire un …	trade off (to)
échanges inter-industriels: tableau *(m)* d' …	input-output table
échantillonnage *(m)* aléatoire	random sampling
échantillonnage *(m)* statistique	statistical sampling
échéance *(f)*	due date
échelle *(f)* des prix	price range
échelle *(f)* mobile	sliding scale
échelle: déséconomie *(f)* d' …	diseconomy of scale
échelle: économie *(f)* d' …	economy of scale
économétrique	econometric
économie *(f)* d'échelle	economy of scale
économie *(f)* des mouvements	motion economy
économique: cycle *(m)* …	business cycle
	trade cycle
économique: durée *(f)* de vie …	economic life
économique: effectif *(m)* de série …	economic batch quantity
économique: étude *(f)* …	economic research
économique: évolution *(f)* …	economic trend
économique: mission *(f)* …	economic mission
économique: quantité *(f)* … à commander	economic order quantity
économique: quantité *(f)* … de production	economic manufacturing quantity
économique: série *(f)* … de fabrication	economic manufacturing quantity
économiste *(m)* d'entreprise	business economist
écran *(m)* visuel	visual display unit (VDU)
écran: recopie *(f)* d' …	hard copy
écrémage: politique *(f)* de prix d'…	prestige pricing
écu *(m)*	ECU (European Currency Unit)
écu *(m)* lourd	hard ecu
éducation *(f)* de la sensibilité	sensitivity training
effectif *(m)* de série économique	economic batch quantity
effectifs *(mpl)*	establishment
	manning
	manpower
	staff

effectifs: gestion *(f)* des ...	manpower management
effectifs: inventaire *(m)* des ...	manpower audit
	staff audit
effectifs: planification *(f)* des ...	manpower planning
	staff planning
effectifs: prévision *(f)* des ...	staff forecasting
effectifs: recrutement *(m)* et gestion *(f)* des ...	staff resourcing
effet *(m)* décourageant	disincentive
effet *(m)* de halo	halo effect
effet *(m)* de levier	gearing
	leverage
efficace	efficient
efficace: coût-...	cost-efficient
efficace: direction *(f)* ...	effective management
efficacité *(f)*	effectiveness
	efficiency
efficacité *(f)* de la direction	managerial effectiveness
efficacité *(f)* organisatrice	organizational effectiveness
efficacité *(f)* publicitaire	advertising effectiveness
efficacité: coût-... *(m)*	cost-effectiveness
efficience *(f)*	efficiency
	productivity
efficience: contrôle *(m)* d'...	efficiency audit
effort *(m)* d'accroissement des ventes	sales expansion effort
effraction *(f)* informatique	hacking
égalité *(f)*	equality
égalité *(f)* des chances	equal opportunity
égalité *(f)* des chances *(fpl)* face à l'emploi	equal employment opportunity
égalité *(f)* des salaires	equal pay
élaboration *(f)* de l'image	imaging
élaboration *(f)* de programmes	programming
élaboration *(f)* des stratégies	strategy formulation
élargissement *(m)* du travail	job enlargement
élasticité *(f)*	elasticity
électronique: bureau *(m)* ...	electronic office
électronique: courrier *(m)* ...	electronic mail (e-mail)

électronique: ensemble *(m)* ... **de gestion**	electronic accounting system
électronique: feuille *(f)* **de calcul** ...	spreadsheet
électronique: traitement *(m)* ... **de l'information (TEI)**	electronic data processing (EDP)
élément *(m)* **du prix de revient**	cost factor
éliminer progressivement	phase out (to)
emballage *(m)*	packaging
embauchage *(m)* **et renvoi** *(m)*	hiring and firing
embauche *(f)*	recruitment
embauche: conditions *(fpl)* **d'** ...	conditions of employment
embaucher	hire (to)
émis: capital *(m)* ...	issued capital
émission *(f)*	issue
emmagasinage *(m)*	storing
	warehousing
empirique	empirical
emploi *(m)* **à mi-temps**	part-time employment
emploi *(m)* **à plein temps**	full-time employment
emploi: accord *(m)* **sur la sécurité de l'** ...	job security agreement
emploi: planification *(f)* **de l'** ...	manpower planning
emploi: prévision *(f)* **de l'** ...	manpower forecast
	manpower forecasting
emploi: sécurité *(f)* **de l'** ...	job security
emplois: classification *(f)* **des** ...	job evaluation
emplois: évaluation *(f)* **des** ...	job evaluation
emplois: ressources *(mpl)* **et** ... **de capitaux**	source and disposition of funds
employé *(m)* **de bureau**	clerical worker
employé *(m)* **qui travaille à mi-temps**	part-timer
employé *(m)* **qui travaille à plein temps**	full-timer
employés: conseil *(m)* **des** ...	employee counselling
employés: relations *(fpl)* **avec les** ...	employee relations
empoigne: foire *(f)* **d'** ...	rat race
empoisonnée: pillule *(f)* ...	poison pill
emporté: ventes *(fpl)* **à l'** ...	hard selling
emprunt *(m)* **à long terme**	loan stock

emprunt *(m)* **parallèle**	parallel loan
emprunt: capital *(m)* **d' ...**	loan capital
emprunt: financement *(m)* **par l' ...**	debt financing
emprunt: source *(f)* **d' ...**	borrowing facility
encadrement *(m)*	management
encadrement: personnel *(m)* **d' ...**	management staff
encouragement: programme *(m)* **de primes d' ...**	bonus scheme
	incentive scheme
endettement: ratio *(m)* **d' ...**	debt ratio
	gearing ratio
engagement *(m)* **d'investissement**	capital commitment
engagement *(m)* **du personnel**	staff commitment
engagements *(mpl)*	liabilities
engineering *(m)*	engineering
engineering *(m)* **industriel**	industrial engineering
engineering *(m)* **des systèmes**	systems engineering
enjeu *(m)*	stake
enquête *(f)* **d'opinion**	attitude survey
	opinion survey
enrichissement *(m)* **du travail**	job enrichment
enseignement *(m)* **assisté par ordinateur (EAO)**	computer-aided learning (CAL)
	computer-based training (CBT)
enseignement *(m)* **automatisé**	computer-assisted teaching (CAT)
enseignement *(m)* **programmé**	programmed instruction
	programmed learning
enseignement *(m)* **séquentiel**	programmed learning
ensemble *(m)* **électronique de gestion**	electronic accounting system
ententes *(fpl)*	agreements
	restrictive practices (*legal*)
entrée *(f)* **de l'ordinateur**	computer input
entrée: données *(fpl)* **d' ...**	input (*data*)
entrées-sorties: analyse *(f)* **...**	input-output analysis
entreposage *(m)*	storage
	warehousing
entreprenant	enterprising
entreprise *(f)*	enterprise
entreprise *(f)* **conjointe**	joint venture
entreprise *(f)* **d'Etat**	public enterprise

entreprise: but *(m)* de l' ...	company goal
	corporate goal
entreprise: comité *(f)* d' ... (CE)	works committee
	works council
entreprise: croissance *(f)* de l' ...	corporate growth
entreprise: culture *(f)* d' ...	corporate culture
entreprise: défaillance *(f)* de l'...	failure of firm
entreprise: économiste *(m)* d' ...	business economist
entreprise: esprit *(m)* d' ...	entrepreneurial spirit
entreprise: formation *(f)* dans l' ...	in-plant training
	training within industry (TWI)
entreprise: gestion *(f)* de l'	business management
entreprise: image *(f)* de l' ...	corporate image
entreprise: jeu *(m)* d' ...	business game
	management game
entreprise: liaisons *(fpl)* dans l' ...	channels of communication
entreprise: modèle *(m)* de l' ...	company model
	corporate model
entreprise: objectif *(m)* de l' ...	corporate objective
entreprise: philosophie *(f)* de l' ...	company philosopy
entreprise: planification *(f)* de l' ...	company planning
entreprise: politique *(f)* de l' ...	corporate policy
entreprise: prévision *(f)* dans l' ...	business forecasting
entreprise: profil *(m)* de l' ...	company profile
entreprise: stratégie *(f)* de l' ...	corporate strategy
entreprise: structure *(f)* de l' ...	company structure
	corporate structure
entreprise: style *(m)* de l' ...	house style
entretien *(m)* de l'équipement	plant maintenance
entretien *(m)* préventif	preventive maintenance
entretien *(m)* productif	productive maintenance
entretien *(m)* en profondeur	in-depth interview
entretien *(m)* systématique	planned maintenance
entretien *(m)* total de l'équipement	total plant maintenance
environnement *(m)*	environment
environnement: analyse *(f)* de l' ...	environmental analysis
environnement: balayage *(m)* de l'...	environmental scan
environnement: prévision *(f)* sur l' ...	environmental forecasting
épuisé	out of stock

équilibré: portefeuille *(m)* ...	balanced portfolio
équipe *(f)* de direction	management team
équipe *(f)* de jour	day shift
équipe *(f)* de nuit	night shift
équipe *(f)* de vente	sales force
équipe: chef *(m)* d' ...	foreman
	team leader
équipe: développement *(m)* d' ...	team-building
équipe: prime *(f)* d' ...	group bonus
	group incentive
équipement: biens *(mpl)* d' ...	capital goods
	investment goods
équipement: budget *(m)* d' ...	capital budget
équipement: entretien *(m)* de l' ...	plant maintenance
équipement: location *(f)* d' ...	plant hire
équipier *(m)*	team player
équitable: rendement *(m)* ...	fair return
ergonomie *(f)*	ergonomics
	human engineering
espérance *(f)* de vie d'un produit	product life expectancy
espionnage *(m)* industriel	industrial espionage
espionnage industriel: contre-... *(m)* ...	industrial security
esprit *(m)* d'entreprise	entrepreneurial spirit
essai: passage *(m)* d'...	test run
essaimage *(m)*	diversification
estimation *(f)*	appraisal
	estimate
estimation *(f)* approximative	guesstimate
estimation *(f)* au jugé	guesstimate
estimation *(f)* des ventes	sales estimate
établir un budget	budget (to)
établir une liste restreinte	shortlist (to)
établissement *(m)* du budget	budgeting
établissement *(m)* des buts	goal-setting
établissement *(m)* des objectifs	target-setting
établissement *(m)* des plannings	planning
établissement *(m)* des prix	price determination
	pricing

établissement *(m)* des prix de revient	costing
établissement: chef *(m)* d' ...	plant manager
	works manager
établissement: déduction *(f)* *(fiscale)* sur frais *(mpl)* d' ...	capital allowance
établissement: frais *(mpl)* d' ...	set-up costs
étalement *(m)* des vacances	staggered holidays
étapes: formation *(f)* par ...	analytical training
	part-analysis training
étapes critiques: graphique *(m)* des ...	milestone chart
état *(m)* d'avancement	progress report
	status report
état *(m)* de l'art	state of the art
état *(m)* financier	financial statement
Etat: entreprise *(f)* d' ...	public enterprise
étendue *(f)* du contrôle	span of control
étendue *(f)* des responsabilités	span of control
étranglement : goulot *(m)* d'...	bottleneck
étude *(f)* de cas	case study
étude *(f)* des charges	cost analysis
étude *(f)* de conception	design engineering
étude *(f)* des écarts	gap study
étude *(f)* de faisabilité	feasibility study
étude *(f)* des implantations	plant layout study
étude *(f)* de marché	market research
	market study
	market survey
étude *(f)* des méthodes	methods engineering
	methods study
étude *(f)* de motivation	motivation research
	motivational research
étude *(f)* des mouvements	motion study
étude *(f)* des périodes	time and motion study
étude *(f)* de point mort	break-even analysis
étude *(f)* préalable	feasibility study
étude *(f)* prévisionnelle	forecast
étude *(f)* de produit	product analysis
	product engineering

étude *(f)* de projet	project analysis
étude *(f)* de projet d'investissement	capital project evaluation
étude *(f)* de rentabilité	investment analysis
	profitability analysis
étude *(f)* des temps	time study
étude *(f)* des temps et des méthodes	time and methods engineering
	time and methods study
étude *(f)* des temps et des mouvements	time and motion study
étude *(f)* du travail	work study
études *(fpl)* économiques	economic research
études *(fpl)* publicitaires	advertising research
études: bureau *(m)* d' …	design office
	research department
euro-obligation *(f)*	Eurobond
eurodevise *(f)*	Eurocurrency
eurodollar *(m)*	Eurodollar
euromarché *(m)*	Euromarket
évaluation *(f)*	appraisal
	assessment
évaluation *(f)* des coûts	costing
évaluation *(f)* des coûts de systèmes	estimating systems costs
évaluation *(f)* de la demande	demand assessment
évaluation *(f)* des dépenses d'investissement	capital expenditure appraisal
évaluation *(f)* des emplois	job evaluation
évaluation *(f)* financière	financial appraisal
évaluation *(f)* du marché	market appraisal
évaluation *(f)* des performances	performance review
évaluation *(f)* du personnel	staff appraisal
évaluation *(f)* des problèmes	problem assessment
évaluation *(f)* de projet	project assessment
évaluation *(f)* de la qualité	quality assessment
évaluation *(f)* des résultats	performance appraisal
évaluation *(f)* des stocks	stock valuation
évaluation: diagnostic *(m)* d' … de gestion	management audit
évaluation: moyen *(m)* d' …	yardstick
évaluation de la qualité: centre *(m)* d' …	assessment centre

évaluer	appraise (to)
	assess (to)
	evaluate (to)
éventail *(m)* de contrôle	span of control
éventail *(m)* de produits	product mix
	product range
	sales mix
éventail *(m)* de salaires	wage range
évolution *(f)* économique	economic trend
évolution *(f)* de produits	product development
examen *(m)* des débouchés	market study
examen *(m)* financier	financial review
examen *(m)* des ressources	resource appraisal
excédent *(m)* de main-d'oeuvre	overmanning
exception: gestion *(f)* par ...	management by exception
exclusif: agent *(m)* commercial ...	sole agent
exécuter	implement (to)
exécution *(f)* de la politique	policy execution
exécution: délai *(m)* d' ...	turnaround time
executive search *(m)*	executive search
exemption *(f)* de la taxe à la valeur ajoutée	zero-rating
exercice *(m)*	financial year
exercice *(m)* comptable	accounting period
exercice *(m)* financier	fiscal year
exercice *(m)* social	fiscal year
exigences *(fpl)* de poste	job challenge
	job requirements
exigibilités *(fpl)*	current liabilities
exigible: passif *(m)* ...	current liabilities
expéditeur: agent *(m)* ...	forwarding agent
expédition *(f)*	dispatching
	forwarding
	shipping
expérimentale: vente *(f)* ...	sales test
expert-conseil *(m)*	consultant
expert: sytème *(m)* ...	expert system
exploitation *(f)* des contacts d'affaires	networking

exploitation *(f)* du logiciel	software application
exploitation *(f)* intensive	intensive production
exploitation: charges *(fpl)* d' ...	operating expenses
	running costs
exploitation: chef *(m)* d' ...	operations manager
exploitation: frais *(mpl)* d' ...	current expenditure
exponentiel: lissage *(m)* ...	exponential smoothing
exponentielle: tendance *(f)* ...	exponential trend
expression *(f)* de la politique	policy formulation
extensible	open-ended
extension *(f)* des tâches	job enlargement
extérieure: formation *(f)* ...	off-the-job training
extérieures: relations *(fpl)* ...	external relations
extérioriser	externalize (to)
extériorités *(fpl)*	externalities
externe	out-house
extraction *(f)* de données	data retrieval
extraction *(f)* de l'information	information retrieval
extraterritorial	offshore
extraterritorial: investissement *(m)*...	offshore investment
extrinsèques: facteurs *(mpl)* ...	hygiene factors

F

fabrication *(f)* à la chaine	flow production
fabrication *(f)* assistée par ordinateur (FAO)	computer-aided manufacturing (CAM)
fabrication *(f)* en série	mass production
fabrication *(f)* intégrée par ordinateur (FIO)	computer-integrated manufacturing (CIM)
fabrication *(f)* par lots	batch production
fabrication *(f)* modulaire	modular production
fabrication *(f)* pilote	pilot production
fabrication: chef *(m)* de ...	production manager
fabrication: comptabilité *(f)* par ...	process costing
fabrication: contrôle *(m)* de ...	manufacturing control
fabrication: directeur *(m)* de ...	production director

fabrication: graphique *(m)* de ...	process chart
fabrication: procédé *(m)* de ...	production process
fabrication: programme *(m)* de ...	production schedule
fabrication: série *(f)* économique de ...	economic manufacturing quantity
fabriqué sur commande *(f)*	custom-made
façonnier *(m)*	computer services bureau
facteur *(m)*	factor
facteur *(m)* de charge	load factor
facteur *(m)* clé d'achat	key buying factor
facteur *(m)* clé de succès	key success factor
facteur *(m)* coût	cost factor
facteurs *(mpl)* extrinsèques	hygiene factors
facteurs *(mpl)* d'hygiène	hygiene factors
facteurs *(mpl)* de production	factors of production
	input
facteurs de profit: analyse *(f)* des ...	profit-factor analysis
factorage *(m)*	factoring
factoring *(m)*	factoring
faire le bilan	debrief (to)
faire un compromis	trade off (to)
faire un échange	trade off (to)
faire la part du feu	cut one's losses (to)
faire le search	head hunt (to)
faire une soumission	tender (to)
faisabilité: étude *(f)* de ...	feasibility study
faisable	feasible
FAO (fabrication *(f)* assistée par ordinateur)	CAM (computer-aided manufacturing)
faux frais *(mpl)* divers	contingencies
favorable: créneau *(m)* ...	window of opportunity
fébriles: capitaux *(mpl)* ...	hot money
feedback *(m)*	feedback
fermée: boucle *(f)* ...	closed loop
fermeture *(f)*	shut-down
feuille *(f)* de calcul électronique	spreadsheet
feuille *(f)* de présence	time sheet
FG (frais *(mpl)* generaux)	overheads
fiabilité *(f)*	reliability
fiabilité *(f)* d'un produit	product reliability

ficelé: bien ...	well-packaged
fichier *(m)* central	computer bank
	data bank
	data base
fidélité *(f)* à la marque	brand loyalty
files d'attente: théorie *(f)* des ...	queueing theory
filiale *(f)*	subsidiary company
finalité *(f)*	objective
financement *(m)*	financing
	funding
financement *(m)* par le déficit	deficit financing
financement *(m)* par l'emprunt	debt financing
financer	finance (to)
financier *(m)* à risque	venture capitalist
financier: contrôle *(m)* ...	financial control
financier: diagnostic *(m)* ...	financial analysis
financier: directeur *(m)* ...	financial director
financier: état *(m)* ...	financial statement
financier: examen *(m)* ...	financial review
financier: exercice *(m)* ...	accounting period
financier: levier *(m)* ...	leverage
financier: plan *(m)* ...	financial plan
	financial planning
financier: rapport *(m)* ...	financial statement
financier: ratio *(m)* ...	financial ratio
financier: tableau *(m)* ...	spreadsheet
financière: analyse *(f)* ...	financial analysis
financière: direction *(f)* ...	financial management
financière: évaluation *(f)* ...	financial appraisal
financière: gestion *(f)* ...	financial administration
	financial management
financière: incitation *(f)* ...	financial incentive
financière: norme *(f)* ...	financial standard
financière: place *(f)* ...	financial market
financière: situation *(f)* ...	financial position
financière: stratégie *(f)* ...	financial strategy
FIO (fabrication *(f)* intégrée par ordinateur)	CIM (computer-integrated manufacturing)
firme *(f)* souple et mobile	flexible firm

fiscal: décalage *(m)* ...	fiscal drag
fiscale: incitation *(f)* ...	tax incentive
fiscale: politique *(f)* ...	fiscal policy
fiscalement: déductible ...	tax-deductible
fixation *(f)* des buts	goal-setting
fixation *(f)* marginale du prix	marginal pricing
fixation *(f)* des objectifs	target-setting
	targeting
fixation *(f)* de prix différents pour un même produit	differential pricing
fixation *(f)* des prix	price determination
	price-fixing
	pricing
fixation *(f)* des prix de transfert	transfer pricing
fixation *(f)* des tâches	job specification
fixer le prix	price (to)
fixes: coûts *(mpl)* ...	fixed costs
fixes: frais *(mpl)* ...	fixed expenses
flambée *(f)* des prix	price escalation
flexible: budget *(m)* ...	flexible budget
fluidisation *(f)*	flow production
flux *(m)* d'affaires	business stream
flux *(m)* de l'information	information flow
focaliser	focus (to)
foire (d) d'empoigne	rat race
follow-up *(m)*	follow-up
fonction *(f)*	function
fonction *(f)* de direction	managerial function
fonction: définition *(f)* de ...	job description
fonction: description *(f)* de ...	job profile
fonction: gestion *(f)* par ...	functional management
fonction: touche *(f)* de ...	function key
fonctionnel	functional
fonctionnel: attaché *(m)* ...	staff assistant
fonctionnelle: analyse *(f)* ... (AF)	functional analysis
fonctionnelle: démarche *(f)* ...	functional approach
fonctionnelle: implantation *(f)* ...	functional layout
fonctionnelle: organisation *(f)* ...	functional organization
	staff organization

fonctionnelle: responsabilité *(f)* ...	functional responsibility
fonctionnelles: liaisons *(fpl)* ...	functional relations
fonctionnement: dépenses *(fpl)* **de** ...	running expenses
fonctions *(fpl)* **complémentaires**	support activities
fonctions: classification *(f)* **des** ...	job classification
fonds *(m)* **d'amortissement**	sinking fund
fonds *(m)* **commercial**	goodwill
fonds *(mpl)* **de prévoyance**	contingency reserve
fonds *(mpl)* **propres réalisables**	equity
fonds *(m)* **de roulement**	circulating capital
	working capital
fonds *(m)* **de roulement net**	net current assets
fonds: allocation *(f)* **des** ...	budget appropriations
fonds: mobilisation *(f)* **des** ...	capital raising
fonds: mouvement *(m)* **de** ...	funds flow
fonds: rationnement *(m)* **des** ..	capital rationing
fonds propres: rendement *(m)* **des** ...	earnings on assets
	return on equity (ROE)
forces et des faiblesses,	SWOT (strengths, weaknesses,
des opportunités et	opportunities and threats)
des menaces: analyse *(f)* **des** ...	analysis
forfait: travail *(m)* **à** ...	work by contract
formation *(f)*	training
formation *(f)* **de capital**	capital formation
formation *(f)* **des cadres**	executive training
	management training
formation *(f)* **dans l'entreprise**	in-plant training
	training within industry (TWI)
formation *(f)* **par étapes**	analytical training
	part-analysis training
formation *(f)* **extérieure**	off-the-job training
formation *(f)* **institutionnelle**	off-the-job training
formation *(f)* **au management**	management development
formation *(f)* **plurimédiatique**	multimedia training
formation *(f)* **pratique**	hands-on training
formation *(f)* **pratique des chefs**	TWI (training within industry)
formation *(f)* **professionnelle**	vocational training
formation *(f)* **sur le tas**	on-the-job training
formation *(f)* **sur le terrain**	on-the-job training

formation: analyse *(f)* des besoins en ...	training needs analysis
formation: besoins *(mpl)* en ...	training needs
formation: directeur *(m)* de ...	training officer
formule *(f)* de marketing	marketing mix
fournir des directives à	brief (to)
fractionner	fractionalize (to)
frais *(mpl)* administratifs	administrative expenses
frais *(mpl)* de courtage	brokerage fees
frais *(mpl)* de démarrage	start-up costs
frais *(mpl)* d'établissement	set-up costs
frais *(mpl)* d'exploitation	current expenditure
	working costs
frais *(mpl)* fixes	fixed expenses
frais *(mpl)* généraux (FG)	overheads
frais *(mpl)* généraux d'administration	administrative overheads
frais *(mpl)* généraux de fabrication	factory overheads
frais *(mpl)* de liquidation	closing-down costs
frais *(mpl)* de représentation	expense account
frais *(mpl)* variables	variable expenses
frais: récupération *(f)* des ...	recovery of expenses
frais: rentrer dans ses ... *(mpl)*	break even (to)
frais: répartition *(f)* des ...	assignment of expenditure
franchisage: contrat *(m)* de ...	franchise
franchise *(f)*	franchise
	franchising
franchiser	franchise (to)
fréquences: distribution *(f)* des ...	frequency distribution
fuite *(f)*	security leak
fusion *(f)*	amalgamation
	consolidation
	merger
fusionner	amalgamate (to)
	merge (to)
fusions *(fpl)* et acquisitions *(fpl)*	mergers and acquisitions (M & A)

G

gâchage *(m)* des prix	price-cutting
gage *(m)*	collateral
gains *(mpl)*	earnings
	pay-off
	profits
gamme *(f)* commerciale	sales mix
gamme *(f)* de produits	product line
gamme: bas *(m)* de ...	down-market
gamme: haut *(m)* de ...	up-market
garantie: titre *(m)* déposé en ...	collateral security
généalogique: arbre *(m)* ...	family tree
général: directeur *(m)* ...	chief executive
	executive director
	general manager
	managing director (MD)
général: directeur *(m)* ... adjoint	deputy managing director
générale: direction *(f)* ...	general management
	top management board
générale: optique *(f)* de la direction ...	top management approach
générateur *(m)* de pertes	loss-maker
généraux: frais *(mpl)* ... (FG)	overheads
générique	generic
gérance *(f)*	management
gérant *(m)*	manager
gerbage *(m)*	palletization
gérer	manage (to)
gestion *(f)*	administration
	management
gestion *(f)* des actifs	asset management
gestion *(f)* automatisée	computerized management
gestion *(f)* du bilan	asset liability management
gestion *(f)* budgétaire	budgetary control
gestion *(f)* cellulaire	divisional management
gestion *(f)* du changement	change management (management of change)

gestion *(f)* commerciale	market management
	sales management
gestion *(f)* de crédit	credit management
gestion *(f)* des crises	crisis management
gestion *(f)* décentralisée	decentralized management
gestion *(f)* par département	departmental management
	divisional management
gestion *(f)* de la distribution physique	physical distribution management
gestion *(f)* des effectifs	manpower management
gestion *(f)* de l'entreprise	business management
gestion *(f)* par exception	management by exception
gestion *(f)* financière	financial administration
	financial management
gestion *(f)* par fonctions	functional management
gestion *(f)* intégrée	integrated project management (IPM)
gestion *(f)* des investissements	investment management
gestion *(f)* des opérations	operations management
gestion *(f)* de portefeuille	portfolio management
gestion *(f)* prévisionnelle	budgetary control
gestion *(f)* de la production	production control
	production management
gestion *(f)* de produit	product management
gestion *(f)* programmée	programmed management
gestion *(f)* de la qualité	quality control
	quality management
gestion *(f)* de la qualité absolue	total quality management (TQM)
gestion *(f)* de réseau	networking
gestion *(f)* des ressources	resource management
gestion *(f)* des ressources humaines	human resource management (HRM)
gestion *(f)* des risques	risk management
	venture management
gestion *(f)* scientifique	scientific management
gestion *(f)* de la sécurité	safety management
gestion *(f)* des stocks	inventory management
	stock control
gestion *(f)* par les systèmes	systems management
gestion *(f)* de trésorerie	cash management
gestion: comptabilité *(f)* de ...	management accounting

gestion: conseil *(m)* de ...	board of directors
gestion: conseil *(m)* en ...	management consultant
gestion: contrôle *(m)* de ...	budgetary control
	management audit
	managerial control
gestion: contrôleur *(m)* de ...	comptroller
	controller
gestion: diagnostic *(m)* d'évaluation de ...	management audit
gestion: ensemble *(m)* électronique de ...	electronic accounting system
gestion: grille *(f)* de ...	managerial grid
gestion: informatique *(f)* de ...	management information system (MIS)
gestion: politique *(f)* de ...	business policy
gestion: procédures *(fpl)* de ...	management practices
gestion: ratio *(m)* de ...	management ratio
gestion: science *(f)* de la ...	management science
gestion: simulation *(f)* de ...	business game
	management game
gestion: système *(m)* intégré de ...	integrated management system
gestion: technique *(f)* de ...	management technique
gestionnaire *(m)*	manager
global: marketing *(m)* ...	global marketing
globale: image *(f)* ...	global image
globale: somme *(f)* ...	lump sum
globalement: introduire ...	roll out (to)
goodwill *(m)*	goodwill
goulot *(m)* d'étranglement	bottleneck
goutte *(f)* à goutte	drip-feeding
grand réseau *(m)*	wide area network (WAN)
graphique *(m)* d'acheminement	flow chart
	flow process chart
graphique *(m)* des activités	activity chart
graphique *(m)* à bâtons	bar chart
graphique *(m)* circulaire	pie chart
graphique *(m)* de circulation	flow chart
	flow process chart
graphique *(m)* en dents de scie	Z chart
graphique *(m)* des étapes critiques	milestone chart

graphique *(m)* de fabrication	process chart
graphique *(m)* en tuyaux d'orgue	bar chart
graphique: traitement *(m)* ...	graphics
grève *(f)* officielle	official strike
grève *(f)* perlée	go-slow
grève *(f)* sauvage	unofficial action
	unofficial strike
grève *(f)* de solidarité	sympathy strike
grève *(f)* surprise	walkout
	wildcat strike
grève *(f)* sur le tas	sit-down strike
grève *(f)* du zèle	work-to-rule
grève: briseur *(m)* de ...	blackleg
	scab
grève: piquet *(m)* de ...	picket
grief *(m)*	grievance
grille *(f)* de gestion	managerial grid
grille *(f)* de produits	product group
grille: structure *(f)* en ...	grid structure
gris: marché *(m)* ...	grey market
groupage *(m)*	bundling
groupe *(m)* d'intervention	task force
groupe *(m)* de produits	product group
groupe *(m)* de réflexion	think-tank
groupe *(m)* de travail	working party
groupe: comptes *(mpl)* de ...	group accounts
groupe: dynamique *(f)* de ...	group dynamics
	methectics
groupe: production *(f)* en ...	batch production

H

habiller le bilan	massage the figures (to)
halo: effet *(m)* de ...	halo effect
harcèlement *(m)* sexuel	sexual harassment
hardware *(m)*	hardware
harmonisation *(f)*	harmonization
harmoniser	harmonize (to)

hausse: marché *(m)* **à la ...**	sellers' market
haussier *(m)*	bull
haussier: marché *(m)* **...**	bull market
haut *(m)* **de gamme**	up-market
haute direction *(f)*	top management
hedging *(m)*	hedging
heures *(fpl)* **supplémentaires**	overtime
heuristique *(f)*	heuristics
hexagonal	French
hiérarchie *(f)*	line of command
	managerial structure
hiérarchie *(f)* **de commandement**	chain of command
hiérarchie *(f)* **des objectifs**	hierarchy of goals
hiérarchique: autorité *(f)* **...**	line authority
hiérarchique: directeur *(m)* **...**	line manager
hiérarchique: organisation *(f)* **...**	line organization
hiérarchique: responsabilité *(f)* **...**	line responsibility
	linear responsibility
hiérarchique: voie *(f)* **...**	line of command
hiérarchiques: liaisons *(fpl)* **...**	line relations
histogramme *(m)*	histogram
holding *(m)*	holding company
horaire *(m)*	schedule
	working hours
horaire *(m)* **à la carte**	flexible working hours
horaire *(m)* **souple**	flexitime
horaire *(m)* **variable**	flexitime
	flexible working hours
horizontale: intégration *(f)* **...**	horizontal integration
horizontale: organisation *(f)* **...**	functional organization
	staff organization
hors-série	one-off
humaines: ressources *(fpl)* **...**	human resources
hygiène: facteurs *(mpl)* **d'...**	hygiene factors
hyperbole *(f)*	hype
hypothèse *(f)*	scenario
hypothèse *(f)* **optimiste**	best-case scenario
hypothèse *(f)* **pessimiste**	worst-case scenario

I

identification *(f)* d'une marque	brand recognition
image *(f)* de l'entreprise	corporate image
image *(f)* globale	global image
image *(f)* de marque	brand image
image *(f)* de produit	product image
image: changer l'...	re-image (to)
image: élaboration *(f)* de l'...	imaging
immatériel: actif *(m)* ...	intangible assets
immobilier: crédit-bail *(m)* ...	equipment leasing
immobilisation *(f)*	shut-down
immobilisation: durée *(f)* d'...	down time
immobilisations *(fpl)*	fixed assets
immobilisations *(fpl)* défectibles	wasting assets
immobilisé: actif *(m)* ...	capital assets
	fixed assets
immobilisées: valeurs *(fpl)* ...	fixed assets
impact *(m)*	impact
implantation *(f)* fonctionnelle	functional layout
implantations: étude *(f)* des ...	plant layout study
importation *(f)* parallèle	parallel import
imposés: prix *(mpl)* ...	resale price maintenance (RPM)
imposition *(f)*	assessment
imposition: suppression *(f)* de la double ...	double taxation relief
impôt *(m)* sur les bénéfices	profits tax
impôt *(m)* négatif sur le revenu	negative income tax
impôt *(m)* sur le revenu	income tax
impôt *(m)* sur les sociétés	corporation tax
impôt: dégrèvement *(m)* d'...	tax relief
imprimante *(f)* à laser	laser printer
imprimante: sortie *(f)* d'...	printout
imprimante: sortir sur ...	print out (to)
impulsif: achat *(m)* ...	impulse buying
imputation *(f)*	apportionment
imputation *(f)* des charges	allocation of costs
incidence *(f)* sur le profit	profit impact

incitation *(f)*	incentive
incitation *(f)* **financière**	financial incentive
incitation *(f)* **fiscale**	tax incentive
incorporation *(f)*	integration
incorporé	built-in
incorporelles: valeurs *(fpl)* ...	intangible assets
incorporer	integrate (to)
incrémentiel *(ordinateur)*	incremental
indemnité *(f)* **de licenciement**	severance pay
indépendant: rendre ...	hive off (to)
indicateur *(m)* **de performance**	performance indicator
indicatif *(m)*	answerback code
indice *(m)*	factor
	index number
indice *(m)* **de charge**	load factor
indice *(m)* **de croissance**	growth index
indice *(m)* **des prix**	price index
indice *(m)* **des prix à la consommation**	consumer price index
indice *(m)* **des prix de détail**	retail price index (RPI)
indice *(m)* **de traitement**	salary grade
indirects: coûts *(mpl)* ...	indirect costs
indirectes: charges *(fpl)* ...	indirect expenses
indirecte: main-d'oeuvre *(f)* ...	indirect labour
industrie *(f)* **en croissance rapide**	growth industry
	sunrise industry
industrie *(f)* **en déclin**	sunset industry
industriels: biens *(mpl)* ...	industrial goods
industriel: contre-espionnage *(m)* ...	industrial security
industriel: engineering *(m)* ...	industrial engineering
industriel: espionnage *(m)* ...	industrial espionage
industriel: génie *(m)* ...	industrial engineering
industrielle: comptabilité *(f)* ...	product costing
industrielle: démocratie *(f)* ...	industrial democracy
industrielle: dynamique *(f)* ...	industrial dynamics
industrielle: psychologie *(f)* ...	industrial psychology
industrielle: sécurité *(f)* ...	industrial safety
industrielles: relations *(fpl)* ...	industrial relations
industriels: déchets *(mpl)* ...	industrial waste

industriels: tableau *(m)* d'échanges inter-...	input-output table
inflation *(f)* par les coûts	cost-push inflation
inflation *(f)* par la demande	demand-pull inflation
inflationniste: pression *(f)* ...	inflationary pressure
influence *(f)*	impact
informaticien *(m)*	computer expert
information *(f)* commerciale	market intelligence
information *(f)* de contrôle	control information
information *(f)* économique	economic intelligence
information *(f)* d'organisation de la gestion	management information
information: flux *(m)* de l'...	information flow
information: manipulation *(f)* de l' ...	information handling
information: récupération *(f)* de l'...	information retrieval
information: réseau *(m)* d'...	information network
information: système *(m)* d'...	information system
information: système *(m)* d'... de management (SIM)	management information system (MIS)
information: système *(m)* d'... par ordinateur	computerized information system (COINS)
information: théorie *(f)* de l'...	information theory
information: traitement *(m)* de l'...	information handling information processing
information: traitement *(m)* électronique de l'... (TEI)	electronic data processing (EDP)
informatique *(f)*	data processing informatics information technology (IT)
informatique *(f)* de gestion	management information system (MIS)
informatique: conseil *(m)* en ...	computer consultant
informatique: effraction *(f)* ...	hacking
informatique: services *(mpl)* en ...	computer services
informatique: traitement *(m)* ...	electronic processing
informatique *(f)*: versé en ...	computer literate
informatique: virus *(m)* ...	computer virus
informatiser	computerize (to)
informelle: organisation *(f)* ...	informal organisation
infrastructure *(f)*	infrastructure

ingénierie *(f)*	engineering
ingénieur *(m)* commercial	sales engineer
ingénieur-conseil *(m)*	management consultant
ingénieur *(m)* en logiciel	software engineer
ingénieur *(m)* système	systems engineer
initié: délit *(m)* d'...	insider dealing
	insider trading
innovateur *(m)*	market leader
innovation *(f)*	breakthrough
	pioneer product
innover	innovate (to)
	pioneer (to)
input *(m)*	input
input *(m)* de l'ordinateur	computer input
installation *(f)* de secours	back-up facility
instantanées: méthode *(f)* des observations ...	random observation method
intégration *(f)*	integration
intégration *(f)* horizontale	horizontal integration
intégration *(f)* verticale	vertical integration
intégré: système *(m)* ... de gestion	integrated management system
intégrée: gestion *(f)* ...	integrated project management (IPM)
intégrer	integrate (to)
intégrés: comptes *(mpl)* ...	integrated accounts
intelligence *(f)* artificielle	artificial intelligence
intendance: services *(mpl)* d'...	ancillary operations
intensité de capital: ratio *(m)* d' ...	capital-output ratio
intensive: exploitation *(f)* ...	intensive production
inter-entreprises: comparaison *(f)* ...	interfirm comparison
inter-industriels: tableau *(m)* d'échanges ...	input-output table
interactif	interactive
interconnecter	network (to)
intéressement *(m)*	financial involvement
	profit-sharing
intérêt *(m)* des tâches	job interest
interface *(f)*	interface
interfacer	interface (to)
intérioriser	internalize (to)

internationaliser	internationalize (to)
interne	in-company
	in-house
interne: audit (m) ...	internal audit
interne: contrôle (m) ...	internal audit
interne: marché (m) ... (de la CE)	single market (of the EC)
interne: services (mpl) de conseil ...	advisory services
interne: taux (m) de rendement ...	internal rate of return (IRR)
intervention: groupe (m) d'...	task force
interview (f) en profondeur	in-depth interview
introduire en bourse	go public (to)
introduire globalement	roll out (to)
intuitif: management (m) ...	intuitive management
inutilisée: capacité (f) ...	idle capacity
	spare capacity
inventaire (m)	stocktaking
inventaire (m) des effectifs	manpower audit
	staff audit
inventaire (m) permanent	continuous stocktaking
inventaire (m) tournant	perpetual inventory
inventer le fil à couper le beurre	reinvent the wheel (to)
investi: capital (m) ...	capital employed
investi: récupération (f) du capital ...	payback
investis: rentabilité (f) des capitaux ... (RCI)	return on capital employed (ROCE)
investissement (m) extraterritorial	offshore investment
investissement: budget (m) d'...	investment budget
investissement: critères (mpl) d'...	investment criteria
investissement: dépenses (fpl) d'...	capital expenditure
investissement: engagement (m) d'...	capital commitment
investissement: évaluation (f) des dépenses d' ...	capital expenditure appraisal
investissement: politique (f) d'...	investment policy
investissement: programme (m) d'...	investment programme
investissement: retour (m) sur ... (RSI)	return on investment (ROI)
investissements: analyse (f) des ...	investment analysis
investissements: appréciation (f) des ...	investment appraisal

investissements: budgétisation (f) des ...	capital budgeting
investissements: gestion (f) des ...	investment management
investissements: rendement (m) des ...	return on investment (ROI)
investissements: rentabilité (f) des ...	return on investment (ROI)
invisibles (mpl)	invisibles
itératif	iterative
itération (f)	iterative process

J

jeu (m) d'entreprise	business game
	management game
jeu (m) de rôles	role-playing
jeu (m) à somme nulle	zero-sum game
jeune cadre (m) dynamique	yuppie
jeune turc (m)	whiz-kid
jeux: théorie (f) des ...	game theory
joie (f) au travail	job satisfaction
jonction (f)	interface
jour: équipe (f) de ...	day shift
jour: mettre à ...	update (to)
jugement (m) d'allure	performance rating
junk bond (m)	junk bond
juste à temps	just in time (JIT)

K

know-how (m)	know-how
krach (m)	crash

L

lancement (m)	launching
lancement (m) (d'un emprunt)	flotation
lancement (m) d'un produit	product launch

lancer sur le marché	market (to)
langage *(m)* commun	common language
langage *(m)* machine	computer language
	machine language
laser: imprimante *(f)* à ...	laser printer
latérale: pensée *(f)* ...	lateral thinking
leader *(m)* du marché	market leader
leader: produit *(m)* ...	core product
leasing *(m)*	leasing
lecture *(f)*	scanning
leverage *(m)*	leverage
levier *(m)* financier	leverage
levier: offre *(f)* de rachat par ...	leveraged bid
levier: rachat *(m)* par ...	leveraged buyout (LBO)
liaisons *(fpl)* dans l'entreprise	channels of communication
liaisons *(fpl)* fonctionnelles	functional relations
liaisons *(fpl)* hiérarchiques	line relations
libéralisation *(f)*	liberalization
licence *(f)*	licence
licence: sous ...	under licence
licences: concession *(f)* réciproque des ...	cross-licensing
licenciement *(m)*	dismissal
	redundancy
licenciement *(m)* abusif	unfair dismissal
licenciement *(m)* sommaire	summary dismissal
licenciement: indemnité *(f)* de ...	severance pay
licencier	fire (to)
lieu *(m)* de travail	workplace
lieu *(m)* de vente (LV)	point of sale (POS)
lieu de vente: publicité *(f)* sur le ... (PLV)	point-of-sale advertising
ligne *(f)* de production	flow line
ligne *(f)* de produits	product line
ligne: en ...	on line
limitation *(f)* d'autorité	contraction of authority
limitation *(f)* des dommages	damage limitation
limite: date *(f)* ... de consommation	use-by date
limite: date *(f)* ... de vente	sell-by date

linéaire: programmation *(f)* ...	linear programming
liquidation *(f)*	liquidation
	winding up
liquidation: frais *(mpl)* **de** ...	closing-down costs
liquider	liquidate (to)
	sell out (to)
	wind up (to)
liquidité *(f)*: **pauvre en** ...	cash-poor
liquidité *(f)*: **riche en** ...	cash-rich
liquidité: coefficient *(m)* **de** ...	current ratio
	liquidity ratio
liquidité: sans ... *(f)*	cash-strapped
liquidité: taux *(m)* **de** ...	liquidity ratio
liquidités *(fpl)*	liquid assets
lissage *(m)* **exponentiel**	exponential smoothing
liste *(f)* **restreinte**	shortlist
listing *(m)*	listing
livraison: délai *(m)* **de** ...	delivery time
	lead time
local: réglementation *(f)* **de contenu** ...	local content rules
local: réseau *(m)* ...	local area network (LAN)
localisation *(f)*	localization
localisation *(f)* **de l'usine**	plant location
location *(f)* **de l'équipement**	plant hire
location *(f)* **longue durée**	contract hire
lock-out *(m)*	lock-out
locomotive *(f)*: **produit** *(m)* ...	star product
logiciel *(m)*	software
logiciel: courtier *(m)* **en** ...	software broker
logiciel: exploitation *(f)* **du** ...	software application
logiciel: ingénieur *(m)* **en** ...	software engineer
logiciel: société *(f)* **en** ...	software company
logistique *(f)*	logistics
logistique	logistical
logistiques: services *(mpl)* ...	extension services
logotype *(m)*	logo
logotype *(m)* **de la société**	company logo
lots: contrôle *(m)* **par** ...	batch control
lots: fabrication *(f)* **par** ...	batch production

lots: traitement *(m)* par ...	batch processing
louer à bail *(m)*	lease (to)
louer: acheter ou ...	lease or buy (to)
loup *(m)*	stag
lourd: écu *(m)* ...	hard ecu
LV (lieu *(m)* de vente)	POS (point of sale)

M

machine *(f)* à traitement de texte	word processor (WP)
machine *(f)* à traitement de texte autonome	stand-alone word processor
machine: langage *(m)* ...	machine language
macro *(m)*	macro
magasinage *(m)*	storage
	warehousing
main-d'oeuvre *(f)*	manpower
main-d'oeuvre *(f)* directe	direct labour
main-d'oeuvre *(f)* indirecte	indirect labour
main-d'oeuvre *(f)* non-spécialisée	unskilled labour
main-d'oeuvre *(f)* professionnelle	skilled labour
main-d'oeuvre *(f)* spécialisée	semi-skilled labour
main-d'oeuvre: ayant un excédent de	overmanned
main-d'oeuvre: à court de	undermanned
main-d'oeuvre: excédent *(m)* de ...	overmanning
main-d'oeuvre: manque *(m)* de ...	undermanning
main-d'oeuvre: mobilité *(f)* de la ...	labour turnover
main-d'oeuvre: notation *(f)* de la ...	personnel rating
maintenir les marges	hold margins (to)
maîtrise *(f)*	middle management
	supervision
	supervisory management
maîtrise: agent *(m)* de ...	supervisor
majoration *(f)* (du prix)	mark-up
majoration *(f)* de prix	price increase
majoritaire: participation *(f)* ...	controlling interest
	majority interest

management *(m)*	management
management *(m)* baladeur	management by walking around
management *(m)* intuitif	intuitive management
management: contrat *(m)* du ...	management contract
management: formation *(f)* au ...	management development
management: système *(m)* d'information de ... (SIM)	management information system (MIS)
managérial	managerial
managérial: style *(m)* ...	managerial style
manipulation *(f)* de l'information	information handling
manipuler les chiffres *(mpl)*	massage the figures (to)
manque *(m)*	shortfall
manque *(m)* de main-d'oeuvre	undermanning
manque *(m)* de personnel	understaffing
manuel: travailleur *(m)* ...	blue-collar worker
manuelle: à commande *(f)* ...	hands-on
manutention *(f)* (des marchandises)	materials handling
marchande: valeur *(f)* ...	market value
marché *(m)* des actions	equity market
marché *(m)* arrivé à maturité	mature market
marché *(m)* à la baisse	bear market
	buyers' market
marché *(m)* -cible	target market
Marché Commun *(m)*	Common Market
marché *(m)* gris	grey market
marché *(m)* à la hausse	sellers' market
marché *(m)* haussier	bull market
marché *(m)* interne *(de la CE)*	single market *(of the EC)*
marché *(m)* marginal	fringe market
marché *(m)* de matières premières	commodity market
marché *(m)* parallèle	grey market
marché *(m)* potentiel	market potential
marché *(m)* tendanciel	market potential
marché *(m)* à terme	forward market
	futures market
marché *(m)* unique	single market
marché: conscience *(f)* du ...	market awareness
marché: couverture *(f)* du ...	sales coverage

marché: dynamique *(f)* de ...	market dynamics
marché: étude *(f)* de ...	market research
	market survey
marché: évaluation *(f)* du ...	market appraisal
marché: lancer sur le ...	market (to)
marché: leader *(m)* du ...	market leader
marché: orientation *(f)* du ...	market trend (*short-term*)
marché: part *(f)* du ...	market share
marché: pénétration *(f)* du ...	market penetration
marché: plan *(m)* de ...	market plan
	market planning
marché: prévision *(f)* du ...	market forecast
marché: prix *(m)* du ...	market price
marché: profil *(m)* du ...	market profile
marché: pronostic *(m)* du ...	market forecast
marché: saturation *(f)* du ...	market saturation
marché: sensible au ...	market-sensitive
marché: strate *(f)* de ...	market segment
marché: stratégie *(f)* de ...	marketing strategy
marché: structure *(f)* du ...	market structure
marché: tendance *(f)* du ...	market trend (*long-term*)
marché: tendances *(fpl)* du ...	market forces
marché: teneur *(f)* de ...	market maker
marché: test *(m)* de ...	test marketing
marchés: analyse *(f)* des ...	market research
marchés: prospection *(f)* des ...	market exploration
marchés: segmentation *(f)* des ...	market segmentation
marge *(f)*	mark-up
	slack
marge *(f)* bénéficiaire	profit margin
marge *(f)* brute	gross margin (GM)
marge *(f)* brute d'autofinancement (MBA)	cash flow
marge *(f)* de sécurité	margin of safety
marge *(f)* nette	net margin
marges: maintenir les ...	hold margins (to)
marginal	incremental
marginal: cash flow *(m)* ...	incremental cash flow
marginal: marché *(m)* ...	fringe market

marginale: analyse *(f)* ...	incremental analysis
	marginal analysis
marginale: comptabilité *(f)* ...	marginal costing
marginale: fixation *(f)* ... du prix	marginal pricing
marginaliser	marginalize (to)
marginaux: coûts *(mpl)* ...	marginal costs
marginaux: méthode *(f)* des coûts ...	marginal costing
marguerite *(f)*	daisy wheel
marketing *(m)*	marketing
marketing *(m)* direct	direct marketing
marketing *(m)* global	global marketing
marketing mix *(m)*	marketing mix
marketing: budget *(m)* de ...	marketing budget
marketing: service *(m)* de ...	marketing department
marque *(f)*	brand
	brand name
marque *(f)* déposée	registered trademark
marque: acceptabilité *(f)* de la ...	brand acceptance
marque: chef *(m)* de ...	brand manager
marque: fidélité *(f)* à la ...	brand loyalty
marque: identification *(f)* d'une ...	brand recognition
marque: image *(f)* de ...	brand image
marque: notoriété *(f)* de la ...	brand awareness
marque: stratégie *(f)* de la ...	brand strategy
marques: portefeuille *(m)* de ...	brand portfolio
marques: positionnement *(m)* de ...	brand positioning
masse *(f)* critique	critical mass
masse *(f)* monétaire	money supply
masse: production *(f)* en ...	mass production
matériel *(m)*	hardware
matériel *(m)* complémentaire	add-on equipment
matériel *(m)* de publicité sur le lieu de vente	point-of-sale material
matérielles: valeurs *(fpl)* ...	tangible assets
mathématique: programmation *(f)* ...	mathematical programming
matière *(f)* grise	creative thinking
matières premières: marché *(m)* de	commodity market
matricielle: structure *(f)* ...	matrix organization

maturité: marché *(m)* arrivé à ...	mature market
mauvaises créances *(fpl)*	bad debts
maximaliser	maximize (to)
maximisation *(f)* du profit	profit maximization
MBA (marge *(f)* brute d'autofinancement)	cash flow
mécanisme *(m)* de taux de change	exchange rate mechanism (ERM)
média *(mpl)*	media
média: analyse *(f)* de ...	media analysis
média: sélection *(f)* des ...	media selection
média *(mpl)* publicitaires	advertising media
médiane *(f)*	median
médiateur: agir en ...	mediate (to)
médiation *(f)*	mediation
mémoire *(f)*	memory
	storage
mémoire *(f)* à accès sélectif	random-access memory (RAM)
mémoire *(f)* morte	read-only memory (ROM)
mémoire *(f)* d'ordinateur	computer memory
mémoire *(f)* passive	read-only memory (ROM)
menottes *(fpl)* dorées	golden handcuffs
mensualisation *(f)*	change to salaried status
menues dépenses *(fpl)*	petty expenses
merchandising *(m)*	merchandising
mère: société *(f)* ...	parent company
mérite: appréciation *(f)* du ...	merit rating
message *(m)* publicitaire	advertising message
mesure *(f)* de performances	performance measurement
mesure *(f)* de la productivité	productivity measurement
mesure *(f)* du travail	ergonometrics
	work measurement
mesure *(f)* du travail par sondage	activity sampling
méthode *(f)* d'actualisation	present value method
méthode *(f)* du chemin critique	critical path method (CPM)
méthode *(f)* du coût proportionnel	direct costing
méthode *(f)* des coûts d'absorption	absorption costing
méthode *(f)* des coûts complets	absorption costing
	full-cost method
méthode *(f)* des coûts directs	direct costing

méthode *(f)* des coûts marginaux	marginal costing
méthode *(f)* des coûts standards	standard costing
méthode *(f)* des observations instantanées	random observation method
méthode *(f)* de qualification par points	points-rating method
méthode *(f)* du simplexe	simplex method
méthode *(f)* des temps prédéterminés	predetermined motion time system (PMTS)
méthodes *(fpl)* administratives	systems and procedures
méthodes *(fpl)* et organisation	organization and methods (O & M)
méthodes: bureau *(m)* des ...	methods study department
méthodes: étude *(f)* des ...	methods engineering methods study
méthodes: étude *(f)* des temps et des ...	time and methods study
métier: risque *(m)* du ...	occupational hazard
mettre en chômage technique	lay off (to)
mettre à jour	update (to)
mettre en veilleuse *(f)*	put on the back burner (to)
mévente *(f)*	sales slump
mi-temps: emploi *(m)* à ...	part-time employment
mi-temps: employé *(m)* qui travaille à ...	part-timer
mi-temps: travail *(m)* à ...	part-time employment
micro *(m)*	micro
micro-éditer	desktop publish (to)
micro-édition *(f)*	desktop publishing
minimiser les risques *(mpl)*	minimize risks (to)
minimum: salaire *(m)* ...	minimum wage
minoritaire: participation *(f)* ...	minority interest
mise *(f)* au courant (*du personnel*)	induction
mise *(f)* à jour	update
mise *(f)* en oeuvre des systèmes	systems engineering
mise au point: réunion *(f)* de ...	debriefing
mission *(f)* économique	economic mission
mission: définition *(f)* de la ...	mission statement
mixte: organisation *(f)* ...	line and staff organization
mobile *(f)*	motivator
mobile *(m)* d'achat	purchasing motivator
mobile: échelle *(f)* ...	sliding scale

mobile: téléphone *(m)* ...	mobile phone
mobilisation *(f)* de fonds	capital raising
mobilité *(f)* de la main-d'oeuvre	labour mobility
mobilité *(f)* du personnel	staff mobility
mode *(m)*	mode
modèle *(m)*	model
modèle *(m)* comptable	accounting model
modèle *(m)* de décision	decision model
modèle *(m)* dynamique de gestion	dynamic management model
modèle *(m)* de l'entreprise	company model
	corporate model
modem *(m)*	modem
modulaire: fabrication *(f)* ...	modular production
modularité *(m)*	modularity
modulateur-démodulateur *(m)*	modem
moindre coût *(m)*	least-cost
moins-value *(f)*	capital loss
	depreciation
mondialisation *(f)*	globalization
mondialiser	globalize (to)
monétaire: masse *(f)* ...	money supply
monétaire: politique *(f)* ...	monetary policy
monétarisme *(m)*	monetarism
monnaie *(f)* commune	common currency
monnaie *(f)* parallèle	parallel currency
monnaie *(f)* unique	single currency
monopole *(m)*	corner
	monopoly
montage: chaîne *(f)* de ...	assembly line
morphologique: analyse *(f)* ...	morphological analysis
mort: étude *(f)* de point ...	break-even analysis
mort: point *(m)* ...	break-even point
mort: temps *(m)* ...	down-time
mot *(m)* dans le vent	buzz-word
motivateur *(m)*	motivator
motivation *(f)*	motivation
motivation *(f)* par le profit	profit motive
motivation: étude *(f)* de ...	motivation research
	motivational research

motivationnel	motivational
motiver	motivate (to)
mouvement *(m)* du personnel	staff turnover
mouvement *(m)* des stocks	stock turnover
mouvement *(m)* de fonds	funds flow
mouvements *(mpl)* sociaux	industrial action
mouvements: économie *(f)* des ...	motion economy
mouvements: étude *(f)* des ...	motion study
mouvements: étude *(f)* des temps et des ...	time and motion study
moyen *(m)* d'évaluation	yardstick
moyens: coûts *(mpl)* ...	average costs
moyen: rendement *(m)* ...	average yield
moyenne *(f)*	average
	mean
moyenne *(f)* pondérée	weighted average
moyenne: recette *(f)* ...	average revenue
moyens *(mpl)* d'action promotionnelle	promotional mix
moyens *(mpl)* de production	factors of production
	input
moyens: cadres *(mpl)* ...	middle management
moyens: répartition *(f)* des ...	resource allocation
multiple: accès *(m)* ...	multi-access
multiple: direction *(f)* ...	multiple management
multiple: régression *(f)* ...	multiple regression analysis (MRA)
multiplet *(m)*	byte
mutation *(f)* dans le personnel	staff transfer
mutation *(f)* du personnel	staff turnover
mutation *(f)* des structures	organizational change

N

nantissement *(m)*	collateral (security)
négoce: programme *(m)* de ...	trading programme
négociable	marketable

négociable: actif *(m)* ...	liquid assets
	quick assets
négociable: option *(f)* ...	traded option
négociation: stratégie *(f)* de ...	negotiation strategy
négociations *(fpl)* collectives	collective bargaining
négociations *(fpl)* des contrats de productivité	productivity bargaining
négociations *(fpl)* au niveau local	plant bargaining
négociations *(fpl)* paritaires	joint negotiation
négociations *(fpl)* salariales	pay talks
négocier	negotiate (to)
net: actif *(m)* ...	net assets
net: bénéfice *(m)* ...	net profit
net: résultat *(m)* ...	bottom line
net: salaire *(m)* ...	take-home pay
nette: marge *(f)* ...	net margin
nette: valeur *(f)* ...	net worth
nette: valeur *(f)* actuelle ...	net present value (NPV)
nettes: valeurs *(fpl)* ...	net assets
niveau *(m)* de notoriété	awareness level
niveau *(m)* des salaires	wage level
niveau *(m)* de vie	standard of living
niveau local: négociations *(fpl)* au ...	plant bargaining
noir: travail *(m)* au ...	moonlighting
noire: caisse *(f)* ...	slush fund
nominal: capital *(m)* ...	authorized capital
non-capitalistique	labour-intensive
non cloisonné	open-plan
non connecté	off line
non-convivial	user-unfriendly
non-distribués: bénéfices *(mpl)* ...	retained profits
non structuré	unstructured
non qualifiés: ouvriers *(mpl)*	unskilled labour
non durables: produits *(mpl)*	non-durable goods
non-linéaire: programmation *(f)* ...	non-linear programming
non-spécialisée: main-d'oeuvre *(f)* ...	unskilled labour
normalisation *(f)*	standardization
normalisation *(f)* quantitative	variety reduction
norme *(f)*	standard

norme *(f)* **financière**	financial standard
norme *(f)* **de prix de revient**	cost standard
norme *(f)* **de production**	production standard
norme *(f)* **de rendement**	performance standard
notation *(f)* **de la main-d'oeuvre**	personnel rating
notoriété *(f)* **de la marque**	brand awareness
notoriété: niveau *(m)* **de ...**	awareness level
nouveaux produits: lancement *(m)* **de ... ...**	new-product launching
novateur	innovative
nuit: équipe *(f)* **de ...**	night shift
numérique	digital
numérique: calculateur *(m)* **...**	digital computer
numérique: commande *(f)* **...**	numerical control
numériser	digitize (to)

O

objectif *(m)*	objective
	target
objectif *(m)* **de l'entreprise**	company objective
	corporate objective
objectif *(m)* **de production**	production target
objectif *(m)* **de profit**	profit target
objectif *(m)* **de vente**	sales goal
objectifs *(mpl)* **globaux de l'entreprise**	overall company objectives
objectifs: définition *(f)* **des ...**	objective-setting
objectifs: direction *(f)* **par ... (DPO)**	management by objectives (MBO)
objectifs: établissement *(m)* **des ...**	target-setting
objectifs: fixation *(f)* **des ...**	targeting
	target-setting
objectifs: hiérarchie *(f)* **des ...**	hierarchy of goals
obligation *(f)*	debenture
obligation *(f)* **pourrie**	junk bond
obligation *(f)* **à risque élevé**	junk bond
obligation: euro-... *(f)*	Eurobond

observations instantanées: méthode (f) des	random observation method
obsolescence (f)	obsolescence
occulte: actif (m) ...	hidden assets
offre (f) publique d'achat (OPA)	take-over bid (TOB)
offre (f) de rachat par levier	leveraged bid
offre (f) de valeur	value proposal
offre: appel (m) d'... (AO)	tender
OP (orientation (f) professionnelle)	vocational guidance
OPA (offre (f) publique d'achat)	TOB (take-over bid)
opération (f) de couverture	hedging operation
opérationnel	operational
opérationnel: attaché (m) ...	line assistant
opérationnel: dirigeant (m) ...	line executive
opérationnelle: direction (f) ...	operating management
opérationnelle: division (f) ...	operating division
opérationnelle: organisation (f) ...	line organization
opérationnelle: recherche (f) ... (RO)	operational research operations research
opérations: contrôle (m) des ...	operations audit
opérations: gestion (f) des ...	operations management
opérations: planification (f) des ...	operational planning
opinion: enquête (f) d'...	attitude survey opinion survey
opportunité: coûts (mpl) d'...	opportunity costs
optimale: quantité (f) ... de commande	economic order quantity
optimisation (f) du profit	profit optimization
optimisation: sous-... (f)	sub-optimization
optimiser	optimize (to)
option (f) d'achat d'actions	stock option
option (f) négociable	traded option
optionnel: plan (m) ... d'achat d'actions	stock option plan
optique (f) de la direction générale	top management approach
or: pont (m) d'...	golden hello
ordinateur (m)	computer
ordinateur (m) analogique	analog computer
ordinateur (m) de bureau	desktop computer

ordinateur *(m)* personnel	personal computer (PC)
ordinateur *(m)* portatif	laptop computer
ordinateur: conception *(f)* assistée par ... (CAO)	computer-aided design (CAD)
ordinateur: enseignement *(m)* assisté par ... (EAO)	computer-assisted learning (CAL) computer-based training (CBT)
ordinateur: fabrication *(f)* assistée par ... (FAO)	computer-aided manufacturing (CAM)
ordinateur: fabrication *(f)* intégrée par ...	computer-integrated manufacturing (CIM)
ordinateur: input *(m)* de l'...	computer input
ordinateur: mémoire *(f)* d'...	computer memory
ordinateur: output *(m)* de l'...	computer output
ordinateur: programme *(m)* d'...	computer program
ordinateur: programmeur *(m)* sur...	computer programmer
ordinateur: simulation *(f)* par ...	computer simulation
ordinateur: système *(m)* d'information par ...	computerized information system (COINS)
ordinateur: terminal *(m)* d'...	computer terminal
ordonnancement *(m)*	scheduling
ordre *(m)* du jour	agenda
organigramme *(m)*	flow diagram organization chart organogram
organigramme *(m)* de données	data flow chart
organique: croissance *(f)* ...	organic growth
organisation *(f)* des bureaux	office management
organisation *(f)* fonctionnelle	functional organization staff organization
organisation *(f)* hiérarchique	line organization
organisation *(f)* horizontale	functional organization staff organization
organisation *(f)* industrielle	industrial engineering
organisation *(f)* informelle	informal organization
organisation *(f)* en matrice	matrix management
organisation *(f)* mixte	line and staff organization
organisation *(f)* opérationnelle	line organization
organisation *(f)* de la production	production management
organisation *(f)* scientifique	scientific management

organisation (f) scientifique du travail (OST)	scientific management
organisation (f) du temps	time management
organisation (f) des ventes	sales management
organisation (f) verticale	line organization
organisation: culture (f) de l'...	organization culture
organisation: méthodes (fpl) et ...	organization and methods (O & M)
organisation: planification (f) de l' ...	organization planning
organisation: structure (f) de l'...	organization structure
organisation: théorie (f) d'...	organization theory
organisatrice: efficacité (f) ...	organizational effectiveness
orientation (f) du client	customer orientation
orientation (f) vers le consommateur	consumer orientation
orientation (f) du marché	market trend (*short-term*)
orientation (f) professionnelle (OP)	vocational guidance
origine: pays (m) d'...	home country
orthographique: correcteur (m) ...	spellcheck
OST (organisation (f) scientifique du travail)	scientific management
outplacement (m)	outplacement
output (m)	output
output (m) de l'ordinateur	computer output
ouvert	open-ended
ouverture (f) préventive	pre-emptive bid
ouvrière: participation (f) ...	worker participation
ouvrières: relations (fpl) ...	labour relations
ouvriers (mpl) non qualifiés	unskilled labour

P

paiement (m) à titre de faveur	*ex gratia* payment
pair (m)	par
pair: au ...	at par
pair: au dessous du ...	below par
pair: au-dessus du ...	above par
palettisation (f)	palletization
panel (m) de consommateurs	consumers' panel
panier (m)	package deal
panier (m) de crabes	rat race

panneau *(m)* d'affichage (*électronique*)	bulletin board
PAO (publication assistée par ordinateur)	desktop publishing
parallèle: emprunt *(m)* ...	parallel loan
parallèle: importation *(f)* ...	parallel import
parallèle: marché *(m)* ...	grey market
parallèle: monnaie *(f)* ...	parallel currency
paramètre *(m)*	parameter
paramétrique: programmation *(f)* ...	parametric programming
parapluie *(m)* doré	golden parachute
parcelliser	chunk down (to)
parcours *(m)* rapide	fast-track
paritaires: consultations *(fpl)* ...	joint consultations
paritaires: négociations *(fpl)* ...	joint negotiations
parité *(f)* du pouvoir d'achat	purchasing power parity
part *(f)* du feu: faire la ...	cut one's losses (to)
part *(f)* du marché	market share
partage *(m)* du travail	job-sharing
partagé: temps *(m)* ...	time-sharing
partager	apportion (to)
participation *(f)*	participation
participation *(f)* aux bénéfices	profit-sharing
participation *(f)* majoritaire	controlling interest
	majority interest
participation *(f)* minoritaire	minority interest
participation *(f)* ouvrière	worker participation
participation: prise *(f)* de ...	*investment in another company*
participative: direction *(f)* ...	participative management
passage *(m)* d'essai	test run
passage *(m)* de production	production run
passer au crible	screen (to)
passer aux profits *(mpl)* et pertes	write off (to)
passerelle *(f)*	gateway
passif *(m)*	liabilities
passif *(m)* exigible	current liabilities
patron directeur *(m)*	owner-manager
pauvre en liquidité *(f)*	cash-poor
payback *(m)*	payback

pays *(m)* d'accueil	host country
pays *(m)* d'origine	home country
PDG (président-directeur *(m)* général)	chairman and managing director
pénétration par la base: politique *(f)* de prix de ...	penetration pricing
pénétration *(f)* du marché	market penetration
pensée *(f)* créatrice	creative thinking
pensée *(f)* latérale	lateral thinking
percée *(f)* commerciale	competitive thrust
	market thrust
perfectionnement *(m)*	development
	training
perfectionnement *(m)* des cadres	executive development
	management development
performance *(f)* du prix des actions	share price performance
performance: contrôle *(m)* de la ...	performance monitoring
performance: contrôler la ...	monitor performance (to)
performance: indicateur *(m)* de ...	performance indicator
performances: appréciation *(f)* des ...	performance appraisal
performances: évaluation *(f)* des ...	performance review
performances: mesure *(f)* de ...	performance measurement
performant	highly efficient
performer	perform (to)
période *(f)* de récupération	payback period
période *(f)* de remboursement	payback period
périodes: études *(fpl)* des ...	time and motion study
périphériques *(mpl)*	peripherals
périphériques: unités *(fpl)* ...	peripheral equipment
perlée: grève *(f)* ...	go-slow
permanent: crédit *(m)* ...	revolving credit
permanent: inventaire *(m)* ...	continuous stocktaking
permanents: capitaux *(mpl)* ...	fixed assets
personnalisé	customized
personnel *(m)*	manning
	staff
personnel *(m)* dirigeant	management staff
personnel *(m)* d'encadrement	management staff
personnel *(m)* du terrain	front-line employees

personnel: administration *(f)* du ...	personnel management
personnel: appréciation *(f)* du ...	personnel rating
personnel: chef *(m)* du ...	personnel manager
	staff manager
personnel: coût *(m)* unitaire du ...	unit labour cost
personnel: développement *(m)* ...	personal growth
personnel: direction *(f)* du ...	personnel department
	personnel management
	staff management
personnel: engagement *(m)* du ...	staff commitment
personnel: évaluation *(f)* du ...	staff appraisal
personnel: manque *(m)* de ...	understaffing
personnel: mouvement *(m)* du ...	staff turnover
personnel: mutation *(f)* du ...	staff turnover
personnel: ordinateur *(m)* ...	personal computer (PC)
personnel: politique *(f)* du ...	personnel policy
personnel: recrutement *(m)* du ...	staffing
personnel: réduction *(f)* du ...	redundancy
	staff cut-back
personnel: registre *(m)* du ...	payroll
personnel: représentation *(f)* du ...	worker representation
personnel: rotation *(f)* du ...	staff turnover
personnel: service *(m)* du ...	personnel department
perspective *(f)* de profit	profit outlook
perspectives *(fpl)* de carrière	job expectations
perspectives *(fpl)* commerciales	market prospects
perte *(f)* sèche	write-off
	dead loss
perte: vente *(f)* à ...	leader merchandising
	switch selling
pertes *(fpl)* du fait de mauvaises créances	bad-debt losses
pertes: générateur *(m)* de ...	loss-maker
pertinence: arbre *(m)* de ...	pertinence tree
petite caisse *(f)*	petty cash
peu élaboré	low-tech
philosophie *(f)* de l'entreprise	company philosophy
physique: gestion *(f)* de la distribution ...	physical distribution management

PIB (produit *(m)* intérieur brut)	GDP (gross domestic product)
pièce: travail *(m)* **à la ...**	piecework
pillage *(m)*	piracy
pillule *(f)* **empoisonnée**	poison pill
pilote: fabrication *(f)* **...**	pilot production
piquet *(m)* **de grève**	picket
pirate *(m)*	hacker
place *(f)* **financière**	financial market
place: test *(m)* **sur ...**	field testing
placement: agence *(f)* **de ...**	employment bureau
plafonnement *(m)* **des salaires**	wage ceiling
plan *(m)*	plan
	planning
plan *(m)* **d'action**	action plan
plan *(m)* **de carrière**	career planning
plan *(m)* **de divisions**	departmental plan
	departmental planning
plan *(m)* **financier**	financial plan
	financial planning
plan *(m)* **de marché**	market plan
	market planning
plan *(m)* **optionnel d'achat d'actions**	stock option plan
plan *(m)* **prévisionnel**	forecast
	plan
plan *(m)* **de projet**	project planning
plan *(m)* **stratégique**	strategic planning
plan *(m)* **tactique**	tactical planning
plan *(m)* **de travail**	schedule
planification *(f)*	planning
planification *(f)* **des bénéfices**	profit planning
planification *(f)* **des bureaux**	office planning
planification *(f)* **à court terme**	short-range planning
	short-term planning
planification *(f)* **des effectifs**	manpower planning
	staff planning
planification *(f)* **de l'entreprise**	company planning
	corporate planning
planification *(f)* **de l'emploi**	manpower planning

planification *(f)* **à long terme**	long-range planning
	long-term planning
planification *(f)* **des opérations**	operational planning
planification *(f)* **de l'organisation**	organization planning
planification *(f)* **du produit**	product planning
planification *(f)* **des ressources humaines**	human resource planning (HRP)
planification *(f)* **des systèmes**	systems engineering
	systems planning
planification *(f)* **des ventes**	sales planning
planification: service *(m)* **de ...**	planning department
planning *(m)*	plan
	planning
planning *(m)* **de distribution**	distribution planning
planning *(m)* **de la production**	production planning
planning: bureau *(m)* **de ...**	planning department
plannings: établissement *(m)* **des ...**	planning
plans *(mpl)* **de remplacement**	management succession planning
plans *(mpl)* **de succession**	management succession planning
planter: se ...	crash (to) (*a program*)
plein rendement *(m)*	full capacity
plein temps: emploi *(m)* **à ...**	full-time employment
plein temps: employé *(m)* **qui travaille à ... ...**	full-timer
plurimédiatique: formation *(f)* **...**	multimedia training
plus-value *(f)*	appreciation
	capital gain
PMTS (méthode *(f)* **des temps prédéterminés)**	PMTS (predetermined motion time system)
PNB (produit *(m)* **national brut)**	GNP (gross national product)
point *(m)* **critique**	break-even point
point *(m)* **focal**	focus
point *(m)* **limite**	cutting edge
point *(m)* **mort**	break-even point
	break-even quantity
point *(m)* **de référence**	benchmark
point *(m)* **de vente**	point of sale (POS)
point: étude *(f)* **de ... mort**	break-even analysis
pointe: technologie *(f)* **de ...**	high-tech

points: qualification (f) par ...	points-rating method
politique (f) de distribution	distribution policy
politique (f) à l'égard des remises	remittance policy
politique (f) de l'entreprise	company policy
	corporate policy
politique (f) fiscale	fiscal policy
politique (f) de gestion	business policy
politique (f) d'investissement	investment policy
politique (f) monétaire	monetary policy
politique (f) du personnel	personnel policy
politique (f) de prix	pricing policy
politique (f) de prix d'écrémage	prestige pricing
politique (f) de prix de pénétration par la base	penetration pricing
politique (f) de promotion	promotional policy
politique (f) salariale	wage policy
politique (f) de vente	sales policy
	selling policy
politique: exécution (f) de la ...	policy execution
politique: expression (f) de la ...	policy formulation
pondérée: moyenne (f) ...	weighted average
pont (m) d'or	golden hello
portage (m) à l'exportation	piggyback
portatif: ordinateur (m) ...	laptop computer
portefeuille (m) d'actifs	asset portfolio
portefeuille (m) d'actions	stock portfolio
portefeuille (m) d'activités	business portfolio
portefeuille (m) équilibré	balanced portfolio
portefeuille (m) de marques	brand portfolio
portefeuille (m) de produits	product portfolio
portefeuille: gestion (f) de ...	portfolio management
portefeuille: sélection (f) de ...	portfolio selection
position (f) concurrentielle	competitive position
positionnement (m)	positioning
positionnement (m) de marques	brand positioning
positive: discrimination (f) ...	positive discrimination
poste: caractéristiques (fpl) de ...	job characteristics
	job description

poste: description *(f)* de ...	job description
	job title
poste: exigences *(fpl)* de ...	job challenge
	job requirements
poste de travail: analyse *(f)* par ...	job analysis
postes: rotation *(f)* des ...	job rotation
potentiel *(m)* **des cadres**	management potential
potentiel *(m)* **de croissance**	growth potential
potentiel *(m)* **de développement**	development potential
potentiel *(m)* **de vente**	sales potential
potentiel: acheteur *(m)* ...	potential buyer
potentiel: cadre *(m)* à haut ...	high-flier
potentiel: cadre *(m)* à moindre ...	low-flier
potentiel: marché *(m)* ...	market potential
potentiel humain: stratègie *(f)* du ...	staff strategy
pouvoir *(m)* **d'achat**	purchasing power
pouvoir d'achat: parité *(f)* du	purchasing power parity
pouvoirs: délégation *(f)* des ...	delegation
pratiques *(fpl)* **restrictives**	restrictive practices
préalable: étude *(f)* ...	feasibility study
prédateur *(m)*	corporate raider
	predator
prédéterminés: méthode *(f)* **des** temps ...	predetermined motion time system (PMTS)
préférentiel: droit *(m)* ... de souscription	rights issue
préférentielle: action *(f)* ...	golden share
premier ordre: valeur *(f)* de ...	blue-chip stock
	gilt
	gilt-edged security
	gilt-edged stock
préparation *(f)* **du budget**	budgeting
préparation *(f)* **des décisions**	preparing decisions
présence: feuille *(f)* de ...	time sheet
présérie *(f)*	pilot production
	pilot run
président *(m)*	chairman
	president
président-directeur *(m)* **général (PDG)**	chairman and managing director (MD)

président: vice-... *(m)*	deputy chairman
	vice-chairman
	vice-president
pression *(f)*	pressure
pression *(f)* **inflationniste**	inflationary pressure
prestation *(f)* **extérieure de services**	contracting out
prestige: publicité *(f)* **de ...**	corporate advertising
prêt-bail *(m)*	lease-lend
préventif: entretien *(m)* **...**	preventive maintenance
préventive: ouverture *(f)* **...**	pre-emptive bid
prévision *(f)*	forecast
	forecasting
prévision *(f)* **budgétaire**	budget forecast
	budget forecasting
prévision *(f)* **de la demande**	demand forecasting
prévision *(f)* **des dépenses d'investissement**	capital budgeting
prévision *(f)* **des effectifs**	staff forecasting
prévision *(f)* **de l'emploi**	manpower forecast
prévision *(f)* **dans l'entreprise**	business forecasting
prévision *(f)* **sur l'environnement**	environmental forecasting
prévision *(f)* **du marché**	market forecast
	market forecasting
prévision *(f)* **technologique**	technological forecasting
prévision *(f)* **de trésorerie**	cash budgeting
	cash forecasting
prévision *(f)* **des ventes**	sales forecast
	sales forecasting
prévisionnel: plan *(m)* **...**	forecast
	plan
prévisionnelle: étude *(f)* **...**	forecast
prévisionnelle: gestion *(f)* **...**	budgetary control
prévoyance: fonds *(m)* **de ...**	contingency reserve
prime *(f)*	bonus
	incentive
	premium
prime *(f)* **collective**	group bonus
	group incentive

prime *(f)* d'équipe	group bonus
	group incentive
prime *(f)* de départ *(m)*	golden handshake
primes: programme *(m)* de ... d'encouragement	incentive scheme
prioritiser	prioritize (to)
prise *(f)* de contrôle	take-over
prise *(f)* de décision	decision-making
prise *(f)* de participation	*investment in another company*
privatisation *(f)*	privatization
privatiser	privatize (to)
privé: secteur *(m)* ...	private enterprise
prix *(m)* au comptant	spot price
prix *(m)* défiant la concurrence	competitive price
prix *(m)* différentiel	differential price
prix *(m)* directeur	price leader
prix *(m)* du marché	market price
prix *(mpl)* imposés	resale price maintenance (RPM)
prix *(m)* standard	standard price
	standard pricing
prix: brader les ...	cut prices (to)
prix: discrimination *(f)* de ...	price discrimination
prix: échelle *(f)* des ...	price range
prix: établissement *(m)* des ...	price determination
	pricing
prix: fixation *(f)* des ...	price determination
	pricing
prix: fixation *(f)* des ... de transfert	transfer pricing
prix: fixation *(f)* marginale du ...	marginal pricing
prix *(m)*: fixer le ...	price (to)
prix: flambée *(f)* des ...	price escalation
prix: gâchage *(m)* des ...	price cutting
prix: indice *(m)* des ...	price index
prix: majoration *(f)* de ...	mark-up
	price increase
prix: politique *(f)* de ...	pricing policy
prix: réduction *(f)* de ...	price-cutting
prix: stratégie *(f)* de ...	pricing strategy

prix: structure *(f)* de ...	price structure
prix d'écrémage: politique *(f)* de	prestige pricing
prix de détail: indice *(m)* des ...	retail price index
prix de pénétration par la base: politique *(f)* de ...	penetration pricing
prix de revient: analyse *(f)* du ...	cost analysis
prix de revient: comptabilité *(f)* de ...	cost accounting
prix de revient: élément *(m)* du ...	cost factor
prix de revient: établissement *(m)* des	costing
prix de revient: norme *(f)* de	cost standard
proactif	proactive
proactive: stratégie *(f)* ...	proactive strategy
probabilités: théorie *(f)* des ...	probability theory
problématique: domaine *(m)* ...	problem area
problème: analyse *(f)* de ...	problem analysis
problème: résolution *(f)* d'un ...	problem solving
problèmes: évaluation *(f)* des ...	problem assessment
procédé *(m)* de fabrication	production process
procédural	procedural
procédure *(f)*	procedure
procédure *(f)* prud'hommale	grievance procedure
procédure *(f)* pour résoudre des griefs	grievance procedure
procédures *(fpl)* de gestion	management practices
processeur *(m)* central	central processing unit (CPU)
processus *(m)* de la décision	decision process
processus *(m)* logistique	logistic process
processus *(m)* de production	production process
processus: commande *(f)* de ...	process control
processus: régulation *(f)* de ...	process control
product-mix *(m)*	product mix
productif	cost-efficient
productif: entretien *(m)* ...	productive maintenance
production *(f)*	output
	yield
production *(f)* à la chaîne	chain production
	line production
production *(f)* continue	continuous-flow production

production *(f)* en groupe	batch production
production *(f)* en masse	mass production
production: capacité *(f)* de ...	manufacturing capacity
production: chaîne *(f)* de ...	chain of production
	production line
production: coûts *(mpl)* de ...	costs of production
	production costs
production: facteurs *(mpl)* de ...	factors of production
	input
production: gestion *(f)* de la ...	production control
	production management
production: ligne *(f)* de ...	flow line
production: norme *(f)* de ...	production standard
production: objectif *(m)* de ...	production target
production: organisation *(f)* de la ...	production management
production: passage *(m)* de ...	production run
production: planning *(m)* de la ...	production planning
production: programmation *(f)* de la ...	production scheduling
production: quantité *(f)* économique de ...	economic manufacturing quantity
production: régulation *(f)* de la ...	production control
production: surveillance *(f)* de la ...	production control
	progress control
production: technique *(f)* de la ...	production technique
production: techniques *(fpl)* de la ...	production engineering
productivité *(f)*	efficiency
	productivity
productivité: campagne *(f)* de ...	productivity campaign
	productivity drive
productivité: contrat *(m)* de ...	productivity agreement
productivité: mesure *(f)* de la ...	productivity measurement
produit *(m)* d'appel	impulse good
	loss-leader
produit *(m)* de base	primary commodity
produit *(m)* dérivé	by-product
produit *(m)* disponible	cash flow
produit *(m)* intérieur brut (PIB)	gross domestic product (GDP)

produit *(m)* leader	core product
produit *(m)* locomotive *(f)*	star product
produit *(m)* national brut (PNB)	gross national product (GNP)
produit: analyse *(f)* de ...	product analysis
produit: chef *(m)* de ...	product manager
produit: comportement *(m)* de ...	product performance
produit: conception *(f)* de ...	product design
produit: conception *(f)* du ...	product conception
produit: cycle *(m)* de vie *(f)* d'un ...	product life cycle
produit: dessin *(m)* du ...	product design
produit: étude *(f)* de ...	product analysis
	product engineering
produit: fiabilité *(m)* d'un ...	product reliability
produit: gestion *(f)* du ...	product management
produit: image *(f)* de ...	product image
produit: lancement *(m)* d'un ...	product launch
produit: planification *(f)* du ...	product planning
produit: profil *(m)* de ...	product profile
produit: rentabilité *(f)* de ...	product profitability
produit: sous-... *(m)*	by-product
produit: stratégie *(f)* de ...	product strategy
produit: suppression *(f)* d'un ...	product abandonment
produit: test *(m)* de ...	product testing
produits *(mpl)* blancs	white goods
produits *(mpl)* bruns	brown goods
produits *(mpl)* chimiques dangereux	hazchem (hazardous chemicals)
produits *(mpl)* de consommation courante	convenience goods
produits *(mpl)* de consommation durable	consumer durables
produits *(mpl)* durables	durables
produits *(mpl)* non durables	non-durable goods
produits: amélioration *(f)* de ...	product improvement
produits: création *(f)* des ...	product generation
produits: développement *(m)* de ...	product development
produits: domaine *(m)* de ...	product area
produits: dynamique *(f)* des ...	product dynamics
produits: éventail *(m)* de ...	product mix
	product range

produits: gamme *(f)* de ...	product line
produits: grille *(f)* de ...	product group
produits: groupe *(m)* de ...	product group
produits: ligne *(f)* de ...	product line
produits: portefeuille *(m)* de ...	product portfolio
produits: publicité *(f)* de ...	product advertising
produits: recherche *(f)* de ...	product research
produits: série *(f)* de ...	product line
professionnalisation *(f)*	professionalization
professionnelle: association *(f)* ...	trade association
professionnelle: formation *(f)* ...	vocational training
professionnelle: main-d'oeuvre *(f)* ...	skilled labour
professionnelle: orientation *(f)* ... (OP)	vocational guidance
profil *(m)* d'acquisition	acquisition profile
profil *(m)* de compétences	personnel specification
profil *(m)* de l'entreprise	company profile
profil *(m)* du marché	market profile
profil *(m)* de produit	product profile
profil *(m)* de risque	risk profile
profit *(m)*	profit
profit sur vente: rapport *(m)* de	profit volume ratio (P/V)
profit: analyse *(f)* coût-...	cost-benefit analysis (CBA)
profit: analyse *(f)* des facteurs de ...	profit-factor analysis
profit: centre *(m)* de ...	profit centre
profit: comptabilité *(f)* par centres de ...	profit centre accounting
profit: incidence *(f)* sur le ...	profit impact
profit: maximisation *(f)* du ...	profit maximization
profit: motivation *(f)* par le ...	profit motive
profit: objectif *(m)* de ...	profit target
profit: optimisation *(f)* du ...	profit optimization
profit: perspective *(f)* de ...	profit outlook
profit: stratégie *(f)* de ...	profit strategy
profits: analyse *(f)* volume-coûts-...	cost-volume-profit analysis
profits: projection *(f)* des ...	profit projection
profits *(mpl)* et pertes: passer aux ...	write off (to)
profondeur: analyse *(f)* en ...	in-depth analysis

profondeur: entretien *(m)* en ...	in-depth interview
profondeur: interview *(m)* en ...	in-depth interview
progiciel *(m)*	programme package
	software package
programmation *(f)*	programming
	scheduling
programmation *(f)* dynamique	dynamic programming
programmation *(f)* linéaire	linear programming
programmation *(f)* mathématique	mathematical programming
	scientific progamming
programmation *(f)* non-linéaire	non-linear programming
programmation *(f)* paramétrique	parametric programming
programmation *(f)* de la production	production scheduling
programme *(m)*	programme
	routine
	schedule
programme *(m)* d'action	action plan
programme *(m)* de développement	development programme
programme *(m)* de diagnostic	diagnostic routine
programme *(m)* de fabrication	production schedule
programme *(m)* d'investissements	investment programme
programme *(m)* de négoce	trading programme
programme *(m)* d'ordinateur	computer program
programme *(m)* de primes d'encouragement	bonus scheme incentive scheme
programme *(m)* secret	hidden agenda
programme *(m)* de stimulants salariaux	incentive scheme
programme *(m)* de travail	work schedule
programmé: enseignement *(m)* ...	programmed instruction
	programmed learning
programmée: gestion *(f)* ...	programmed management
programmer	program (to)
	programme (to)
programmes: direction *(f)* par ...	programmed management
programmeur *(m)* sur ordinateur	computer programmer
progrès: à la pointe du ...	state of the art
progressivement: adopter ...	phase in (to)
project management *(m)*	project management

projection *(f)*	projection
projection *(f)* des profits	profit projection
projet *(m)*	blueprint
projet *(m)* et contrôle *(m)* de la production	production planning and control
projet: chef *(m)* de ...	project manager
projet: étude *(f)* de ...	project analysis
projet: évaluation *(f)* de ...	project assessment
projet: plan *(m)* de ...	project planning
promesse *(f)* unique de vente	unique selling point (USP)
	unique selling proposition (USP)
promoteur *(m)*	developer
promotion *(f)*	promotion
promotion *(f)* des cadres	executive advancement
	executive promotion
promotion *(f)* (de vente) discrète	soft sell
promotion *(f)* des ventes	sales promotion
promotion: politique *(f)* de ...	promotional policy
promotionnel	promotional
pronostic *(m)* du marché	market forecast
prophète *(m)* de malheur	doomwatcher
proportionnel	*pro rata*
proportionnel: méthode *(f)* du coût ...	direct costing
proposition *(f)* d'affaires	business proposition
propres: capitaux *(mpl)* ...	shareholders' equity
prospect *(m)*	prospective customer
prospecter	canvass (to)
prospection *(f)* des marchés	market exploration
prospection *(f)* sur le terrain	field research
protection *(f)* du consommateur	consumer protection
protection *(f)* des données	data protection
provision *(f)* pour amortissement	depreciation allowance
prud'hommale: procédure *(f)*	grievance procedure
prud'hommes: conseil *(m)* de ...	*conciliation board*
psychologie *(f)* industrielle	industrial psychology
psychométrique: test *(m)* ...	psychometric testing
public: secteur *(m)* ...	public enterprise
public: service *(m)* ...	public utility

publication *(f)* **assistée par ordinateur (PAO)**	desktop publishing
publicitaire: efficacité *(f)* ...	advertising effectiveness
publicitaire: message *(m)* ...	advertising message
publicitaire: thème *(m)* ...	advertising theme
publicitaires: études *(fpl)*...	advertising research
publicitaires: média *(mpl)* ...	advertising media
publicitaires: supports *(mpl)* ...	advertising media
publicité *(f)* **directe**	direct mail
publicité *(f)* **sur le lieu de vente (PLV)**	point-of-sale advertising (POS)
publicité *(f)* **de prestige**	corporate advertising
publicité *(f)* **de produits**	product advertising
publicité *(f)* **subliminale**	subliminal advertising
publicité: agent *(m)* **de** ...	advertising agent
publicité: budget *(m)* **de** ...	advertising budget
publicité: campagne *(f)* **de** ...	advertising campaign
	advertising drive
publicité: directeur *(m)* **de la** ...	advertising manager
publipostage *(m)*	mailing
	mail merge
publique: offre *(f)* ... **d'achat (OPA)**	take-over bid (TOB)
publiques: relations *(fpl)* ... **(RP)**	public relations (PR)
puce *(f)*	chip
	microchip
puce: carte *(f)* **à** ...	smart card
punch *(m)***: avoir du** ...	be a go-getter (to)

Q

qualification *(f)* **par points**	points-rating method
qualification *(f)* **du travail**	job evaluation
qualité: centre *(m)* **d'évaluation de la** ...	assessment centre
qualité: cercle *(m)* **de** ...	quality circle
qualité: contrôle *(m)* **de la** ...	quality assurance
	quality control

qualité: évaluation *(f)* de la ...	quality assessment
qualité: gestion *(f)* de la ...	quality control
	quality management
qualité: gestion *(f)* de la ... absolue	total quality management (TQM)
quantitative: analyse *(f)* ...	quantitative analysis
quantitative: normalisation *(f)* ...	variety reduction
quantité *(f)* économique à commander	economic order quantity
quantité *(f)* économique de production	economic manufacturing quantity
quantité *(f)* optimale de commande	economic order quantity
quota *(m)* de ventes	sales quota
quotient *(m)*	quotient

R

R et D (recherche *(f)* et développement *(m)*)	R & D (research and development)
rachat *(m)* d'une entreprise par ses cadres	management buyout (MBO)
rachat *(m)* d'une entreprise par ses employés	employee buyout
	worker buyout
rachat *(m)* par levier	leveraged buyout (LBO)
rachat: offre *(m)* de ... par levier	leveraged bid
raison *(f)* sociale	trade name
raisonnable: concurrence *(f)* ...	fair competition
raisonnement *(m)*	rationale
ralentissement *(m)*	downturn
rapide: parcours *(m)* ...	fast-track
rapide: voie *(f)* ...	fast-track
rappel *(m)*	follow-up
rapport *(m)* cours-bénéfices	price-earnings ratio (P/E)
rapport *(m)* dettes-actions	debt-equity ratio
rapport *(m)* financier	financial statement
rapport *(m)* profit sur ventes	profit-volume ratio (P/V)
rapport *(m)* sur la solvabilité	status report
rassemblement *(m)* de données statistiques	data gathering

ratio *(m)* **administration-production**	administration-production ratio
ratio *(m)* **comptable**	accounting ratio
ratio *(m)* **d'endettement**	debt ratio
	gearing ratio
ratio *(m)* **financier**	financial ratio
ratio *(m)* **de gestion**	management ratio
ratio *(m)* **d'intensité de capital**	capital-output ratio
ratio *(m)* **de liquidité**	current ratio
ratio *(m)* **de trésorerie**	cash ratio
rationalisation *(f)*	rationalization
rationalisation *(f)* **des choix budgétaires (RCB)**	*planning, programming, budgeting system (PPBS)*
	functional costing
	output budgeting
	performance budgeting
	programme budgeting
rationaliser	rationalize (to)
	streamline (to)
rationnement *(m)* **de capitaux**	capital rationing
rationnement *(m)* **des fonds**	capital rationing
RCB (rationalisation *(f)* **des choix budgétaires)**	*PPBS (planning, programming, budgeting system)*
RCI (rentabilité *(f)* **des capitaux investis)**	ROCE (return on capital employed)
réactif	reactive
réaction *(f)*	feedback
réactive: stratégie *(f)* ...	reactive strategy
réalisable	feasible
réalisable: actif *(m)* ...	current assets
	liquid assets
	quick assets
réalisation: délai *(m)* **de** ...	lead time
réalisations *(fpl)* **comparées aux projets**	performance against objectives
réaliser (*un portefeuille***)**	realize (to) (*profit*)
	sell out (to)
recentrage *(m)*	refocusing
réceptivité *(f)* **des consommateurs**	consumer acceptance

récession *(f)*	slump
recette *(f)* moyenne	average revenue
recherche *(f)* des besoins des consommateurs	consumer research
recherche *(f)* des buts	goal-seeking
recherche *(f)* commerciale	marketing research
recherche *(f)* documentaire	desk research
recherche *(f)* et développement *(m)* (R et D)	research and development (R & D)
recherche *(f)* opérationelle (RO)	operational research (OR)
	operations research (OR)
recherche *(f)* de produits	product research
recherche *(f)* sur le terrain	field research
recherche: service *(m)* de ...	research department
réciproque: reconnaissance *(f)* ...	mutual recognition
reclassement *(m)* (*de main-d'oeuvre*)	redeployment
reconfiguration *(f)*	reconfiguration
reconnaissance *(f)* réciproque	mutual recognition
reconstitution *(f)* de la société	company reconstruction
recopie *(f)* d'écran	hard copy
recouvrement *(m)* des dépenses	recovery of expenses
recrutement *(m)*	recruiting
	recruitment
recrutement *(m)* du personnel	staffing
recrutement *(m)* et gestion *(f)* des effectifs	manpower resourcing
	staff resourcing
recruter	recruit (to)
recueil *(m)* de données statistiques	data gathering
récupération *(f)* (*du capital investi*)	payback
récupération *(f)* des frais	recovery of expenses
récupération *(f)* de l'information	information retrieval
récupération: délai *(m)* de ...	payback period
récupération: période *(f)* de ...	payback period
récupération: valeur *(f)* de ...	break-up value
recyclage *(m)*	booster training
	recycling
	retraining
recycler	recycle (to)
redéployer	redeploy (to)

redressement: délai *(m)* **de ...**	turn-around time
redresser	turn around (to)
réduction *(f)* **des coûts**	cost reduction
réduction *(f)* **du personnel**	redundancy
	staff cut-back
réduction *(f)* **de prix**	price cutting
réel: revenu *(m)* **...**	real income
réel: temps *(m)* **...**	real time
réévaluation *(f)* **des actifs**	revaluation of assets
réexécuter	rerun (to)
référence: année *(f)* **de ...**	base year
référence: point *(m)* **de ...**	benchmark
référence: temps *(m)* **de ...**	standard time
réflexion: cellule *(f)* **de ...**	think-tank
réflexion: groupe *(m)* **de ...**	think-tank
refus *(m)* **de vente**	refusal to supply
régime *(m)* **de croisière**	on stream
registre *(m)* **du personnel**	payroll
règle *(f)* **du jeu**	name of the game
règlement *(m)*	regulation
réglementation *(f)* **de contenu local**	local content rules
réglementer	regulate (to)
régler	regulate (to)
régression *(f)*	regression
régression: analyse *(f)* **de ...**	regression analysis
régression *(f)* **multiple: analyse** *(f)* **de ...**	multiple regression analysis (MRA)
régulation *(f)* **de processus**	process control
régulation *(f)* **de la production**	production control
réinvesti: bénéfice *(m)* **...**	ploughback
relais: travail *(m)* **par ...**	shiftwork
relations *(fpl)* **d'affaires**	business relations
relations *(fpl)* **avec les employés**	employee relations
relations *(fpl)* **extérieures**	external relations
relations *(fpl)* **humaines**	human relations
relations *(fpl)* **industrielles**	industrial relations
relations *(fpl)* **ouvrières**	labour relations
relations *(fpl)* **professionnelles**	industrial relations
relations *(fpl)* **publiques (RP)**	public relations (PR)

relations *(fpl)* syndicales	industrial relations
relations *(fpl)* du travail	labour relations
remboursement: période *(f)* de ...	pay-back period
remises: politique *(f)* à l'égard des ...	remittance policy
remplacement: coûts *(mpl)* de ...	replacement costs
remplacement: plans *(mpl)* de ...	management succession planning
remue-méninges *(m)*	brainstorming
rémunération *(f)*	remuneration
rémunération *(f)* des cadres	executive compensation
	executive remuneration
rémunération: écart *(m)* de ...	earnings differential
rendement *(m)*	efficiency
	output
	productivity
	profit performance
	return
	yield
rendement *(m)* de capital	return on capital
rendement *(m)* équitable	fair return
rendement *(m)* des fonds propres	earnings on assets
	return on equity (ROE)
rendement *(m)* des investissements	return on investment (ROI)
rendement *(m)* moyen	average yield
rendement *(m)* standard	standard performance
rendement *(m)* au travail	job performance
rendement: norme *(f)* de ...	performance standard
rendement *(m)*: plein ...	full capacity
rendement: salaire *(m)* au ...	incentive wage
rendement: taux *(m)* de ...	rate of return
rendement: taux *(m)* de ... interne	internal rate of return (IRR)
rentabilité *(f)*	earnings performance
	pay-off
	productivity
	profitability
	rate of return
rentabilité *(f)* des capitaux investis (RCI)	return on capital employed (ROCE)

rentabilité *(f)* d'investissements	return on investment
rentabilité *(f)* de produit	product profitability
rentabilité *(f)* des ventes	return on sales
rentabilité: amélioration *(f)* de la ...	profit improvement
rentabilité: analyse *(f)* de la ...	profitability analysis
rentabilité: étude *(f)* de ...	investment analysis
	profitability analysis
rentabilité: seuil *(m)* de ...	break-even point
	cut-off point
rentable	cost-effective
rentrer dans ses frais	break even (to)
rémunération *(f)* des cadres	executive compensation
renvoi: embauchage *(m)* et ...	hiring and firing
renvoyer	fire (to)
réorganisation *(f)*	redeployment
	reorganization
réorganiser	redeploy (to)
répartir	apportion (to)
répartition *(f)*	allocation
	apportionment
répartition *(f)* des capitaux	capital structure
répartition *(f)* des charges	cost apportionment
répartition *(f)* des frais	assignment of expenditure
répartition *(f)* des moyens	resource allocation
répartition *(f)* des responsabilités	allocation of responsibilities
repasser	rerun (to)
répercussion *(f)* sur les bénéfices	profit implication
repère *(m)*	benchmark
répondeur *(m)* téléphonique	answerphone
représentation *(f)* analogique	analog(ue) representation
représentation *(f)* de personnel	worker representation
représentation: frais *(mpl)* de ...	expense account
reprise *(f)*	upturn
réputation *(f)* de solvabilité	credit rating
réseau *(m)* de communication	communications network
réseau *(m)* de distribution	distribution channels
	distribution network
réseau *(m)* d'information	information network

réseau *(m)* local	local area network (LAN)
réseau: analyse *(f)* de ...	network analysis
réseau: gestion *(f)* de ...	networking
réseau *(m)*: grand ...	wide area network (WAN)
résistance *(f)* des consommateurs	consumer resistance
résolution *(f)* d'un problème	problem solving
responsabilité *(f)* fonctionnelle	functional responsibility
responsabilité *(f)* hiérarchique	line responsibility
	linear responsibility
responsabilité: centre *(m)* de ...	responsibility centre
responsabilité: zone *(f)* de ...	jurisdiction
responsabilités: étendue *(f)* des ...	span of control
responsabilités: répartition *(f)* des ...	allocation of responsibilities
responsable *(m)*	manager
ressort *(m)*	accountability
	jurisdiction
ressources *(fpl)*	assets
ressources *(fpl)* humaines	human resources
ressources: affectation *(f)* des ...	resource allocation
ressources: allocation *(f)* des ...	resource allocation
ressources: examen *(m)* des ...	resource appraisal
ressources: gestion *(f)* des ...	resource management
ressources humaines: développement *(m)* des	human resource development (HRD)
ressources humaines: gestion *(f)* des	human resource management (HRM)
ressources humaines: planification *(f)* des	human resource planning (HRP)
ressources *(fpl)* et emplois *(mpl)* de capitaux	source and disposition of funds
restreinte: liste *(f)* ...	shortlist
restriction *(f)* du crédit	credit squeeze
restriction *(f)* sur le commerce	trade restriction
restrictives: pratiques *(fpl)* ...	restrictive practices
restructuration *(f)*	reorganization
	restructuring
restructuration *(f)* du travail	work structuring
restructurer	restructure (to)

résultat *(m)* net	bottom line
résultat *(m)* de sortie	output
résultats: évaluation *(f)* des ...	performance appraisal
retombée *(f)*	spill-over effect
	spin-off effect
retour *(m)* sur investissement (RSI)	return on investment (ROI)
retraite *(f)*	retirement
retraite: prendre sa ...	retire (to)
retraite *(f)* anticipée	early retirement
rétroaction *(f)*	feedback
réunion *(f)* du conseil d'administration	board meeting
réunion *(f)* de mise au point	debriefing
revendicative: action *(f)* ...	industrial action
revenu *(m)* disponible	disposable income
revenu *(m)* réel	real income
revenu: impôt *(m)* sur le ...	income tax
réviser	review (to)
révision *(f)* comptable	audit
révision *(f)* des traitements	salary review
revoir	review (to)
riche en liquidité *(f)*	cash-rich
risque *(m)* du métier	occupational hazard
risque: capital *(m)* à ...	risk capital
risque: financier *(m)* à ...	venture capitalist
risque: profil *(m)* de ...	risk profile
risques: analyse *(f)* des ...	risk analysis
risques: appréciation *(f)* des ...	risk assessment
risques: gestion *(m)* des ...	risk management
	venture management
RO (recherche *(f)* opérationnelle)	OR (operational research, operations research)
robot *(m)*	robot
robotique *(f)*	robotics
robotiser	robotize (to)
rôles: jeu *(m)* de ...	role-playing
ronds: en chiffres *(mpl)* ...	in round figures
rotation *(f)* des capitaux	asset turnover
rotation *(f)* du personnel	staff turnover

rotation *(f)* des postes	job rotation
rotation *(f)* des stagiaires	trainee turnover
rotation *(f)* des stocks	inventory turnover
	stock turnover
roulants: capitaux *(mpl)* ...	circulating capital
roulement: fonds *(mpl)* de ...	circulating capital
	working capital
router	route (to)
routine *(f)*	routine
RP (relations *(fpl)* publiques)	PR (public relations)

S

saisie *(f)* de données	data acquisition
salaire *(m)* lié aux bénéfices	profit-related pay
salaire *(m)* minimum	minimum wage
salaire *(m)* net	take-home pay
salaire *(m)* à prime de rendement	premium bonus
salaire *(m)* au rendement	incentive wage
	payment by results
salaire *(m)* stimulant	incentive wage
salaires: blocage *(m)* des ...	pay pause
	wage freeze
salaires: dérive *(f)* des ...	wage drift
salaires: écart *(m)* de ...	wage differential
salaires: égalité *(f)* des ...	equal pay
salaires: éventail *(m)* de ...	wage range
salaires: niveau *(m)* des ...	wage level
salaires: plafonnement *(m)* des ...	wage ceiling
salaires: structure *(f)* des ...	salary structure
	wage structure
salariale: politique *(f)* ...	wage policy
salariales: négociations *(fpl)* ...	pay talks
salle *(f)* du conseil	boardroom
sans liquidité *(f)*	cash-strapped
satisfaction *(f)* du consommateur	consumer satisfaction
satisfaction *(f)* au travail	job satisfaction
saturation *(f)* du marché	market saturation

sauvage: grève *(f)* ...	unofficial action
	unofficial strike
savoir-faire *(m)*	know-how
science *(f)* du comportement	behavioural science
science *(f)* de la gestion	management science
scientifique: gestion *(f)* ...	scientific management
scientifique: organisation *(f)* ... du travail (OST)	scientific management
scission *(f)* d'actif	divestment (of assets)
scrutation *(f)*	scanning
SdT (simplification *(f)* du travail)	job simplification
	work simplification
search *(m)*: faire le ...	head-hunt (to)
secours: installation *(f)* de ...	back-up facility
secret: programme *(m)* ...	hidden agenda
secteur *(m)* de croissance	growth area
secteur *(m)* privé	private enterprise
secteur *(m)* public	public enterprise
secteur *(m)* de vente	trading area
secteur: chef *(m)* de ...	area manager
sections: comptabilité *(f)* des ...	responsibility accounting
sécurité *(f)* de l'emploi	job security
sécurité *(f)* industrielle	industrial safety
sécurité: accord *(m)* sur la ... de l'emploi	job security agreement
sécurité: gestion *(f)* de la ...	safety management
sécurité: marge *(m)* de ...	margin of safety
sécurité: stock *(m)* de ...	safety stock
segmentation *(f)*	segmentation
segmentation *(f)* des marchés	market segmentation
segmenter	segment (to)
sélectif: accès *(m)* ...	random access
sélectif: mémoire *(f)* à accès ...	random-access memory (RAM)
sélection *(f)* de portefeuille	portfolio selection
sélection *(f)* des média	media selection
sélectionner	screen (to)
	shortlist (to)
semi-conducteur *(m)*	semiconductor
semi-variable: coûts *(mpl)* ...	semi-variable costs

sensibiliser	sensitize (to)
sensibilité: éducation *(f)* de la ...	sensitivity training
sensible au consommateur	consumer-responsive
sensible au coût	cost-sensitive
sensible au marché	market-sensitive
séquentiel: enseignement *(m)* ...	programmed learning
séquentielle: analyse *(f)* ...	sequential analysis
série *(f)* chronologique	time series
série *(f)* économique de fabrication	economic manufacturing quantity
série *(f)* de produits	product line
série: effectif *(m)* de ... économique	economic batch quantity
série: fabrication *(f)* en ...	mass production
série: pré ... *(f)*	pilot production
	pilot run
service *(m)* après-vente	after-sales service
service *(m)* à la clientèle	customer service
service *(m)* de marketing	marketing department
service *(m)* du personnel	personnel department
service *(m)* de planification	planning department
service *(m)* planning	planning department
service *(m)* public	public utility
service *(m)* de recherche	research department
service *(m)* technique	engineering and design department
service: chef *(m)* de ...	departmental manager
services *(mpl)* commerciaux	sales department
services *(mpl)* comptables	accounting department
services *(mpl)* de conseil interne	advisory services
	management services
services *(m)* d'état-major	management services
services *(m)* fonctionnels	management services
services *(mpl)* en informatique	computer services
services *(mpl)* d'intendance	ancillary operations
services *(mpl)* logistiques	extension services
seuil *(m)* de rentabilité	break-even point
	cut-off point
sexuel: harcèlement *(m)* ...	sexual harassment
siège *(m)* social	head office
significatif	meaningful
	significant

SIM (système *(m)* d'information de
  management)
      MIS (management information
      system)
simplexe: méthode *(f)* du ...
      simplex method
simplification *(f)* du travail (SdT)
      job simplification
      work simplification

simulation *(f)*
      simulation
simulation *(f)* de gestion
      business game
      management game

simulation *(f)* par ordinateur
      computer simulation
simuler
      simulate (to)
situation *(f)* financière
      financial position
SME (Système *(m)* Monétaire
  Européen)
      EMS (European Monetary System)

social: capital *(m)* ...
      authorized capital
social: conflit *(m)* ...
      industrial dispute
social: exercice *(m)* ...
      fiscal year
social: siège *(m)* ...
      head office
sociale: analyse *(f)* ...
      social analysis
sociale: raison *(f)* ...
      trade name
sociaux: avantages *(mpl)* ...
      fringe benefits
sociaux: mouvements *(mpl)* ...
      industrial action
société *(f)* affiliée
      associate company
société *(f)* apparentée
      affiliate company
      associate company
société *(f)* commerciale
      business corporation
société *(f)* cotée en bourse
      publicly listed company
      quoted company
société *(f)* d'exploitation en
  commun
      joint-venture company
société *(f)* de logiciel
      software firm
société *(f)* mère
      parent company
société *(f)* en nom collectif
      partnership
société *(f)* non inscrite à la cote
      unlisted company
société *(f)* de portefeuille
      holding company
société *(f)*: attaquer une ...
      raid a company (to)
société: logotype *(m)* de la ...
      company logo
société: reconstitution *(f)* de la ...
      company reconstruction
socio-culturel
      socio-cultural
socio-économique
      socio-economic

sociométrique	sociometric
software *(m)*	software
solidarité: grève *(f)* de ...	sympathy strike
solide	robust
solvabilité: rapport *(m)* sur la ...	status report
solvabilité: réputation *(f)* de ...	credit rating
sommaire: licenciement *(m)* ...	summary dismissal
somme *(f)* globale	lump sum
somme nulle: jeu *(m)* à	zero-sum game
sommet *(m)*: du ... à la base	top-down
sondage *(m)* aléatoire	random sampling
sondage: mesure *(m)* du travail par ...	activity sampling
sortie *(f)* d'imprimante	printout
sortie *(f)* de l'ordinateur	computer output
sortie: résultat *(m)* de ...	output (data)
sortir sur imprimante	print out (to)
souci *(m)* du client	customer care
soumission *(f)* concurrentielle	competitive tendering
soumission: faire une ...	tender (to)
souple: disque *(m)* ...	floppy disk
source *(f)* d'emprunts	borrowing facility
sourcing *(m)*	outsourcing
souris *(f)*	mouse
sous licence	under licence
sous-capacité *(f)*	undercapacity
sous-capitalisé	undercapitalized
sous-chef *(m)*	assistant manager
sous-directeur *(m)*	assistant manager
	vice-president
sous-optimisation *(f)*	sub-optimization
sous-performer	underperform (to)
sous-produit *(m)*	by-product
sous-traitance *(f)*	subcontracting
sous-traiter	contract out (to)
	subcontract (to)
souscription: droit *(m)* préférentiel de ...	rights issue
souscrit: capital *(m)* ...	issued capital
spécial	one-off

spécialisée: main-d'oeuvre *(f)* ...	semi-skilled labour
sponsoring *(m)*	sponsorship
stagflation *(f)*	stagflation
stagiaires: rotation *(f)* des ...	trainee turnover
standard *(m)*	standard
standard *(m)* budgétaire	budget standard
	budgetary standard
standard *(m)* de vie	standard of living
standard: prix *(m)* ...	standard price
standard: rendement *(m)* ...	standard performance
standard: temps *(m)* ...	standard time
standardisation *(f)*	standardization
standardiser	standardize (to)
standards: coûts *(mpl)* ...	standard costs
standards: méthode *(f)* des coûts ...	standard costing
standing *(m)*	credit rating
star *(m)*	high-flier
station *(f)* de travail	workstation
statistique: contrôle *(m)* ...	statistical control
statistique: échantillonage *(m)* ...	statistical sampling
statistiques: recueil *(m)* de données ...	data gathering
stimulant *(m)*	incentive
stimulant *(m)* compétitif	competitive stimulus
stimulant: salaire *(m)* ...	incentive wage
stimulants salariaux: programme *(m)* de	incentive scheme
stock *(m)* de sécurité	safety stock
stock *(m)* tampon	buffer stock
	safety stock
stocks: contrôle *(m)* des ...	inventory control
	stock control
stocks: évaluation *(f)* des ...	stock valuation
stocks: gestion *(f)* des ...	inventory control
	inventory management
	stock control
stocks: mouvement *(m)* des ...	stock turnover
stocks: rotation *(f)* des ...	inventory turnover
	stock turnover
strate *(f)* de marché	market segment

stratégie *(f)* des affaires	business strategy
stratégie *(f)* des cadres	executive manpower strategy
stratégie *(f)* commerciale	marketing strategy
stratégie *(f)* concurrentielle	competitive strategy
stratégie *(f)* de croissance	expansion strategy
	growth strategy
stratégie *(f)* défensive	defensive strategy
stratégie *(f)* de diversification	diversification strategy
stratégie *(f)* de l'entreprise	company strategy
	corporate strategy
stratégie *(f)* d'expansion	expansion strategy
stratégie *(f)* financière	financial strategy
stratégie *(f)* de marché	marketing strategy
stratégie *(f)* de la marque	brand strategy
stratégie *(f)* de négociation	negotiation strategy
stratégie *(f)* du potentiel humain	staff strategy
stratégie *(f)* de prix	pricing strategy
stratégie *(f)* proactive	proactive strategy
stratégie *(f)* de produit	product strategy
stratégie *(f)* du profit	profit strategy
stratégie *(f)* réactive	reactive strategy
stratégie *(f)* de survie	survival strategy
stratégie *(f)* de l'utilisateur	user strategy
stratégie: application *(f)* de ...	strategy implementation
stratégies: élaboration *(f)* des ...	strategy formulation
stratégique: alliance *(f)* ...	strategic alliance
stratégique: plan *(m)*...	strategic plan
	strategic planning
structuration *(f)*	structuring
structure *(f)*	structure
structuré	structured
structure *(f)* d'autorité	authority structure
structure *(f)* des coûts	cost structure
structure *(f)* de l'entreprise	company structure
	corporate structure
structure *(f)* en grille	grid structure
structure *(f)* du marché	market structure
structure *(f)* matricielle	matrix organization
structure *(f)* de l'organisation	organization structure

structure *(f)* des prix	price structure
structure *(f)* des salaires	salary structure
	wage structure
structuré: non ...	unstructured
structurer	structure (to)
structures: mutation *(f)* des ...	organizational change
style *(m)* de direction	leadership
	management style
style *(m)* de l'entreprise	house style
style *(m)* managérial	managerial style
style *(m)* de vie	lifestyle
subordonnés *(mpl)*	down the line
subsidiarité *(f)*	subsidiarity
succès: facteur *(m)* clé ...	key success factor
succession: plans *(mpl)* de ...	management succession planning
succursale *(f)*	branch office
suggestions: système *(m)* de ...	suggestion scheme
suivi *(m)*	follow-up
suivre	follow up (to)
supérieurs: cadres *(mpl)* ...	top management
supplémentaires: heures *(fpl)* ...	overtime
supports *(mpl)*	media
supports *(mpl)* audio-visuels	audiovisual aids
supports *(mpl)* publicitaires	advertising media
supression *(f)* de la double imposition	double taxation relief
suppression *(f)* d'un produit	product abandonment
surcapacité *(f)*	excess capacity
	overcapacity
sur-capitalisé	overcapitalized
surprise: grève *(f)* ...	walk out
	wildcat strike
surveillance *(f)* de la production	production control
	progress control
surveillance: conseil *(m)* de ...	supervisory board
surveillant *(m)*	supervisor
surveillant *(m)* de premier niveau	first-line manager
surveiller	monitor (to)
	supervise (to)

survie: stratégie *(f)* **de ...**	survival strategy
syndical: délégué *(m)* **...**	trade union representative
syndicales: relations *(fpl)* **...**	industrial relations
syndicat *(m)*	syndicate
	trade union
synergie *(f)*	synergism
	synergy
systématique: entretien *(m)* **...**	planned maintenance
systématisée: direction *(f)* **...**	systems management
systématiser	systematize (to)
système *(m)*	system
système *(m)* **de direction**	management system
système *(m)* **expert**	expert system
système *(m)* **d'information**	information system
système *(m)* **d'information de management (SIM)**	management information system (MIS)
système *(m)* **d'information par ordinateur**	computerized information system (COINS)
système *(m)* **intégré de gestion**	integrated management system
Système *(m)* **Monétaire Européen (SME)**	European Monetary System (EMS)
système *(m)* **des salaires**	wage system
système *(m)* **de suggestions**	suggestion scheme
système: ingénieur *(m)* **...**	systems engineer
systèmes: analyse *(f)* **des ...**	systems analysis
systèmes: conception *(f)* **des ...**	systems design
systèmes: engineering *(m)* **des ...**	systems engineering
systèmes: gestion *(f)* **par les ...**	systems management
systèmes: mise *(f)* **en oeuvre des ...**	systems engineering
systèmes: planification *(f)* **des ...**	systems engineering
	systems planning
systèmes: théorie *(f)* **des ...**	systems theory

T

tableau *(m)* **de bord**	management chart
tableau *(m)* **d'échanges inter-industriels**	input-output table

tableau 234

tableau *(m)* financier	spreadsheet
tableur *(m)*	spreadsheet
tâches: affectation *(f)* des ...	job assignment
tâches: amélioration *(f)* des ...	job improvement
tâches: analyse *(f)* des ...	job analysis
tâches: conception *(f)* des ...	job design
tâches: décomposition *(f)* des ...	job breakdown
	operations breakdown
tâches: extension *(f)* des ...	job enlargement
tâches: fixation *(f)* des ...	job specification
tâches: intérêt *(m)* des ...	job interest
tactique *(f)* concurrentielle	competitive tactic
tactique: plan *(m)* ...	tactical plan
	tactical planning
TAD (traitement *(m)* automatique des données)	ADP (automatic data processing)
tampon: stock *(m)* ...	buffer stock
	safety stock
tangibles: valeurs *(fpl)* ...	tangible assets
tard: date *(f)* au plus ...	latest date
tas: formation *(f)* sur le ...	on-the-job-training
tas: grève *(f)* sur le ...	sit-down strike
taux *(m)* de base	base rate
taux *(m)* de base bancaire (TBB)	bank rate
taux *(m)* de change	exchange rate
taux *(m)* de change à terme	forward exchange rate
taux *(m)* de charge	load factor
taux *(m)* de couverture	cover ratio
taux *(m)* de liquidité	liquidity ratio
taux *(m)* pour les opérations à terme	forward rate
taux *(m)* de price-earnings	price-earnings ratio (P/E)
taux *(m)* de rendement	rate of return
taux *(m)* de rendement interne	internal rate of return (IRR)
taux *(m)* en vigueur	going rate
taux *(m)* zéro	zero-rating
taux de change: mécanisme *(m)* de ...	exchange rate mechanism (ERM)
taxe *(f)* à la valeur ajoutée (TVA)	value added tax (VAT)
taxe *(f)* à la valeur ajoutée (TVA): exemption *(f)* de la ...	zero-rating

TBB (taux *(m)* de base bancaire)	bank rate base rate
technique: directeur *(m)* ...	technical manager works manager
technique *(f)* de gestion	management technique
technique *(f)* de la production	production technique
technique: service *(m)* ...	engineering and design department
techniques *(fpl)* marchandes	merchandising
techniques *(fpl)* de la production	production engineering
technologie *(f)* de pointe	high-tech
technologie: transfert *(m)* de ...	technology transfer
technologique: prévision *(f)* ...	technological forecasting
TEI (traitement *(m)* électronique de l'information)	EDP (electronic data processing)
télé-enseignement *(m)*	distance learning
téléconférence *(f)*	teleconference
télécopie *(f)*	facsimile fax
télécopier	fax (to)
télécopieur *(m)*	fax machine
télémarketing *(m)*	telemarketing
télématique *(f)*	electronic communication telematics
téléphone *(m)* arabe	grape vine
téléphone *(m)* mobile	mobile phone
téléphone *(m)* sans fil	cellphone
téléphone *(m)* de voiture	car phone
téléphone: vente *(f)* par ...	telesales
téléphonique: répondeur *(m)* ...	answerphone
télévente *(f)*	telesales
temps *(m)* de bon fonctionnement	uptime
temps *(m)* mort	down time
temps *(m)* partagé	time-sharing
temps *(m)* réel	real time
temps *(m)* de référence	standard time
temps *(m)* standard	standard time
temps: étude *(f)* des ...	time study
temps: étude *(f)* des ... et des méthodes	time and methods engineering time and methods study

temps: étude *(f)* des ... et des mouvements	time and motion study
temps: organisation *(f)* du ...	time management
tendance *(f)*	trend
tendance *(f)* du marché	market trend (*long-term*)
tendance *(f)* exponentielle	exponential trend
tendances *(fpl)* du marché	market forces
tendanciel: marché *(m)* ...	market potential
teneur *(m)* de marché	market maker
tension *(f)* due au travail	work stress
terme: contrat *(m)* à ... d'instruments financiers (CATIF)	financial futures
terme: contrats *(mpl)* à ...	futures
terme: échange *(m)* financier à ...	forward swap
terme: emprunt *(m)* à long ...	loan stock
terme: marché *(m)* à ...	forward market
	futures market
terme: taux *(m)* de change à ...	forward exchange rate
terminal *(m)*	terminal
terminal *(m)* d'ordinateur	computer terminal
terrain: personnel *(m)* du ...	front-line employees
terrain: prospection *(f)* sur le ...	field research
terrain: recherche *(f)* sur le ...	field research
territoire *(m)* de vente	sales area
	sales territory
	trading area
territoire: défense *(f)* de son ...	turf protection
test *(m)* d'aptitude	aptitude test
test *(m)* de marché	marketing test
test *(m)* sur place	field testing
test *(m)* de produit	product testing
test *(m)* psychométrique	psychometric testing
test *(m)* de vente	market test
têtes: chasseur *(m)* de ...	head-hunter
texte: traitement *(m)* de ...	word processing
thème *(m)* publicitaire	advertising theme
théorie *(f)* administrative	administrative theory
théorie *(f)* des communications	communications theory
théorie *(f)* de la contingence	contingency theory

théorie *(f)* des décisions	decision theory
théorie *(f)* des files d'attente	queueing theory
théorie *(f)* de la gestion de l'entreprise	management theory
théorie *(f)* de l'information	information theory
théorie *(f)* des jeux	game theory
théorie *(f)* d'organisation	organization theory
théorie *(f)* des probabilités	probability theory
théorie *(f)* des systèmes	systems theory
tiers *(m)*	third party
titre *(m)* déposé en garantie	collateral security
titre de faveur: paiement *(m)* à ...	*ex gratia* payment
titres *(mpl)*	securities
titrisation *(f)*	securitization
titriser	securitize (to)
tôt: date *(f)* au plus ...	expected date
touche *(f)* de fonction	function key
tournant: inventaire *(m)* ...	perpetual inventory
traficoter	fiddle (to)
traitement *(m)* automatique des données (TAD)	automatic data processing (ADP)
traitement *(m)* des données	data processing
traitement *(m)* graphique	graphics
traitement *(m)* électronique de l'information (TEI)	electronic data processing (EDP)
traitement *(m)* de l'information	information handling information processing
traitement *(m)* informatique	electronic processing
traitement *(m)* par lots	batch processing
traitement *(m)* de texte	word processing
traitement: indice *(m)* de ...	salary grade
traitement: unité *(f)* centrale de ...	mainframe
traitement de texte: machine *(f)* à ...	word processor
traitements: révision *(f)* des ...	salary review
traiter	process (to)
tranches: découper un projet en ...	chunk a project (to)
transaction *(f)* au comptant	cash deal
transactionnel	transactional
transactionnelle: analyse *(f)* ...	transactional analysis (TA)

transfert *(m)* électronique de fonds au point de vente	EFTPOS (electronic funds transfer at point of sale)
transfert *(m)* de technologie	technology transfer
transfert: fixation *(f)* des prix de ...	transfer pricing
transitaire *(m)*	forwarding agent
transitionnel	transitional
travail *(m)* en cours	work in progress
travail *(m)* à forfait	work by contract
travail *(m)* à mi-temps	part-time employment
travail *(m)* au noir	moonlighting
travail *(m)* à la pièce	piecework
travail *(m)* par relais	shiftwork
travail: accident *(m)* du ...	industrial injury
travail: adaption *(f)* du ... à l'homme	ergonomics
	human engineering
travail: analyse *(f)* par poste de ...	job analysis
travail: charge *(f)* de ...	workload
travail: compétence *(f)* dans le ...	job competence
travail: conflit *(m)* du ...	labour dispute
travail: contenu *(m)* du ...	job content
	work content
travail: cycle *(m)* de ...	work cycle
travail: élargissement *(m)* du ...	job enlargement
travail: enrichissement *(m)* du ...	job enrichment
travail: étude *(f)* du ...	work study
travail: groupe *(m)* de ...	working party
travail: joie *(f)* au ...	job satisfaction
travail: lieu *(m)* de ...	workplace
travail: mesure *(f)* du ...	ergonometrics
	work measurement
travail: mesure *(f)* du ... par sondage	activity sampling
travail: organisation *(f)* scientifique du ... (OST)	scientific management
travail: partage *(m)* du ...	job-sharing
travail: plan *(m)* de ...	schedule
travail: programme *(m)* de ...	work schedule
travail: qualification *(f)* du ...	job evaluation
travail: relations *(fpl)* du ...	labour relations

travail: rendement *(m)* au ...	job performance
travail: restructuration *(f)* du ...	work structuring
travail: satisfaction *(f)* au ...	job satisfaction
travail: simplification *(f)* du ...	job simplification
(SdT)	work simplification
travail: tension *(f)* due au ...	work stress
travailler en indépendant	freelance (to go)
travailleur *(m)* manuel	blue-collar worker
trésorerie: budget *(m)* de ...	cash budget
trésorerie: coefficient *(m)* de ...	cash ratio
trésorerie: gestion *(f)* de ...	cash management
trésorerie: prévision *(f)* de ...	cash budgeting
	cash forecasting
trésorerie: ratio *(m)* de ...	cash ratio
trouver un débouché pour	market (to)
truquage *(m)* *(du bilan)*	window-dressing
turc *(m)*: jeune ...	whiz-kid
tuyaux d'orgue: graphique *(m)* en ...	bar chart
TVA (taxe *(f)* à la valeur ajoutée)	VAT (value added tax)

U

uniformiser	standardize (to)
Union *(f)* Monétaire Européenne	European Monetary Union (EMU)
unique: marché *(m)* ...	single market
unique: monnaie *(f)* ...	single currency
unique: promesse *(f)* ... de vente	unique selling point (USP)
	unique selling proposition (USP)
unitaires: coûts *(mpl)* ... du personnel	unit labour costs
unité *(f)* d'affichage	display unit
unité *(f)* centrale de traitement	mainframe
Unité *(f)* de Compte Européenne (ECU)	European Currency Unit (ECU)
unité *(f)* de disques	disk drive
unité *(m)* de visualisation	visual display unit (VDU)
unités *(fpl)* périphériques	peripheral equipment
us *(mpl)* et coutumes *(fpl)*	custom and practice

usine: capacité *(f)* de l' ...	plant capacity
usine: directeur *(m)* d' ...	plant manager
	works manager
usine: localisation *(f)* de l' ...	plant location
utilisateur: stratégie *(f)* de l'...	user strategy
utilisateurs: attitude *(f)* des ...	user attitude
utilisation *(f)* de la capacité	capacity utilization
utilisation *(f)* de la capacité: coefficient *(m)* d'	load factor

V

vacances: étalement *(m)* des ...	staggered holidays
valable	viable
valeur *(m)* des actifs	asset value
valeur *(f)* actuelle nette	net present value (NPV)
valeur *(f)* ajoutée	value added
valeur *(f)* comptable	book value
valeur *(f)* marchande	market value
valeur *(f)* nette	net worth
valeur *(f)* non cotée	unlisted security
valeur *(f)* de premier ordre	blue-chip stock
	gilt
	gilt-edged security
	gilt-edged stock
valeur *(f)* de récupération	break-up value
valeur: analyse *(f)* de la ...	value analysis (VA)
valeur *(f)*: augmenter de ...	appreciate (to)
valeur: chaîne *(f)* de ...	value chain
valeur: concept *(m)* de ...	value concept
valeur: offre *(f)* de ...	value proposal
valeur: taxe *(f)* à la ... ajoutée (TVA)	value added tax (VAT)
valeurs *(fpl)*	securities
valeurs *(fpl)* immobilisées	fixed assets
valeurs *(fpl)* incorporelles	intangible assets
valeurs *(fpl)* matérielles	tangible assets
valeurs *(fpl)* nettes	net assets

valeurs *(fpl)* **tangibles**	tangible assets
value: moins- *(f)* **...**	capital loss
value: plus- *(f)* **...**	capital gain
variables: coûts *(mpl)* **...**	variable costs
variance: analyse *(f)* **de ...**	variance analysis
vendre moins cher	undercut (to)
vente *(f)* **agressive**	hard sell
vente *(f)* **d'appel**	impulse sale
vente *(f)* **de choc**	impulse sale
vente *(f)* **par correspondance (VPC)**	mail order
vente *(f)* **directe**	direct selling
vente *(f)* **expérimentale**	market test
	sales test
vente *(f)* **à perte**	leader merchandising
	switch selling
vente *(f)* **par téléphone**	telesales
vente: arguments *(mpl)* **de ...**	sales talk
vente: équipe *(f)* **de ...**	sales force
vente: lieu *(m)* **de ...**	point of sale (POS)
vente: objectif *(m)* **de ...**	sales goal
vente: point *(m)* **de ...**	point of sale (POS)
vente: politique *(f)* **de ...**	sales policy
	selling policy
vente: potentiel *(m)* **de ...**	sales potential
vente: promesse *(f)* **unique de ...**	unique selling point (USP)
	unique selling proposition (USP)
vente: refus *(m)* **de ...**	refusal to supply
vente: service *(m)* **après-...**	after-sales service
vente: territoire *(m)* **de ...**	sales area
	sales territory
	trading area
vente: test *(m)* **de ...**	market test
ventes *(fpl)* **anticipées**	sales expectations
ventes: administration *(f)* **des ...**	sales management
ventes: analyse *(f)* **des ...**	sales analysis
ventes: animation *(f)* **des ...**	sales drive
ventes: chef *(m)* **de ...**	sales manager
ventes: direction *(f)* **des ...**	sales department
	sales management

ventes: effort *(m)* **d'accroissement des ...**	sales expansion effort
ventes: estimation *(f)* **des ...**	sales estimate
ventes: organisation *(f)* **des ...**	sales management
ventes: planification *(f)* **des ...**	sales planning
ventes: prévision *(f)* **des ...**	sales forecast
	sales forecasting
ventes: promotion *(f)* **des ...**	sales promotion
ventes: volume *(m)* **de ...**	sales volume
ventes: quota *(m)* **de ...**	sales quota
ventes: rentabilité *(f)* **des ...**	return on sales
vérificateur *(m)* **de comptes**	auditor
	comptroller
	controller
vérification *(f)* **de comptes**	audit
	auditing
vérifier	verify (to)
vérifier un compte	audit (to)
versé en informatique	computer literate
versement des dividendes: politique *(f)* **de ...**	dividend policy
verticale: intégration *(f)* **...**	vertical integration
verticale: organisation *(f)* **...**	line organization
viabilité *(f)*	viability
vice-président *(m)*	deputy chairman
	vice-president
vidéo *(f)*	video
vidéotex *(m)*	viewdata
vidéotex *(m)* **diffusé**	teletext
vidéotrace *(f)*	hard copy
vie *(f)* **d'un produit**	product life
vie: courbe *(f)* **de ... (d'un produit)**	product life cycle
vie: coût de la ...	cost of living
vie: cycle *(m)* **de ... (d'un produit)**	product life cycle
vie: durée *(f)* **de ...**	shelf-life
vie: espérance *(f)* **de ... (d'un produit)**	product life expectancy
vie: niveau *(m)* **de ...**	standard of living
vie: standard *(m)* **de ...**	standard of living
vie: style *(m)* **de ...**	lifestyle

vie économique: durée *(f)* de ...	economic life
vieillissement *(m)*	obsolescence
vigueur: taux *(m)* en ...	going rate
virus *(m)* informatique	computer virus
viseur *(m)*	window
vision *(f)*	vision
vision: définition *(f)* de la ...	vision statement
visuel *(m)*	visual display unit (VDU)
visuel: écran *(m)* ...	visual display unit (VDU)
vocation *(f)* de la société	corporate mission
voie *(f)* hiérarchique	line of command
voie *(f)* rapide	fast-track
voies *(fpl)* de communication	channels of communication
	communication channels
voiture: téléphone *(m)* de ...	car phone
volume *(m)*	volume
volume *(m)* de ventes	sales volume
VPC (vente *(f)* par correspondance)	mail order

W

winchester: disque *(m)* ...	Winchester disk

Y

yuppie *(m)*	yuppie

Z

zèle: grève *(f)* du ...	work-to-rule
zéro défaut	zero defects
zéro: budget *(m)* base ...	zero-base budget
zéro: taux *(m)* ...	zero-rating
zone *(f)* critique	problem area
zone *(f)* de responsabilité	jurisdiction